Explicating Maxine Greene's Notion of Naming and Becoming

Imagination and Praxis: Criticality and Creativity in Education and Educational Research

Series Editors

Tricia M. Kress (*The University of Massachusetts Boston, Boston, MA, USA*)
Robert L. Lake (*Georgia Southern University, Statesboro, GA, USA*)

Editorial Advisory Board

Peter Appelbaum (*Arcadia University, Philadelphia, PA, USA*)
Roslyn Arnold (*University of Sydney, Australia*)
Patty Bode (*Ohio State University, Columbus, OH, USA*)
Cathrene Connery (*Ithaca College, Ithaca, NY, USA*)
Clyde Coreil (*New Jersey City University, Jersey City, NJ, USA*)
Michelle Fine (*CUNY Graduate Center, New York, NY, USA*)
Sandy Grande (*Connecticut College, New London, CT, USA*)
Awad Ibrahim (*University of Ottawa, Ottawa, ON, Canada*)
Vera John-Steiner (*University of New Mexico, Albuquerque, NM, USA*)
Wendy Kohli (*Fairfield University, Fairfield, CT, USA*)
Carl Leggo† (*University of British Columbia, Vancouver, BC, Canada*)
Donaldo Macedo (*University of Massachusetts Boston, MA, USA*)
Martha McKenna (*Lesley University, Boston, MA, USA*)
Ernest Morrell (*Columbia University, New York, NY, USA*)
William Reynolds (*Georgia Southern University, Statesboro, GA, USA*)
Pauline Sameshima (*Lakehead University, Thunder Bay, ON, Canada*)

VOLUME 15

The titles published in this series are listed at *brill.com/ipcc*

Explicating Maxine Greene's Notion of Naming and Becoming

"I Am ... Not Yet"

By

Christine Debelak Neider

BRILL

LEIDEN | BOSTON

All chapters in this book have undergone peer review.

Library of Congress Cataloging-in-Publication Data

Names: Neider, Christine Debelak, author.
Title: Explicating Maxine Greene's notion of naming and becoming : "I am
   ... not yet" / by Christine Debelak Neider.
Description: Leiden ; Boston : Brill, [2021] | Series: Imagination and
   praxis : criticality and creativity in education and educational
   research, 2542-9140 ; volume 15 | Includes bibliographical references
   and index.
Identifiers: LCCN 2021032817 | ISBN 9789004499843 (hardback) | ISBN
   9789004499874 (paperback) | ISBN 9789004499881 (ebook)
Subjects: LCSH: Greene, Maxine. | Teaching--Philosophy. |
   Education--Philosophy. | Reflective teaching. | Critical discourse
   analysis. | Educators--United States--Biography.
Classification: LCC LB885.G682 N45 2021 | DDC 371.1--dc23
LC record available at https://lccn.loc.gov/2021032817

Typeface for the Latin, Greek, and Cyrillic scripts: "Brill". See and download: brill.com/brill-typeface.

ISSN 2542-9140
ISBN 978-90-04-49987-4 (paperback)
ISBN 978-90-04-49984-3 (hardback)
ISBN 978-90-04-49988-1 (e-book)

Copyright 2021 by Koninklijke Brill NV, Leiden, The Netherlands.
Koninklijke Brill NV incorporates the imprints Brill, Brill Nijhoff, Brill Hotei, Brill Schöningh, Brill Fink, Brill mentis, Vandenhoeck & Ruprecht, Böhlau Verlag and V&R Unipress.
All rights reserved. No part of this publication may be reproduced, translated, stored in a retrieval system, or transmitted in any form or by any means, electronic, mechanical, photocopying, recording or otherwise, without prior written permission from the publisher. Requests for re-use and/or translations must be addressed to Koninklijke Brill NV via brill.com or copyright.com.

This book is printed on acid-free paper and produced in a sustainable manner.

Contents

Acknowledgments VII

Introductory Letter to My Reader 1

1 **Letters to Maxine** 6
 1 Prelude 6
 2 Mindset 7
 3 Journey toward Maxine: Troubling Epistemology 12
 4 Imaging Ontological Possibilities 21
 5 Naming and Being 28
 6 Naming, Learning, and Social Imagination 41

2 **Letters to My Colleague** 57
 1 Toward a Method of Inquiry for a Teacher 57
 2 (Re)Claiming Interpretation: Currere 61
 3 Engaging Teachers in Inquiry: Teacher Lore 66
 4 Logics of a Naming Study 73

3 **Letters to New Teachers** 93
 1 Teaching Vignettes 94
 2 Disturbances 135
 3 "We" Know: Beginnings of Discursive Naming 143
 4 Naming a Feminized Profession 150
 5 Naming Hidden Work and (Mis)Understanding 156
 6 Being Ethical 170
 7 Becoming Possibilities 177

Interlude: Today 190

Concluding Letter to Fellow Teachers 191
 1 Becoming Together 197

Bibliography 201
Index 216

Acknowledgments

For the academic endeavor, I am indebted to the kind, inspiring and deeply provocative mentoring of Noreen Garman; the transformative educational encounters created by/with Michael Gunzenhauser; the collegiality and companionship of Matthew Rhodes and Bryan Stephany; the supportive critique of Jean Ferguson Carr, Patricia McMahon, and Robert Lake; and the faithful reads and edits of Leah Lederman and Emily Parrino.

For the realization of this study as a book, I am grateful to my editors, Robert Lake and Tricia Kress, for their enthusiasm for and guidance of my work; and to the publication team at Brill who patiently navigated deadlines with me through the ups and downs of my chronic illness and lent me such professional expertise, especially Evelien van der Veer, Alessandra Giliberto, and Jolanda Karada.

For the nourishing stories and personal-professional companionship, I thank the staff of Birchwood School of Hawken and my teacher friends, especially Hannah Birchman, Beth Driehaus, Eileen Hannigan, Pam Quinlan, Megan Sweet, Hannah Bontje, Grace Wang, and Theresa Tropp.

For surrounding me with communion in my life during this time, I honor the friends and family who cared for my family and my heart: Peter Debelak, Thawivann Spalding, Marianne Uechi, Cindy McNaughton, Jessica Carlton-Humenik, Cecily Routman, Susanna Nadeau, Paul Neider, Jonalea Neider, Kristen Cliffel, Joe and Emily Parrino, and Ann Masterson.

For the initiation, process, and partnering in this book and my Becoming, I deeply love my parents, Chuck and Helene Debelak, who inspire and live a Becoming life as educators; my children, Jonah and Phoebe, whose very presence prompted me to find the most loving and respectful way to be human; and my husband, Samuel Neider, who Becomes together with me, always.

Introductory Letter to My Reader

> Far more is possible for individuals than is ordinarily recognized, but they do not reach out for fulfillment if they do not feel impeded somehow, and if they are not enabled to name the obstacles that stand in their way.
>
> MAXINE GREENE (*The Dialectic of Freedom*, 1988, 5)

∴

Dear Reader,

This book evolved as a study in what troubled me as a teacher, and the concept upon which I began to find hope and create a new way of being as a teacher (and a human being!) lies in the quote above.

… Name the obstacles that stand in their way

While I embarked on my career in teaching with great enthusiasm and a strong sense of purpose, I discovered myriad obstacles which blocked my ability to embody my ideals. Over and over again, and from all sides—including from within me!—I felt confused, frustrated, saddened, devastated, angry, resentful and self-pitying as a teacher. How could this be?! I loved my work with children and colleagues, but …

This book is a study in the "but." Specifically, this concept of Naming in the work of Maxine Greene revealed itself over time as quite promising for the challenging and uncomfortable "but" in the way of teachers finding the purposeful fulfillment we imagined might be ours in our profession. I gave myself the task of explicating this concept in the prolific work of Greene, preeminent philosopher and pioneer in the field of education, because I sensed she had a powerful way of seeing teachers and children as human beings and would address our needs and desires from that perspective. Once I came to some understanding of her meaning of Naming, I knew I couldn't teach or live the same way again. Her work contributed to a massive shift in the way I perceived education, myself as a teacher, and my posture toward life. Thus, I enacted in this work a study upon myself, wondering if, in Naming my own experiences as a teacher (as a Naming praxis), I might engage in the fulfilling promise of a life lived with integrity to my ethical commitments and ideals. Furthermore, I hoped that what I found through my study might be a boon to my current and future colleagues.

But I was less clear when I began ...

⋯

I suspect you are a teacher or very nearly one. I am over two decades a teacher—a career or half a career depending on your longevity as a teacher yourself. The years matter, don't they? They are our wisdom; they are our weight—badges both battle-worn and of great honor.

About ten years in, I decided to pursue a doctorate to better understand our dilemma as teachers and to find a way to strengthen us in our practice to honor and live out the ideals that led us to teaching in the first place, especially in the challenging circumstances the new millennium brought us.

This book, however, is a work of scholarship, not practice. See how I just made teaching and scholarship two different things? That's how I felt as I studied and wrote, though the dualism challenged me. In fact, I suspected that part of the root of my frustrations was the idea that teachers don't have time for deep reading, or worse they weren't intelligent enough for it. Some of this came from my own sense of self. My brother is the family intellect, so my inner story goes, who highlights Herman Hesse and Foucault in his leisure time. My story continued—I was practical and gifted interpersonally, which made teaching a natural fit as opposed to more "intellectual" endeavors.

The field of education, especially teacher education, promotes this idea. How many philosophy and history of education classes did you take for your licensure? How many "practical" courses did you take or "impractical" ones were you told to avoid? Methods, methods, methods. Content. "experience." Seems about the right proportions for what we were required to "master," right? And then there is the way we organized—a union instead of a professional organization—quite telling about our collective self-perception. Not to mention our history and present circumstances slowly, and then quite rapidly in the last two decades, removed most creative agency from teachers, as those in authority suspected our inability to do the intellectual work of curriculum, teaching, reflection, learning and re-creation.

Should I even start discussing the ways in which social-cultural-political attitudes toward teachers have diminished concurrently with professional condescension?

As I studied, and especially as I wrote, I carried and then resisted the powerful weight of this personal and professional frame negating teachers as intellectuals, possessing wisdom and with much to add to the work of educating children. In large part, I drew strength from the imagination and work of Maxine Greene and other scholar-practitioners, especially in the fields of Curriculum Studies and Social Foundations of Education. Their research and conceptual studies resonated deeply, articulating what troubled and awed me about teachers, teaching, learning and schooling. In that resonance, I recognized that I KNEW something valuable. What I had garnered through my own experience and professional study was SOMETHING—something which I did not need to be TOLD. This *knowing* of mind and heart became my impetus for further, deeper, and original study through dialogue with these scholars, other practitioners, and peers.

And yet, throughout, a single question threatened to undermine everything and provided layers of existential angst:

Who do you think you are?

Ah, reader, it took me ten years and three pregnancies to birth this book as my body, mind, and heart found the courage to rise to answer:

A TEACHER! UNIQUELY SUITED TO THIS TASK, WITH THE RIGHT AND RESPONSIBILITY TO UNDERSTAND WHAT SHE KNOWS AND MAKE IT PUBLIC IN SERVICE OF HER COLLEAGUES AND STUDENTS!

Having written this work, I now know what I know, and I could write it much differently. In the assurance of my knowing, having completed the study, I would be direct and unapologetic. I would be less hesitant. I wouldn't feel the need to justify myself beyond the warrants which must be satisfied by the collective agreement of our field of scholarship. Perhaps there would be fewer asides, pop culture references and one less emoji!

Instead, what this text represents as a whole is the present effort of a teacher to grow into and embody the bridge between scholar and practitioner. It represents, in Maxine Greene's words, my own Becoming and demonstrates that this work cannot be done in two parts: scholarship or practice, personal or professional. What it required was finding a third (middle) way, a passage into and through the paradoxes.

Cultivating and trudging that path was, and always is, messy or convoluted. It's peppered with triumphant "aha's!" and bits of crushing angst. It was especially thus as it involves these "interior" matters of heart and relationship, of "being" and not simply "possessing" knowledge. I felt as the mystic Teresa of Avila expressed in her long introductory remarks of her seminal work *Interior Castle*.

> These interior matters are so obscure for our minds that anyone who knows as little as I will be forced to say many superfluous and even foolish things in order to say something that's right. Whoever reads this must have patience, for I have to have it in order to write about what I don't know.[1]

For me, I didn't know what I knew; I wrote to make meaning of my experience. (Narrative research scholar, Laurel Richardson, strengthened my resolve by her assertion that writing, in fact, is a way of coming to know). I believe you will feel this in the text of this book beginning with the way I framed it as conversation in letters. Except for the introductory and concluding letters, which are written to you, dear Reader, I directed each letter to a private individual: educational scholar Maxine Greene, a close teacher friend, and two friends who were new teachers. This move allowed a certain sense of security as I stepped into the ring of scholarship with trepidation and vulnerability. Of course, I assumed these letters were also public, thus each recipient might be privy to the other letters. The letters then both stand alone and yet also rely on one another to expound my meaning-making. My hope is that I've also written in a way that invites you to enter the conversation as my journey unfolds; in this way, again, I endeavored to make my tone approachable and the chapter endnotes useful in highlighting the reflexive union of practice and scholarship for teachers like me.

In the first section of this book, I address my letters to Maxine Greene. I dialogue with her because it was my initial engagement with her work which began to transform my visioning of teachers and myself; her work resonated with both my experience and that which I imagined my experience could be. My tone in our discussion genuflects to her, and here you see my vulnerability in tone again. I dared not overinterpret her work, and so I diligently collected her thoughts so that I uttered my understanding in her voice with as much fidelity as possible. Letters to her unfold from my mindset as a teacher encompassing hopes, commitments, and troubles. Through discursive deliberation I represent the encounters in my study which disturbed and disrupted this mindset. I described, in dialogue with her, the alternatives she presented to my thinking and to my Being in the world, which ultimately brought me to this study of Naming within her work and which I found potentially useful and purposeful to myself and other teachers.

Then, I spend the entire second section in letters to my colleague and friend justifying teacher knowledge as valuable and critical to the field of education because I needed the affirmation, because teachers need the assurance, and because policy makers, teacher education curriculum constructors and other "authority" figures apparently need more evidence. I discuss with Kathy our shared understanding of research and the way that understanding troubles our confidence that we can trust our teacher knowledge born through reflective, critical understanding of our practice. As I speak directly to my fellow teacher and myself, I lay considerable and firm groundwork in research discourses to assure us both that our teacher knowledge can be legitimate; that intentional cultivation of our understanding through practice may be significant to who we are as Beings and teachers; that attention to our Becoming in this way may impact our ethical relationships with children.

Through letters to new teachers, in the third chapter, I attempt to model my delight in fellow teachers, especially those at the outset of their careers, as well as my desire to walk alongside such colleagues with my own experience. In this section, I tried to avoid the "I've been through so much and now I have the answers" sentiment toward these teachers as well as for myself. What good does it do me to believe I have arrived and am not also growing as they are? In these letters, I enact the Naming study I posit in the first two chapters. I narrate vignettes of my early teaching experiences, mostly those that bothered me unexpectedly. Weaving together discourses in the fields of Curriculum Studies and Social Foundations of Education, I create a rich fabric of multiple interpretations through which I study my experiences and Name them. I discover and explore the ethical possibilities which Naming as a praxis engenders.

I wrote the final chapter at the same time as this first introduction, three years from the time of my doctoral defense. Perhaps there are fewer "extra" things as I "try to say something that is right." Ah, perspective. In those three years, in addition to teaching children, I continued in a leadership role working alongside teachers, intentionally mentoring within the framework established through this study. Thus, in my last letter to you, I offer entry points to Naming within your own Becoming process as a teacher in your reflective and critical practice, and I reflect on the possibilities of Naming within one's whole life.

Dear Reader, respected colleague, we are in this together. I hope our conversation through this book engages you further toward your own Becoming and supports your noble work. Please write in response to expand and enrich this dialogue.

Together with you,

Christy Neider

Note

1 Teresa of Avila, "Interior Castles," 290.

CHAPTER 1

Letters to Maxine

1   Prelude

Dear Maxine,

I learned of your passing today. And I wept. Isn't it odd? We never met, and yet I mourn. I think this speaks to the power of the dialogic. My engagement with your work, your text, was an engagement with you; thus, I was changed by knowing and being with you. You see, in your work, I found the language to Name what troubled my heart and inspired my avocation.

> A teacher in search of his/her own freedom may be the only kind of teacher who can arouse young persons to go in search of their own … and children who have been provoked to reach beyond themselves, to wonder, to imagine, to pose their own questions are the ones most likely to learn to learn.[1]

Your personal reflection embodies the path before me. "Who am I? I am … not yet."[2]

I am thankful today for your life and work, and I join many, many scholars who wish to honor you in some way. What I can do, I realize, is to continue to do what you inspired when I first encountered you. I can honor you and your work by pressing on with my own, facing forward to the questions and disquietude, expecting then to find openings for greater and richer possibilities for living and working together with my fellows—teachers, students, friends, and citizens alike.

As I attempt to craft a study framed by your work, I find I simply must talk to you. Objectivity and functional, formal academic writing do not permit me to access both my rational and intuitive considerations for this project. Aesthetically, the traditional tools of academia do not suit the personal-professional Becoming that I hope this study will represent. By writing to you, I hope to enter the on-going dialogic engagement among you and scholars so vividly portrayed in the personal, public letters of Robert Lake's edited collection *Dear Maxine*.[3] Rather than morbid fascination, I hope this work addressed to you recalls the imaginative mode you heralded as a necessity for teachers like me.

Sincerely,

Christine Debelak Neider
June 2014

2   Mindset

> Like Jonas himself I find myself traveling toward my destiny in the belly of a paradox.[4]

Dear Maxine,

I embark upon this study with no small amount of trepidation. Not only is this my first foray into formal scholarship, but I have chosen to explicate a concept in *your* educational philosophy. Maxine Greene! I might as well be an NBA recruit attempting to refine the jump shot of LeBron James. In public. I recognize my hubris. Your work, Maxine, both prolific and profound, shaped scholarship and practice in a number of discourses and disciplines in the field of education, especially in philosophy of education, curriculum studies, and aesthetic education. For me to interpret a concept, "Naming," which you yourself did not explicitly expound, despite its emergent presence in expression after expression of your thought, decade after decade—is an enormous responsibility.[5] In my discomfort and grappling, I recalled some thoughts of Madeleine L'Engle's, which I read the summer before my study began.

> The artist is a servant who is willing to be a birth giver ... but the artist must be obedient to the work, whether it be a symphony, a painting, [an aesthetic work of scholarship!] or a story for a small child. I believe that each work of art whether it is a work of great genius or something very small, comes to the artist and says, "Here I am. Enflesh me. Give birth to me."[6]

L'Engle shares wisdom from author Jean Rhys in support of this thought.

> Listen to me. All of writing is a huge lake. There are great rivers that feed the lake, like Tolstoy and Dostoyevsky. And there are mere trickles, like Jean Rhys. All that matters is feeding the lake. I don't matter. The lake matters. You must keep feeding the lake.[7]

I read this in contemplation of my impending journey with this study. A great deal of angst arose as I considered my work and how I might change the world or at least the things that troubled me. Reclining on my porch, I sighed to dispel the tightness in my chest. For a moment, I listened. The sun bathed me, and I drew soul-warmth from my grandmother's shawl. The trees rustled the quiet of my backyard. A calm rested on me. And the still, small voice in my heart lifted a request: *I just want to serve.*

For me, that lake—the writing, the art, the creation—was about each of us doing our part toward speaking and living a human experience that contributed to the well-being of humanity. Service. The lake was an ethical commitment. I understood my part, as it unfolded presently, to be doctoral study and a future career at the intersection of education and humanity. And in this sense, if this was a way to be of service, then I and my shaky self-esteem didn't matter. My experiences, beliefs, and attitudes had brought me to this point and they would serve me moving forward, positioning me for the coming Work.

But even though I was clear about a calling to serve, I came into graduate school conflicted. While I was so sure about the problems I encountered in my practice, I was uneasy about my attitudes toward the people I'd encountered within it. My own actions and rumblings and disturbances from my practice-oriented past thrust uncomfortably into my clear-minded solutions to the problems in American education.

Doctoral inquiry seemed the next logical step in a quest to fix the problems I had encountered as a practitioner. The drumbeat of my quest had been "Teachers need to be critical thinkers."[8] Teachers who think critically would be the antidote to what ails K-12 education, the relief to my mindset and frustrations with teachers, schools, and learning. If teachers thought critically, then they wouldn't be so narrow-minded and rootless, hitching their practice to each trendy educational bandwagon as it passed. Historical context and discernment would ground their decision-making. If teachers thought critically, they would know their subject well; they would be facile with engaging the depth and breadth of their discipline according to students' abilities and interests. Teachers who thought critically would also be aware of how their pedagogy, content, and classroom environment fit into a larger whole within a school's system of education. All of this mattered because children need to be critical thinkers. Critical thinking is an essential component of democratic citizenry and an essential component of engagement in one's own well-lived life. How could a teacher create experiences to engender and develop critical thinking if she herself was not familiar with the process, rewards, and pitfalls of thinking critically about her own life and practice?

I saw plenty of teachers who fell short of these aspirations. In my undergraduate experience, we history majors read multiple books a week, learning to synthesize and analyze historically as we wrote paper after paper in our seminars. You can imagine how we looked with condescension on the education majors who just seemed to do a lot of coloring. As I watched them make math games, carefully cutting patterns, I felt affirmed. I selected my major for the intellectual rigor the education courses would "never" afford. I proudly entered Teachers College, Columbia University because it promised to elevate the education of teachers to a more rigorous level, in my mind, than most teacher education programs. As a teacher, I witnessed colleagues shun historical context in favor of the latest fad in math education. Others refused to engage in school-wide conversations about students' educational experiences in favor of their pet curricular choices or to avoid any contention at work. At professional conferences, a surprising number of faculty goofed around in the back of auditoriums, dying for lunch and free time. Most of my colleagues (and I) complained a lot about the conditions in which we taught, the administrators and the parents who didn't support us professionally, the way no one listened to us or had our best interests at heart. Victims. Unable to even muster the will to try things differently.[9]

There were a few teachers who represented my aspirations every day. Their gumption and thoughtful probing were the thorns in the side of, well, everyone. When they observed issues problematic to their concept of quality education, they wouldn't let them go. They derailed faculty meeting agendas to force conversations beyond dress code to issues of significance, like cohesion across disciplines and grade levels. They tried to coordinate with each other for the kids' sake. They operated from clearly articulated theories about science pedagogy and what it cultivates in middle school children, for example. They stayed on top of their field, wisely choosing, separating wheat from chaff in research and pedagogy. Despite honorable work and intentions, they had to fight so hard to be heard. This was especially poignant when I substituted in the public schools at the inception of No Child Left Behind.[10] Based upon their experience working with children in the classroom, teachers had little trouble explaining cogent rationale for why high stakes accountability would not get every child reading. Most of them, however, would only talk about it among themselves. A few spoke up in faculty meetings. Even fewer teachers at this time spoke publicly. No one asked them. But a critical thinker would recognize her responsibility to bring to the light the piece that only she could see, I believed.

My focus on teachers was virtually all-consuming. When I thought about students, I had two reactions. First, by default they were the impetus for my moral call to train teachers to be critical thinkers. They are the object of all educational endeavors: we do it for the children, of course! But secondly, I tried not to think about them too much specifically. I definitely rejoiced when old students reached out, but for the most part, I had feelings I couldn't identify related to a number of children in my care. Either way, my feelings were stuffed so far down, they appeared not to affect my intellectual thinking. Intellectual, rational, logical thinking was what mattered anyway.

My clarity in doctoral study was forcefully claimed. I came to the program desirous to support teachers but also embarrassed by and judgmental of them. To be frank, I had participated in much of the positive and negative experiences I just described. I was both fulfilled and ashamed of myself as a teacher. Throughout my teaching, I was driven by similar emphatic clarity, but I also experienced a confounding paralysis when it came to asserting myself for change. In fact, I had even experienced disillusion. By the time I embarked on doctoral study, I had no way to hold these apparent contradictions in my hands at the same time. My certitude about teachers as critical thinkers masked disquietude. Educator Parker Palmer illuminates my dilemma in *The Promise of Paradox*.

> Contradiction, paradox, the tension of opposites: these have always been at the heart of my experience, and I think that I am not alone. I am tugged one way and then the other. My beliefs and actions often seem at odds. My strengths are sometimes canceled by my weaknesses. Myself, and the world around me, seem more a study in dissonance than a harmony of the integrated whole.[11]

And Palmer's further note on contradictions reveals my own response to them is not uncommon but resounds in much of humanity.

> [She] really did have a choice. Instead of accepting, she could have rejected the complexity and contradictions of life, trying—as many people and belief systems, secular as well as religious do—to reduce it to a few variables to create the illusion that things are simple and we are in charge.[12]

Ah! How could we acquiesce and yet stringently claim ideological certitude? When I encountered you in *The Dialectic of Freedom*, I found promise in the paradox as I discovered Naming in the context of your philosophy. There was resonance within me. And even more—there was intangible hope.

> Far more is possible for individuals than is ordinarily recognized, (but) they do not reach out for fulfillment if they do not feel impeded somehow, and if they are not enabled to name the obstacles that stand in their way.[13]

The Work came to me.

You spoke of critical thinking but you wrote about more than thinking and knowing, you illustrated Being.[14] You wrote about Becoming in connected ways with others and for the sake of greater justice. At the time, in my first semester of study, I could not articulate or even understand what your ideas meant to me. In retrospect, L'Engle best describes the resonance.

Instead of understanding—that intellectual understanding which we are so fond of—there is a feeling of rightness, of knowing, knowing things which we are not yet able to understand.[15]

Repeatedly in the ensuing six years of coursework the theme of an ontological commitment to educational practice emerged. Within various concepts I studied: Noreen Garman's dialogic classroom, Alexander Sidorkin's dialogic ways of knowing and being, William Pinar's notion of study, John Dewey's democratic ways of being together, Michael Gunzenhauser's creative intersubjectivity, and Parker Palmer's emotional intelligence[16]; I identified my ethical commitments and ontological framework for practice. Only in your work, Maxine, did these notions fit together holistically with the paradoxical tensions of my mindset. Through your work I recognized the significance of Naming the paradoxes of my Being (personally and professionally) to the kind of freedom that may render the larger commitment to living and teaching possible. The study that unfolded—and continued to do so from my comprehensive exams to the overview proposal to the study and final manuscript—has been an attempt to understand, to enflesh understanding in language, and give birth through language to insight I could only once feel but am coming to embody as I write.

To this point, my study begins perhaps solipsistically, Maxine. Of what relevance is my experience to the practice and scholarship of education? The more I engaged with you, Maxine, the more I felt your resounding affirmation of the relevance of paying attention to my experience. At the heart of this affirmation is your belief that education refers to "multiple modes of becoming, of confronting life's situations, of engaging with others, of reflecting, forming, choosing, struggling to be."[17] To be educated, then, is to make my own way as a person. I am educated so that I may create myself. Therefore, a teacher,

> must engage ... fully in the classroom life so that she can deal with each student as an individual with her own particular structure of cognitive capabilities. She must be ready to take the risk of making decisions without support and, frequently, without hope of justifying them in any final sense. At the very least, she must make decisions authentically and sincerely; she must take responsibility for every act which she performs.[18]

It is incumbent upon me to take account. As a teacher, it is imperative to understand and engage in the lived experiences, the curriculum, which my consciousness has chosen for making sense and lending direction to my Being.[19] I hope that my narrative exploration of that experience might speak to an essence of truth in the heart and work I share with my fellow teachers, which is why this study is comprised of letters to my colleagues as well. The stories we tell ourselves about our work and our lives invite the paradox, the truth, the ethics of our living amongst each other, while they provide space for the possibility of our living with one another in greater freedom of Being. My story, then, is just another rivulet to feed that lake.

Excited to embark with you,

Christine

3   Journey toward Maxine: Troubling Epistemology

> To say that man's essence is his rationality is to say nothing about the existing being, with all his shifting moods, feelings, impulses, fantasies, who is struggling to cope with the world.[20]

Dear Maxine,

As I write, I consciously join numerous scholars and teachers in dialogue with you across time and space.[21] Alive or beyond this world, you speak through your work, always inviting and provoking your readers to attend to our conscious being-in-the world as teachers. We who endeavor to live in the space of "not yet" find in your work profound ideas that speak to our ontological engagement with the world, enabling us to grapple with our ethical and moral commitments. In this letter, Maxine, I would like to explore with you the possibility of an ontological commitment to teaching as opposed to an epistemological one.

I met you through *The Dialectic* in my first semester of doctoral study, and I read this book as a divided soul. Personally, I had begun to run up against previously unseen obstacles to reaching my adult ideals—the ugly side of religion, cracking marital ideals, infertility, addiction, voices in my head intensifying in the "shoulds" of a well-lived life. Because some of these began to surface, I began to "see" life differently than I had imagined it. Thus, in the summer before entering doctoral study, I lived in a tension of frustration/disillusionment and new possibility.

Professionally, I was divided in my concern for my fellow teachers. I had become disgusted by a victim mentality in my colleagues and our profession as a whole, driven, I surmised, by a lack of critical thinking about our work and our own lives. I was equally compelled, however, to be a support to teachers. I greatly admired these people for responding to an ethical calling in a profession robbed of resources, autonomy, and honor. I wanted to help them be everything they wanted and needed to be in service to children. My chorus rang in "if only's." If only they were equipped with the knowledge and skills and habits of mind. If only they practiced them in their own lives as well as in their teaching practice. If only they could bring children into the same acquisition and practice of knowledge skills and habits of mind that we hope will equip and lead children into a well-lived life in our democratic society.

I wanted to help teachers according to this perspective, and in order to provide the necessary support, I needed to arm myself through doctoral study. I intended to take coursework and/or study history of education, history of the disciplines and their habits of mind, institutional history of schools, psychology, or studies that helped me consider not only the mind but also the culture and background of children in schools. All of this, I hoped, would help me to shape teacher education practice in ways that would introduce teachers to the ways of thinking that would, in turn, better help them be effective, ethical educators.

My encounter with you in some ways affirmed my assumption about the relationship between the teachers' lives and experiences and their effect on the children they taught. As I mentioned in my first letter, I was delighted to find this thought in your work:

> A teacher in search of his/her own freedom may be the only kind of teacher who can arouse young persons to go in search of their own ... and children who have been provoked to reach beyond themselves, to wonder, to imagine, to pose their own questions are the ones most likely to learn to learn.[22]

I was aware that I did not know exactly what that meant. I took freedom to mean something related to democracy, but I felt I was onto something that both confirmed my intuition about critical thinking and yet opened a door to something richer and more profound than I could yet imagine. This quote from *The Dialectic* became bedrock for my studies; I derived from it a certainty about my intuition that I previously doubted.

As I mentioned in my previous letter, I gleaned another idea from my first read of your book. It wove its way in and out of my studies and became a profound way of seeing in my personal life as well.

> Far more is possible for individuals than is ordinarily recognized ... but they do not reach out for fulfillment if they do not feel impeded somehow, and if they are not enabled to name the obstacles that stand in their way.[23]

This thought about intentionally articulating, or putting language to what troubled me, was intriguing—even more intriguing was that the act of creating these words created new possibilities. Again, I did not know quite what I was touching, but I could not put it down. Over time, I found that what drew me was the way in which Naming honored my Being.

> Accepting loss becomes the very force of learning, and what one loves when lovely knowledge is lost is the promise of thinking and doing otherwise.[24]

Maxine, my journey through doctoral study, framed by my initial reading of your work in the first semester, could very well be described by Patti Lather in the quote above. At the inception of doctoral study, mine was an *epistemological* position,[25] no, commitment to the teaching profession. Frankly, I wouldn't have known the term "epistemological" at the time, but I was resolute in this commitment. If teachers had enough of the right kind of knowledge and ways of thinking about their profession, then they could do what was best for the children in their care and bring respect to the profession. I was not alone. I knew critical thinking scholars supported this epistemological position toward ethics.[26]

Through my doctoral coursework, I studied the discourses of Instruction and Learning,[27] which represented the very best thinking in this epistemological vein. In an effort to uplift the profession and provide a skilled workforce in the schools, Deborah Ball, rooted in the work of Lee Shulman,[28] developed with others an epistemological framework for "the work of teaching: the core tasks teachers must execute to help children learn."[29] The following really captures this professional perspective, Maxine:

> No one balks at "medical training" or blinks at disciplinary scholars—from historians to mathematicians—who refer to the skills, habits of mind and ways of asking and answering questions that they developed through their "training." Far from reducing practice in these realms to

"mindless routines," this kind of "systematic instruction and exercise" defers to the highly skilled nature of professional practice ... *Training*—a term embraced with ease in other professions-is in fact fully worthy of the intricate demands of teaching.[30]

Numerous scholars have built and are building currently on this premise—accumulation of the right knowledge and right habits of mind—within the discourse of Teaching and Learning. In an attempt to capture the knowledge that is unique to teachers, differing from those in a discipline field but not a teacher of that discipline, Ball created six realms of knowledge that teachers need to know to be effective.[31] Hiebert and colleagues suggest an inquiry stance rooted in the scientific method.[32] Putnam and Borko create new knowledge domains and construct teacher learning activities accordingly.[33] Fernandez has popularized a Japanese teacher learning activity called "lesson study" in which teacher colleagues conduct their own learning within their practice with this scientific method.[34]

The standards for this epistemological commitment to the work of teaching seemed rigorous and exemplary, worthy of the high calling and ethical responsibilities of teaching in my mind.[35] They were delivered to me by professors and researchers with a no-nonsense urgency. There was no room for talk of teaching as an art. Those days were over. Those days robbed children of high quality teachers. This epistemological work was for the sake of children; it was ethical work.[36] In discovering these discourses, Maxine, you would have thought I'd found my people, my justification, and a rich mine of treasure for my passion. But I was troubled as I confronted the very best articulations of my problem and my assumed solutions.

• • •

Fortunately, I had encountered conversations which complicated[37] my epistemological entrenchment in the fields of Social Foundations of Education and Curriculum Studies.[38] Scholars and discourses claimed by these fields had begun to reorient my seeing, as experiences in my personal life had begun to do prior to doctoral study. Road signs emerged through study and helped me Name my disquietude with the epistemological commitment to teaching.[39] In fact, the idea of putting language to my troubled soul, found in my initial reading of *The Dialectic*, became a practice and dialogical tool in my study. As I Named, my grip released on lovely knowledge, my need to be right diminished, my compassion emerged, and I learned to honor and follow my intuitive, ethical inklings into new ways of Being.

Maxine, I will briefly mention some of those signs that directed me toward you, toward an ontological commitment to teaching through Naming. The first sign was my own discomfort, and Parker Palmer gave me permission to direct my attention to that "feeling." Those scare quotes are for the lack of respect I held for emotions in scholarly, or even just educational, encounters. Feelings were not substantive enough to even be recognized without a caveat. Palmer's argument, however, in his article on the new aims of education, gave me permission to explore the troubled feeling and shook my ingrained deference to the rational, logical, "intellectual," ways of knowing.[40] I was *not* comfortable after engaging with this epistemological argument for teaching. I *felt* disturbed. Palmer allowed me to ask "Why?" And Palmer urged me to honor that feeling, and so I took the time to mine my thoughts *and* emotions.[41]

Through reflection, I recalled my professional experience. I knew a number of highly intellectual teachers, disciplined in their practice, critical thinkers.[42] But I saw some of them close their classroom doors so that they could teach without the noise of politics in the halls, offices, and polls beyond. Grumblings slipped out: that no one listened, that they couldn't change anything but the minds of children in their care, anyway. Staying quiet, or being silenced, about the experiences of children in our care didn't quite seem right. In these considerations, Noreen Garman's imperative resonated, delivered drip-by-drip in study group dialogue and always evoking the wince of my soul:

> We force students, by law, to go to a place each day for years of their lives, a place where some children learn that they are very good, some learn that they are adequate, and some learn that they are failures. We have designed these places. Schools are contrived structures for learning and we tend to forget that. I see this as a moral dilemma that we are obliged to struggle with.[43]

We are *morally* obligated to our students. This was my second sign; students are *children*, and in many epistemological discourses merely represented as tools for assessing whether teachers have done their job, as the end product of our social experiment. Morality or ethics were assumed, tied to the acquisition of knowledge in the articulation of the epistemological framework. This second sign gave me pause, though I could not yet understand how knowing enough was not *enough*.

The field of Social Foundations of Education introduced me to critical theory and critical pedagogy.[44] My goodness, what an eye-opener, Maxine. The critical perspective awakened me to the political, institutional, socioeconomic, cultural, and historical structures that inhibited individuals from realizing their full potential and exercising their democratic capacities. This was something new for me, steeped in a culture that saw the rise or fall of a person's life as the sole responsibility of that individual. I shared the American Dream idealism: If you really want it and work hard enough, you can make something of yourself. You can "pull yourself up by your bootstraps."[45] I saw in these discourses the moral imperative to confront and speak to the social injustice. That knowledge, as well as the habits of mind of the critical theorists, struck a blow to my sense of self. My good heart and noble aspirations for children and a democratic citizenry were a bit like a fairy tale and even naive. I recognized the profound need to include this knowledge and critical habits of mind into teacher education—perhaps added to the epistemological framework. Teachers had to understand what it was they were walking into! They needed the habits of mind to critique their circumstances and not take things at face value.

Ball's genres of knowledge did not include a framework for social justice and it certainly did not account for these domains of knowledge, but critical educators like Gloria Ladson-Billings and Lisa Delpit brought the critical stance out of theory and into the relentless practical world of teaching and learning.[46] Nevertheless, within the discourses and field of Instruction and Learning even the efforts to learn enough and ask the right questions for the right perspective felt confining. In some ways, I had added another knowledge realm to my epistemological stance, though perhaps a more pointedly ethical one.

I was troubled by the addition of greater standards of knowledge acquisition, and your good friend William Pinar gave me pause, language, and another sign. I was captivated and bothered incessantly by his counter to a basic cultural/professional premise:

> ... [A]ttention to pedagogy, teaching, instruction ... sets intellectual and political traps for the teacher. Power and responsibility accompany the command of attention. It becomes the teacher upon whom the student depends in order to learn: that is the intellectual trap. It is the teacher who becomes responsible for student learning: that is the political trap. The locus of responsibility, the very site of education, is the teacher, then, not the student. But the truth is quite different. Teachers provide educational opportunities; students are responsible for taking them.[47]

In this light, the effort to thoroughly and precisely develop the epistemological framework for teaching serves to strengthen the historical tendency toward social engineering and instrumental rationality. In essence, the framework says, "If we only make the proper adjustments in teaching, learning, assessment, then we'll get the right product in the end." While I greatly admire the work of Ball and her colleagues and (still) believe it has a place in the work of teaching, I had to see the sign. An epistemological approach in this vein ultimately emphasizes the process rather than the human Beings and their respective responsibilities.[48]

Pinar pointed me to another sign. His turn to the concept of "study" struck a deep chord for me, loosing a binding thread. Study, as differentiated from teaching and learning which disseminate knowledge, enables understanding. It is the means by which we "impose our character upon our roles in life ... It is grounded in individuality, autonomy, and creativity ... and [allows us to] refashion ourselves by engaging freely and creatively with our circumstances."[49]

My mind returned to *The Dialectic of Freedom*, to the morning dew expectancy of something new rising in my soul. Something is different; yet reminiscent of my own parents' nurturing view to strive for a well-lived life, beyond the grades, the knowledge and the skills. Pinar reminded me of my original call to teaching. He reminded me of my first scholar-friend Dewey. His belief that education is life itself was my own.[50] Formal, intentional education should only avail to the human being engaged in it the opportunity to grow along human lines of possibility: to thrive, to grow, to become more human in the most beautiful ways (to borrow a notion from Aristotle as well).[51]

Your good friend, William Ayers, affirmed my commitment to the intellectual work of teaching, but he also pointed me toward these philosophical roots when considering my ethical commitment, which inched me even closer to an ontological stance toward teaching. He wrote,

> Schools are set up to induct the young, and so, whatever else they do, they enact partial answers to humanity's enduring questions: What does it mean to be human? What is society good for? What is the meaning of life and what is "the good life"? What can we hope for?[52]

The epistemological discourses in Instruction and Learning, with the exception of critical pedagogy, did not ask me to do this, but I took these questions to heart and reexamined my understanding of my old friend Dewey in this light. I had taken the social aim, educating for democracy, to be rooted in a political notion of selfhood. I taught toward democracy so that the individuals in my classroom could be good citizens to promote and protect democracy. But a deeper reading of Dewey illuminated democracy as an ethical ideal and a way of being together. Specifically, I found his notion of "function," the partnership between an individual's capacities and a particular environment, provocative.[53] Because, in Dewey's estimation, procuring another's identity was an impossibility, realization of selfhood could only occur by the self. However, the process of self-realization was entirely social.[54] As you know, Maxine, in "Ethics of Democracy," Dewey suggested society offered the individual the "full significance of personality ... in objective form" and was the "chief stimuli and encouragement to realization of personality."[55] An individual could only understand herself in the context of her society by identifying the possibilities for her growth and the avenues and environments by and in which she might engage in growth. An individual was free when she was exercising her function. Situating herself within a place in society, dedicated to realizing her well-being through the development of common interests with other members of society who situated and dedicated themselves similarly, an individual found positive freedom.[56] Her enactment of Being in freedom opened possibilities for others to do the same, thus upholding the ethical ideal in her very existence.

This study supported a growing understanding of your idea of freedom, Maxine, in terms of a situated, connected person being able to participate in her life by choosing.[57] This work also recalled your emphasis on dialogue among others who share a common interest in social/cultural context. I tingled, as neurons connected for me slowly but surely between my old friend Dewey, my new friend—you, Maxine Greene, and my own intuition of what felt true. This sign, through Ayers and Dewey, pointed me toward Being and Being together, toward an ethics within this dialectic.

I was thrilled then to help create a pedagogical encounter crafted by another friend of yours and my doctoral mentor, Noreen Garman, which sought to nurture the capacities for democracy referenced by Dewey. Together with our study group of Social Foundations' teaching fellows[58], she nudged me to look beyond the intellectual capacities to the human will. The dialogic classroom, an intentionally created pedagogical encounter for democratic, deliberative dialogue around issues of social justice in education, relied on the willingness of its participants. Supported by Jerome Bruner's assertion that education should also serve as a strengthener of the will to explore alternate versions of the world,[59] Noreen writes, "Although class members embody (these) rich capacities ... they may, for whatever reason lack the will to bring them to the group."[60]

Yes, I could see the lack of will to contribute to the whole, especially in ethical capacities and contexts. In the Social Foundations classroom, we were concerned with social justice. The intent of the educational encounters was to bring to light the injustice of what is rather than the possibilities of what could be. And this is where frustration came and I saw Noreen's point. With some degree of surprise, similar to my alarm when I entered the profession and witnessed the same in myself and colleagues, I observed my bright, idealistic students, hoping to be teachers, shrink from engaging with complicated, or complex, issues in education. As we read Jean Anyon, Michael Apple, Joel Spring, Phil Jackson, and others, many of my students became disillusioned rather than enlivened and impassioned by the injustice.[61] A resounding urge to blame the individual and their families or cultures echoed semester after semester among my mostly white, female, middle class students. I was honestly flabbergasted at the unwillingness to look at multiple perspectives, or themselves, in an effort to think more critically about our democracy and the education that was meant to support it. This matter of the will was a critical sign. Unaddressed, it didn't matter how much good knowledge one accumulated or skills one developed. Teachers still had to exert their will to use that framework to enact thoughtful, ethical, even efficient practice. I too had to resist an overwhelming sense of defeat as I sensed the enormity of tackling immovable, invisible structural forces. My teaching memories of knowing the "right thing" and the lack of will to do the "right thing" intensified my fear of facing even greater challenges to my ethical commitments.

Oh Maxine, the lovely knowledge lost. As I traversed the doctoral journey, these signs were transformative in terms of orienting me toward something other than an epistemological commitment. That commitment represented something hard and fast, a demand, a mold. But all of the other knowledge I accumulated, the critical habits of mind, these were not the entire picture either. In some ways, I had only enlarged the epistemological framework. In doing so, I had created an even higher standard. I had placed another demand upon teachers. And my experience as a teacher taught me that teachers already come into the profession with lofty goals and intentions to reach their very best for the sake of the children in their care. But a worrisome, tiring, frustrating, and sad number of times, we who are teachers simply could not follow through with our best intent. We could not BE who we wanted to BE and so could not ACT according to our best ethical, thoughtful selves. And I could not ignore this any longer.

Sharon Todd confirmed this for me. Her thought hammered the last nail in the coffin of the preeminence of epistemology to teaching and learning for me. And it set me on my path with you to find a way of Being that matched my ethical commitments. Her concern is that ethics in education is built upon the assumption that teachers act based upon their knowledge: knowledge of the good, knowledge of the best outcomes, or knowledge of others and their concerns.[62] Ethical action based on teachers' knowledge creates the potential for violence, Todd implies as she writes. "Exercising my knowledge over the Other ... the Other becomes an object of my comprehension, my world, my narrative, reducing the Other to me." [63]

This wasn't an epistemological problem. It was an ontological, relational problem. What was in the way of our Being? Further study elicited more signs toward Naming within an ontological stance in teaching, and I will address these in coming correspondence.

Sincerely,

Christine

4   Imaging Ontological Possibilities

> Looking back, I attribute my choosing of questions to my being a woman (and a wife and mother), to my involvement with literature and the other arts, to the persisting conversations with students, to my friendships, and to my awareness of the darkness, of the silence that greets or longing for some cosmic meaning, for a "truth."[64]

Dear Maxine,

This sense that I was coming to a reckoning with vague standards was new, professionally, but I had had some experience grappling with unseen forces in my personal life. There was a time when the standards for motherhood, my work, and, frankly, my womanhood were principles to stand for, live from, and defend. As I matured and found new ways to look at the world, the pendulum would swing. Women should stay home with their young children! (Just like my mom and other Christian women did). Women should work! (I exclaimed as I graduated college and found the world my oyster). But each version of an ideal became a demanding, confining standard, too high and too far to meet. And at either end, I could never listen to my fear. It was too dangerous. If I gave in to a fear, I might knock myself off a "correct" path. Or by listening I might see my confinement and confirm my paralysis, thereby increasing the suffocating power of a standard. It was too scary to let fear speak. Until it was too scary not to. As I mentioned in my earlier letter on my personal journey, by engaging in dialogue, I found a way through the dichotomies, the standards of being, and paralyzing fear to a sense of selfhood. I didn't have this phrase "engaging in dialogue" through most of this process but I did, in fact, confront each standard (and sometimes I faced the sources of these standards). I listened to its voice, questioned its arguments and persuasions, held them up against my experience with them, and made determinations about whether the standard actually reflected something I wanted to Be or Become.

At this time, I began to recognize my fear as my friend, a rich resource communicating understanding of my "self." I saw that whenever I acted based upon my fear, I could bank on that action adversely affecting my "self." That fear exposed my vulnerability; it cautioned me, "Someone may expect something from you that you are not able to give, Christy. What are you going to do?" By hearing this fear, I recognized the red flag and examined, by habit now, what forces were at work. I found in my head my parents, my professors, and some kind of personal-spiritual duty each urging me to think and act from a particular perspective. Even further, I interpreted that I should (this word is another red flag in my process) "be" a certain way if I am to retain love, acceptance, and respect. Having faced this fear over and over through the course of the last ten years or so, I know this fear can be irrational but my experiences also proved there was some truth within the fear. And yet, I also know *now* that I don't want to live beholden to fear and others' perceptions of me. I began to see that a conversation with the voices of the "shoulds" in my life was a way to take care of my "self." I felt more, less condemned, less isolated, less defensive. I think, I live more fully and I am more able to care for others meaningfully and genuinely.

I found scholarship that helped me to understand this personal process. My work with Noreen and our study group prompted further study of a Bakhtinian notion of the dialogic, which Sidorkin attempted to clarify as an ontological notion. These ideas provided language and a sign, toward Being rather than merely Knowing. Dialogue, he argues, is not merely a method of communication; rather, it is the very essence of human existence. Dialogic ontology claims an individual values her existence and understands it in relation to how she makes sense of the existence of other individuals. An individual transcends her own situatedness within familial, social and cultural contexts and identifies with others on the basis of shared humanity. For Bakhtin, that transcendence and connectedness allows individuals to discover new and integral aspects of being human. Ideas are birthed at the point of dialogue between human beings. Sidorkin believes those points of contact where different voices meet is where the "truth about myself is born." Self-realization cannot be produced from within an individual but by being open to the polyphony of human voices. For Sidorkin, those voices exist within and without the individual. Our ability to make moral choices, he says, relies on a multitude of perspectives available to us through internalization of views and voices that belong to "our significant others" which have the ability to reason and persuade. The growth, development, and learning of individuals, then occur within dialogic relations. Thus, while humans can exist biologically, full existence occurs when humans know and value the dialogic relation. The authentic human is in an open process, not unlike Dewey's concept of function, of tuning in to one's unique position among other people by the peculiarities of every particular dialogue with particular human others.[65]

I don't want to sound like I'm lecturing you on theory here, Maxine! However, this ontological theory deeply resonated with me. Here I am, a single entity and yet, I make sense of myself to the extent that I am aware and engaged with others in a conversation that could potentially alter my Being in the world! I mean, holy smokes! Does this not sound like my personal experiences, Maxine? It also clarified some of my discomfort with critical theory. While the claims to political oppression ring true, as an individual, I do not experience them as oppressive in their overarching meta-narratives, critiques of narratives though they may be. I experience them in embodied form, within my immediate community and in my own head. I could Name them and what I perceive they stand for. I could engage with them and find openings for alternate ways of seeing them or their confining argument.

Further into study, Foucault helped me to see that oppression does not necessarily take the form of overt political limitations on my freedom. His concept of subjectivity, constructed through the norming of my being-in-the-world by the exercise of disciplinary power relations, resonated.[66] So much of my existential pain seemed to come from my understanding of the world in terms of standards—standards that often times I experience as embodied but at other times seem to be "just the way things are." This was clear personally and professionally. Zembylas described what was happening to me in my teacher role. I "learned to internalize and enact roles and norms assigned to [me] by school culture through what are considered 'appropriate' expressions and silences."[67] Oh my goodness, Maxine, this explained so much of my professional experience: trying to be a good teacher!

The explanation of normative assumptions in this light could have made me feel powerless; instead, my study of Foucault profoundly relieved me. One of my mentors, Michael Gunzenhauser, contends that we "underestimate our complicity with normalization" for our exercise of power equates to our choosing among possibilities.[68] He argues that resistance is not simply reactive, rather it "emerges from critique ... exposing the historicity of normalizing practices."[69] Here again, I found critique as a way of creating openings toward freedom; the kind of freedom you suggest, Maxine, that allows for choosing oneself among a multitude of possibilities. The "it's just the way things are" argument was built layer by layer historically through language, structures, and habit, all of us contributing knowingly or not. Foucault posited that we, as constituted subjects, have a choice creatively to constitute or be constituted by power relations at work in our lives. Name or be named.[70] These nameless, personally experienced oppressions now had language and discourse around them. It made sense to me with my critical thinker's background, supported by critical theorists' charge, that I could question them! I could get to the root of them! I could decide if I wanted to give them power or if I wanted to live by alternate standards or ideals. Foucault's work, as a sign, suggests knowing the "right" only indicates the recognition of a standard, of a normed understanding of the possibilities for one's Being. In a Foucauldian sense, knowledge could be relevant in so far as it opened alternate possibilities for a subject's Being.

And yet, even Foucault troubled me. I could not completely buy the post-structuralists' argument that contributed to the death of the "subject," that we are only an accumulation of power relations operating upon us.[71] This came from my engagement with feminist discourses and my growing feminist self—another sign, pointing me toward an ontological stance and away from the prioritization of the epistemological. I think, Maxine, that you might understand this journey of mine. I will digress just a bit to share a significant feminist Naming experience, supported by these discourses, most importantly those embodied in Adrienne Rich's poem "Diving into the Wreck."[72]

> ... I came to explore the wreck
> The words are purposes.
> The words are maps.
> I came to see the damage that was done
> and the treasures that prevail ...
>
> the thing I came for:
> the wreck and not the story of the wreck
> the thing itself and not the myth ...

In a "ways of knowing" course in the Philosophy of Education, I wrote a response to the epistemological question: How do *you* know? I read the "you" as emphasized. In this question, I read aggression. I read, "Who do you think you are to make these claims of truth and reality?" I read, "Your claims are suspect because of how you come to know." I read this question and I was vulnerable. My vulnerability stemmed from several roots. Most deeply, I held an old understanding that there is only one way to come to know. That way has several names: the rational, the logical, the analytical ... By any name, I saw it in my father, my brother, and my husband. This way of knowing is linear; it has little use for narrative; it directly leads to a point; the point has inherent value and is privileged as the way to understand whatever spare description precedes it.

We joke in my family about how long it takes my mother and I to tell a story; my sister and I call each other specifically to luxuriate in the communication of the minutia of our lives. As one of us—my mother, myself or my sisters—inevitably becomes side tracked by another story, which we believe has some merit in the larger narrative, it's typical for one of us to point out how we could only do so because we are talking to each other. And we quickly affirm one another: we want to hear it all! If it is important enough for you to talk about, if you want to talk about it, then it is meaningful ... It is meaningful to me. But we can only do this among ourselves because we know it isn't the most logical way to talk, and we believe it isn't worth hearing outside of our relationship. There is inherent devaluing of how we make meaning and what is meaningful for us. As a result, I attempted for many years to be something other than I am. I tried very hard to be logical, to get to the point, and to avoid descriptive narrative, especially in a clearly demarcated intellectual realm and especially around men. I was never safe, never comfortable in my own skin and thus, I think, detached and unable to make "real" sense out of my experiences in those environments. Usually, I found I had a grasp on something if a peer or friend or my husband gave me the space to talk it out. Journals became useful tools as well; my entries were imagined conversations, reflections upon my experiences.

In addition to a learned way of knowing through family relations, I believe that those experiences also reflected an inherent dichotomy of the masculine and feminine. A sociocultural, historical privileging of the masculine reinforced my family's way of Being and my learned way of knowing. While I had begun to recognize my need to talk to understand, I truly embraced it in the last few years after I had my son. The complexities of motherhood dynamically affected me and compelled me to talk to other women more frankly and authentically than I ever had before. I found in most other mothers willing and grateful companions in dialogue about the experience of motherhood. The minutia MATTERS in mothering. The implications of every little mothering move feel enormous, almost too much to bear alone. And many of us found that fathers, our husbands and partners in many ways, did not experience parenting in the same way. The isolation could not be borne and, in this way, I found kinship in strangers, depth in acquaintances, and mutuality in friends. Through sharing experience and finding those experiences shared, we reflected together. We made sense of our lives. Our relation encouraged particular values that imbued our way of being with meaning. And we came to appreciate, even rely upon, this particular way of knowing together. About the same time, I began to read feminists and read about feminism for school. I engaged in a deeper way than ever before because I was coming to honor women's ways of Being and knowing in the world.[73] I read to understand myself, my friends, and our historical moment. The discourses, both in their historical formation and their arguments, affirmed me.[74] For centuries, women have been gathering together, talking and reflecting on their experiences as a way of knowing, to Name and/or to change their historical moment. The scholarship of women in the last century demonstrates women's ways of being and knowing as meaningful and valuable in myriad circumstances. As I have read, written, and thought about these discourses, I have come to value myself, my way of making sense of the world, and I am becoming more and more intentional and creative in my way of Being in the world.

And so Maxine, I could not fully embrace the constituted subject. Nel Noddings Named my frustration and wrote that many feminists questioned with me: Just as I am beginning to claim my subjectivity, the subject is "dead"?! These feminists claim instead "a partially constituted subject—one who is shaped in large part by her situation in time and place but also at least in part by her own decisions and actions."[75] Thus, I searched for a notion of Being which engaged the dialogic, a critical stance, and a personal intuitive inkling toward the world.

I felt so very near a sacred truth in my Being (and experience) as I read Freire, a final and confirming sign toward an ontological notion of teaching and learning. His work teased my memories of *The Dialectic*: ontology, freedom, language in Naming/dialogue and personal/social transformation. Freire establishes the need for an ontological commitment and a praxis of Naming. I want to specifically call forth his related ideas because you align yourself closely with them.

> Humans, however, because they are aware of themselves and thus of the world—exist in a dialectical relationship between determination of limits and their own freedom ... [I]t is not the limit-situations in and of themselves which create a climate of hopelessness, but rather how they are perceived by women and men at a given historical moment: whether they appear as fetters or as insurmountable barriers.[76]

Therefore, ontologically, we require Naming:

> To exist, humanly, is to name the world, to change it. Once named, the world in its turn reappears to the namers as a problem and requires of them a new naming. Human beings are not built in silence, but in word, in work, in action-reflection.[77]

Naming, though, occurs within dialogue with others who want to Name the world and who have taken it upon themselves to speak their word. Thus, one cannot Name the world for another.

> Dialogue imposes itself as the way by which they achieve significance as human beings ... It is an act of creation.[78]

Freire goes on to suggest that dialogue is mediated by the world, which must be confronted to be transformed.

> Reflection upon situationality is reflection about the very condition of existence: critical thinking by means of which people discover each other to be "in a situation." Only as this situation ceases to present itself as a dense, enveloping reality or a tormenting blind alley, and they can come to perceive it as an objective-problematic situation—only then can commitment exist. Humankind emerge from their submersion and acquire the ability to intervene in reality as it is unveiled ... a step forward from emergence.[79]

Both personally and professionally, as a woman and a teacher specifically, Naming and human freedom resonated with me.[80] And like my encounters with Sidorkin and Foucault, I thought initially that I had discovered my philosophical kindred spirit in Freire. But with each, there was a space unaddressed or overlooked, slightly off from the ethical project that tugged at my heart. Sidorkin's dialogic ontology caused me to re-imagine Being, but ultimately, he focused on the web of relations as opposed to individuals. Foucault's subject, historically constituted, was fruitful to my seeing; missing from his work, however, was the visceral experience of the "single one," and therefore also missing was the effect on emotion and will in the existential crisis that was proving central to my way of Being in the world. Freire, too, rooted in Marxist critical theory, focused on the oppression evolving from socioeconomic class. Though ontologically he addressed individuals, he does so primarily within a political framework, humans as political beings. Dewey's reconstruction of experience within his democratic theory enticed me in what I thought was the end of my search. Ultimately, his faith and prioritization of a scientific method of self-creation for social ends over the on-going challenge of human beings choosing themselves were not closely enough aligned with my concerns.[81] Noreen listened as I groped for a firm philosophical foundation and, knowing how often I returned to you, encouraged me to read more of your work. I cannot wait to discuss with you my engagement with it!

Sincerely,

Christine

5   Naming and Being

> A self is not something static, tied up in a pretty parcel and handed to the child, finished and complete. A self is always becoming. *Being* does mean becoming, but we run so fast that it is only when we seem to stop—that we are aware of our own *is*ness, of being.[82]

> When language is limited, I am thereby diminished, too.[83]

Dear Maxine,

To this point, I've described my interpretive journey through doctoral study. Moving forward, I imagine us in deeper conversation, perhaps in your living room "salon." Had this privilege been mine, I might have heard you speak from the breadth and depth of your work. My own engagement would have been reflected in what my interpretive lens brought forward from the landscape of your work. Thus, here, in the remaining portion of my letters to you, I am using quotations of your work as one might in an academic article; however, for me, these quotes represent your voice in our conversation. And I respond. My interpretive lens has framed the meaning I have made of your work.[84]

As I delved into your work, I found you were concerned, as am I, with "the single one." This did not discount the external structures addressed by critical theorists or the Foucault's exercise of power relations both of which foregrounded forces at work in human freedom or self-creation. I hear you suggest, they are not determinant, rather:

> No external categorization, naming or definition can touch that crucial awareness; each man relates himself to the world around from a perspective that is within.[85]

You focused on the need for the existing individual to create herself, inwardly conscious of her own Being and, yet as a being-in-the-world, obliged to relate herself to the situations marking her life in time.[86] Consciousness, phenomenologically speaking, helped you to explain the dialectical relation of the individual to the world.[87] Constituting one's world becomes a search for coherence in response to the existential sense of incompleteness or meaninglessness. The existential response is to confront the unease, "the inevitability of such feelings and moods and to live them as aspects of the human condition.[88] An individual in opposition to this stance would merely exist as one of many. This kind of person becomes automatic, thinking in stereotypes, unable to learn or become. And you call my attention to our interpretations of the world.

The crucial point is that we, as conscious beings, constitute the world we inhabit through the interpretations we adopt or make for ourselves. To take that work for granted as predefined or objectively there is to be uncritical, submissive, and submerged.[89]

The emphasis in existential thought discourse and in your own is that self-creation, this Becoming, is intentional. You address this by the existential fundamental project, first. Just as my parents urged me, "put yourself in circumstances that will help you grow and become who you are, Christy!" the existentialists' fundamental project is the intentionally created or demarcated space and conditions for self-creation.

Early in your writing, you define your space of study within the lives and work of teachers. Maxine, you had me at "hello." Yes! I agree that individuals who choose to teach must see teaching as you say,

> His fundamental project, his means of creating himself ... [for] his effectiveness, like his authenticity, depends to some degree upon the nature of his personal commitment. He must acknowledge he cannot live in two domains-private and professional ... [And thus a] true account of teaching is one which can take into account the intention of the living individual who is making choices, guiding discoveries, identifying possibilities.[90]

But, Maxine, in my own life, somehow, deciding to make teaching my fundamental project was not enough. Conversely, I began to see that my *desire* to live my life to its fullest and continue to grow was not enough to overcome some roadblocks in my teaching. Professionally, I discovered that my best effort to be an effective, caring teacher was not enough to navigate through politics, my colleagues' opinions, and parents' and students' needs and still make choices that aligned with my ethical and professional commitments. It is only in hindsight that I recognize this as my experience. At the time, and for years, what I felt was nagging discomfort after making a decision, feeling, somehow, I did not care for the student adequately and yet convinced I had no other way to act in the circumstance. I felt diminished in some way. I know I mentioned earlier that personally, as I matured into adulthood, I experienced oppression, marginalization of my own sense of Being. "Shoulds" and "musts," principles of a well-lived life for a woman, wife, mother, daughter, student, Christian, citizen, embodied in the voices of people I loved and respected all echoed in my head, even arguing with one another. The cacophony disturbed my ability to make decisions. I felt paralyzed by contradictory, opposing, or sometimes just different versions of who I was or was supposed to be. I fought depression and addiction, actively, but many times resigned myself to a smaller existence than what I had hoped for.

This was my central frustration: this slip into submergence, this inability to become what one imagines possible. "Apathy, withdrawal, paralysis" this, too, has been your deep concern through the length of your work. How can one move from the decision of the fundamental project to actual participation in one's Becoming within the framework of the project? You detail the possible obstacles, where freedom leaks out. They may be mundane habits or routine[91] or the experiences of human suffering. What Hannah Arendt calls "the rule of Nobody," which you believe is exacerbated by that positivistic separation between knower and known and the subsequent link to "technological controls," contributes to this feeling of imposition.[92] This results in "the sense that the self as participant, as inquirer, as creator of meanings has been obliterated."[93] You feared individuals would numb themselves and not take responsibility for their own creation. You borrowed Freire's term *false consciousness*, "a confinement of experience, a restriction of meaning," to further illuminate this point.[94]

Maxine, your specific illustrations of the dilemma of teachers in this light provoked me. I am saddened that your description of this dilemma as early as 1967 has only intensified in the era of neo-liberal, high-stakes accountability and the corporatization of public schools.[95] Their "individual potency is somehow drained away [as] ..."

> They have faced apathy and withdrawal in their classrooms; they have felt the disenchantment of children who cannot "believe." They have been asked to govern their curriculum planning with considerations of "national policy" rather than thorough consultation of the requirements of the individual child. They have administered countless tests; they have grouped and classified in ever more elaborate categories. They have become aware of moral ambiguities and the rejection of traditional codes ...[96]

Yes, I shake my head in recognition and am stirred by your clear identification of the problem, in compassionate and rousing tones, about the oppression of teachers from without.

> Because teachers are living beings, they suffer objectification like other members of society; they are also thrust into molds (and) play roles in many ways defined by others, although their interpretations of these roles must in some manner be grounded in an understanding of themselves.[97]

Ah, the problem of our cultural machinations and teachers' internalization of cultural expectations are both are to blame!

When I hear the language of "best practices," I am reminded of your emphasis on educational talk as a significant barrier to becoming. These days, we are supposed to think of ourselves as "facilitators." You know, we don't deposit knowledge; we facilitate students' acquisition of it. *eye roll* I can see why, in your opinion, this kind of language reduces teaching work to images too solidified to be questioned, too trite to render much meaning to teachers' work but that nevertheless provide a safe and superior rational for apathy. The language hangs like veils between the teacher, with the capacity for existential response, and "the phenomenology of the situation."[98]

Later, you highlighted the education and credentialing of teachers as problematic in this vein, referring to the latter as inhuman in that it sorts and ranks people according to market demand. In an era when national accreditation is a coup for a teacher, and competency can be evaluated from several videotaped lessons with accompanying standards-based lesson plans, your words from so long ago do not ring hollow. Technical training or a "competency-based approach" may cause teachers to see themselves as "mere transmission belts or clerks."[99] You also worried that, facing myriad issues that children bring to the classroom as the result of the depersonalizing of society, teachers will become "drifters" or "authoritarians," unable to cope with the unimaginable difficulties of the students' and their circumstances. Finally, the increasing pressure on teachers, demanding "basics, discipline, and preparation for the world of work" obscures the purpose of education that addresses "the question of their students' endangered selves."[100] This kind of oppression, you insisted, has led many teachers to take on a "rock-like self, the more he identifies with a doctrine, a single idea ... and we are left with a thousand unresolved questions. Is it possible to transcend "chance, circumstances, [and] the time?"[101]

I propose the angry coalition of educators that is the Badass Teachers Association as evidence of the maddening frustration and paralysis of policies and practices you identified decades ago.[102] Teachers post in the online forum, weeping and screaming, the conditions of their working environment and the effect of policy on the children they teach. While the mission of the organization is to resist these policies, day after day their online presence represents teachers' inability to richly Become.

And herein the existential condition of freedom leaps to the fore, demanding attention.

> There is the question of being *able* to accomplish what one chooses to do. It is not only a matter of the capacity to choose; it is a matter of the power

to act to attain one's purposes. We shall be concerned with intelligent choosing and, yes, humane choosing, as we shall be with *the kinds* of conditions necessary for empowering persons to act on what they choose.[103]

You first address the intentional work toward freedom when you moved in your work to explicate Schutz's notion of "wide-awakeness." The opportunity to live fully cannot be grasped without attention to the possibilities of freedom. Early in your work you note his definition:

> Heightened consciousness and reflectiveness are meaningful only with respect to human projects, human undertakings, not in a withdrawal from the intersubjective world … Human beings define themselves by their projects and that wide-awakeness contributes to the creation of the self.[104]

When I think of wide-awakeness, I imagine myself inhaling, eyes forward, spine outstretched, tippy-toes engaged, expectant, watching. For what? For freedom: its opportunities and impediments for my Being. The inclusion of wide-awakeness in your philosophy seemed to me to be your pedagogical move to "awaken people to their freedom."[105] But later in your life, Maxine, you spoke to your good friend Janet Miller and clarified your meaning of wide-awakeness.

> It's a matter of breaking with the natural attitude, the passive acceptance of the way things are, of what those around us keep insisting is normal … We have to move beyond the moments of mere passive empathy, working through if, at all possible, our own feelings of unease, of helplessness or blindness, along with our longings to take refuge somehow at the center. It's what I draw from Schutz, that emphasis on wide-awakeness. Consciousness is not an inner state. Acts of consciousness grasp the appearance of things, jut into the world. Consciousness always OF something, never empty. So, wide-awakeness, for me, is not just awareness, but more like Freire's ability to name the world and act on it.[106]

Wide-awakeness, then, is a specific action of attention but it is also one of critical interpretation and action. This comes to light specifically as "Naming" when you directly addressed freedom in *The Dialectic of Freedom*.

Prior to this work, primarily in conversation with teachers over the course of your scholarship, you include freedom as both the goal and the condition of human Becoming, but your emphasis was different. From whetting our imaginations with the possibilities of the existential life, to prompting our intentional stance as stranger to unshackle ourselves from preconceived notions, from painting a phenomenological picture of attention to our Becoming to urging us into countless aesthetic encounters to imagine our lives, our teaching, and our world differently, Maxine, you endeavored to lift our eyes beyond our circumstances to ignite the striving within each of us. You provided myriad opportunities to engage in our Becoming. But it was not until *The Dialectic* that your vision of freedom and its key were brought to the fore. Maxine, within several paragraphs of *The Dialectic*, you announce vivid concern for a precise notion of freedom in relation to the existential project of human becoming individually and socially, drawing as you do on the work of colleagues, history, and literature.

Rather than the contemporary definitions of freedom, "untethered" notions which entitle humans to be left alone and unengaged with themselves or their communities, Maxine, your focal interest is "in the capacity to surpass the given and look at things as if they could be otherwise" with others who share this project.[107] Drawing on Foucault's notion of thought as freedom, I hear you suggest:

> Thought, after all grows through language; without thought or "freedom in relation to which one does," there is little desire to appear among others and speak in one's own voice.[108]

And it is here that my kinship with you grew, Maxine, because you write that we do not grow or change or become different simply by our desire to do so. You remind us that many of us experience ourselves as limited and overwhelmed, "victimized and powerless." But how are we to counter what Foucault called "'power,' that which inheres in prevailing discourse, in knowledge itself?"[109] I hear your response,

> There is general agreement that the search for some kind of critical understanding is an important concomitant of the search for freedom. There is also agreement that freedom ought to be conceived of as an achievement within the concreteness of lived social situations rather than as a primordial or original possession. We might, for the moment, think of it as a distinctive way of orienting the self to the possible, of overcoming the determinate, of transcending or moving beyond in the full awareness that such overcoming can never be complete.[110]

In your work, it seems, we know the experience of freedom when we are able to choose and act within and in response to our social and cultural context.

Enacting this praxis, which you borrow from Freire, we see not only our own fuller Becoming, but the possibilities for social transformation as well.[111]

Now, Maxine, some refer to your concept of Imagination as this praxis, this re-orienting of our Beings. Of course, you spend much time in your scholarship on "Imagination" as a requirement of hope. But, Maxine, you do not talk about Imagination explicitly in this carefully articulated argument for a definitive notion of freedom in the same way you discuss "Naming." Instead, Imagination and Naming are distinct yet interdependent parts in the existential project of Becoming, an important dialectic for freedom I believe you argue throughout your work. Is this an accurate assessment? You begin with the Existentialist's use, with Sartre:

> For Sartre, they do not reach out for fulfillment if they do not feel impeded somehow, and if they are not enabled to *name* the obstacles that stand in their way. At once the very existence of obstacles depends on the desire to reach toward wider spaces for fulfillment, to expand options, to know alternatives.[112]

Anyone who has studied your thought to some degree may easily see your notion of Imagination in this second sentence. And certainly, the significance of nurturing the aspirational qualities of our Becoming cannot be over-emphasized. Curiously, however, not many have elaborated on this verb or action "Name," as they have done with "Imagination."[113] You are not surreptitious with its use in *The Dialectic* and once noted, it is hard not to see this concept throughout your work.

Building on Sartre, Dewey, and later Charles Taylor, you initiate discussion of "Naming" in the context of perception and acceptance. Situated freedom necessitates the acceptance of our defining circumstances as ours.[114] You acknowledge the substantive barrier of fear in facing such circumstances; however, once owned, aspects of the lived world as experienced by the individual can then be perceived as resistant to the freedom required for one's Becoming.[115] Naming, as critical interpretation, "reveals lacks and deficiencies ... and may open the way to surpassing and repair."[116]

Naming, then, is a kind of understanding enabled through calling out the dialectic, its themes and symbols, in language. Maxine, you want to dismantle dichotomy, highlighting instead "a dialectical relation marking every human situation: the relation between subject and object, individual and environment, self and society, outside community, living consciousness and phenomenal world."[117] I know you emphasize that while these are distinct, apparently opposite poles, we can presuppose a mediation between them. In using language, your hope is to bring to light the tension within the mediation, not as a problem to be solved; rather, you write that "freedom is dependent on understanding these ambiguities and developing a kind of critical distance with respect to them."[118] Often times, you refer to whether or not one can "feel the weight." With Sartre, you suggest, "All have ... to be perceived as obstacles, if freedom is to be achieved ..."[119]

As we have come to expect from you, Maxine, much of this book is comprised of aesthetic encounters that help us to "see" what you mean. Vividly, you illustrate through history and literature individuals reaching for freedom through Naming. You explain your purpose in writing *The Dialectic*:

> We are going to look at how some of them, *naming* what stood in the way of their becoming, were able to posit openings in what appeared to most observers to be closed situations, openings through which they could move.[120]

First, there is Hannah Arendt's portrayal of the French Resistance, as remembered by René Char.

> He spoke of the ways in which the members of his group came together ... how they felt they had been visited for the first time in their lives by an "apparition of freedom." [T]hey had become challengers, had taken initiative upon themselves and therefore, without knowing or even noticing it, had begun to create that public space between themselves where freedom could appear. They had, as it were, posited what the Nazis were doing in France as obstacles to their own projects, affronts to their own chosen principles, barriers to their self-realization ... By *naming* the atrocities and the repression as obstacles to their shared existential undertaking, they focused attention on them as factors to be resisted, to be fought, perhaps to be overcome.[121]

In this, we see a reaching for freedom: the weight felt by each one, the taking of responsibility for themselves situated in their lived world, "seeing" these aspects as resistant to their Becoming, the importance of Being together for their own projects, and this Being together initiated a shared, social project as well.

With the example of *The Color Purple,* you clearly demonstrate the significance of Naming obstacles in order to perceive alternate ways of Being, to freedom in Becoming.

> Through connection, [Walker] moves Celie not only to put questions to her familiar world, but to begin to name it and act so that she can transform, through her own actions, her own life ... Not noticing, she could not question. When she questions, a space opens for her; she knows she has to take initiatives, that she has to name the "man" if she is to see. She has been, in some familiar and deadly way, oppressed.[122]

In the instance of the Civil Rights movement, Maxine, I noticed the emphasis on the shared project, toward what you would later call "social imagination."

> [Martin Luther King, Jr. and Rosa Parks] came together to name the obstacles—the unjust laws, the segregation codes, the fire hoses, the clubs, the power structures themselves. Having named them, having found them obstacles to their own becoming, they took action together to overcome ... they chose themselves in all their diversity as morally responsible for kindred goals.[123]

How these pieces fit together in a holistic view of your scholarship comes up in conversation with Janet Miller, again. She explains,

> In relation to "wide-awakeness," Maxine conceptualizes actions taken in naming the world as grounded in what she calls social imagination.[124]

In your elaboration, you assert the importance of the individual's Becoming to social imagination. "Let it begin with me," if you will.

> Social imagination has to do with the recognition of the need for and shaping of a social vision. It has to do with the possibilities of desirable changes in the social world—the fight for justice, for equality, for a decent and humane way of living together. *I want people to become wide-awake enough* to come together to act on the possibility of repair.[125] (emphasis mine)

If in fact, Naming is so central to what you and I claim to be *the* project of human existence, then *what does it look like*? I found clear direction in your illustrations of the work of women in *The Dialectic*: you frame the project as "telling the truth" because the "not yet" is always to a degree "concealed" until a "human being tries to tell the truth and act on it."[126]

> The first step, as all, is (to use Martin Heidigger's term) to "unconceal" (1971, p. 54 ff). Concealment does not simply mean hiding; it means dis-

sembling, presenting something as other that it is. To "unconceal" is to create clearings, spaces in the midst of things where decisions can be made. It is to break through the masked and the falsified, to reach toward what is also half-hidden or concealed.[127]

You suggest making one's lived world visible and questionable through language by the categories and labels which organize it.[128] You encourage engagement with the dialectic in this sense.

Surely, it would have made a difference if they came to realize that what they took for granted as "natural" and inexorable was a human construction, susceptible to reinterpretation and change. It would have made a difference if they could reconstitute their own internalized visions of themselves. We are back to the dialectic, back to the subject/object relationship and the realization that freedom can be achieved only in an ongoing transaction, one that is visible and legible to those involved.[129]

You want to draw attention to the growing capacity to express thought and by such expression become more and more aware of what is there. "I am eager to think in terms of the inner experience of language ... to view it as a gradual, cumulative overcoming of inarticulateness, a breaching of boundaries, a bringing of the world (or aspects of the world) into visibility."[130] Earlier in your work, without using the word "Naming," you describe this process phenomenologically in your understanding of consciousness.

Consciousness does, however, have the capacity to return the precognitive, the primordial, by "bracketing out" objects as customarily seen. The individual can release himself into his own inner time and rediscover the ways in which objects arise, the ways in which experience develops. Not only may it (interior journey) result in the effecting of new syntheses within experience; it may result in an awareness of the process of knowing, of believing, or perceiving. It may even result in an understanding of the ways in which meanings have been sedimented in an individual's own personal history.[131]

How does one identify what so often are normative ways of being? Where the desire to be different may not be enough ... where does one start? You write earlier in the book and in your work of the feelings associated with naming: *weight, disquietude, tension.* These emotional responses to one's lived world are "flags" beckoning attention. In this chapter, you also address other emotional responses that may be indicators of obstacles. For example, the Grimke sisters,

19th century activists for abolition and women's rights, take action toward an alternate envisioning of their world, prompted by "their own observations," coupled with *shame*. It seems the negative emotional response, such as shame or *fear*, is an intuitive nudge to attend to our Becoming. Likewise, frustration, which so easily surfaced as women began to write their own stories in the nineteenth century, could be seen as another such nudge.

> The truth about themselves, when revealed, had to do with what it meant to struggle against confinement and constriction ... of daily life. They were unlikely to name their men as their oppressors, nor the inequitable system that deprived them of civil rights and equality of regard. It was, most often, the infinity of small tasks, the time consuming obligations of housework and child care that narrowed spaces in which they could choose.[132]

At other times, it is in the *futuring* of consequences[133] or at times, the *reflection* upon those experienced that direct us to see our relations as confining. Your inclusion of James' *Portrait of a Lady* serves as a warning. The main character, Isabel,

> did not realize that she had been caught in the "traps and treacheries" of a moneyed and stratified society until she suddenly became privy to Gilbert's (her husband) intimacy with her admired friend Madame Merle—and recognized that she been betrayed, actually "sold." Only then did she allow herself to name her predicament and acknowledge her unhappiness. Only then did she see that she had ushered herself, her felt autonomy, into "the house of darkness."[134]

It was also useful to me that you consider "gaps" as obstacles as well. My journey through doctoral study might be framed as such. That, in fact, it may not be that one experiences "outright coercion" or even "walls." Instead, there may simply be a *sense of something missing*. In writing of the struggles of minority writers who found ways to tell their stories, you conclude:

> In most cases, they felt and named a gap between what they were and what they desired to be; and, making an intentional effort to cross the gap, knowing it was an alternative to remaining where they were, they felt provisionally free.[135]

Finally, through your stories of the work of women and later as you present the American struggle for civil rights, Maxine, it is clear how significant *multiple perspectives* are to human Becoming for the purpose of identifying the obstacles that stand against individual and social freedom. Multiple interpretations of shared worlds enlighten one's own experience, presenting itself as possibly resistant to the individual's free pursuit of Becoming.

> Human consciousness is always situated; and the situated person, inevitably engaged with others, reaches out and grasps the phenomena surrounding him/her from a particular vantage point and against a particular background consciousness.[136]

Further, you argue, Naming begins with the individual's own landscape, which by nature is limited and requires multiple perspectives for the opening of possibilities.

> On the ground of pre-reflective landscape or understanding, the individual develops or learns to take a variety of perspectives on the world. The perspectives available are always partial. The individual sees profiles, aspects of the building entered in the morning, the school or the agency ... There is always something more to be discovered each time he/she focuses attention. As important, each time he/she is with others—in dialogue, in teaching-learning situations, in mutual pursuit of a project—additional new perspectives open; language opens possibilities of seeing, hearing, understanding. Multiple interpretations constitute multiple realities; the "common" itself becomes multiplex and endlessly challenging, as each person reaches out from her own ground toward might be, should be, is not yet.[137]

Maxine, in fact, you encourage the intentional taking of alternative positions in order to counter one's own perspective, "to see" what was previously invisible, to *make strange the familiar*.[138] Of your own journey toward Becoming, you write, "I came to see that the taking of odd or unaccustomed perspectives can indeed make a person 'see' as never before,"[139] and so:

> I wanted to see through as many eyes and from as many angles as possible; and I believe I deliberately sought visions for a long time that might enable me to look from the other side of the looking glass, to begin to feel what Alfred Schutz called the multiple realities or provinces of meaning that mark lived experience in the world.[140]

Multiple perspectives for you are always embodied, however. They always occur through connection. For women, you look to Carol Gilligan's work and explain that the existential risk incurred by Naming requires experiences of friendship and sisterhood in order for them to question their world. While mutuality and care may not be enough to enable the freedom of your concern, you determine that spaces for freedom, public spaces, must be established "so that what is indecent can be transformed and what is unendurable may be overcome."[141] Maxine, your examples in history and literature of people defying oppression represent individuals who come together or who are provoked by their connection with others. They are people who felt victimized but "acted to make a space for themselves in the presence of others."[142]

Herein we see a vision of social imagination. The requirement of multiple perspectives for the individual's Naming toward Becoming also creates a space for shared visioning of social responsibility, a project of Imagination and Naming. The mutuality of individual and social Becoming is made quite palpable in your telling of the narrator's decisions and perspective at the end of Ellison's *The Invisible Man*.

> He says that "the mind that has conceived a plan of living must never lose sight of the chaos against which that pattern was conceived. That goes for societies as well as individual" (p. 502). What he speaks of as "chaos" may be the weight of what cannot be changed but can be understood: the deceptions of upward mobility; the plunging "out of history" on the part of so many the falsifications of ideologies; the dead ends of violence. His determination to invent a plan of living represents his refusal to be what the world has made him. And, it may be, because he speaks again of social responsibility, that his plan will bring him into a changed relationship with others to challenge what has been taken for granted and to transform the world.[143]

I believe, in a sort of conversation with you in your work, I've laid out a clear picture to this point of how central the concept of Naming is to your overall existential and phenomenological philosophy. In partnership with Imagination, Naming—critical interpretation and understanding through language—becomes a way of Being toward realizing the freedom required for existential Becoming. It is an action to be taken, where lack of will, apathy or paralysis may otherwise stand. Once taken, once one sees differently, choices open where there was once only a normative way of Being. And it is within this experience of freedom, in which the individual may continue to choose to create himself. I would contend, however, and I think you'd agree, Maxine, that praxis, as Naming, is in itself a choice to Become. It is the choice to be in the "not yet" of our Becoming.[144] It is resistance to stasis and the blasphemy that we are finished. It is an act of honoring our Being and its possibility.

In my next letter, I want to address how you have explicitly addressed the concept of Naming within educational encounters. I am excited to "do" philosophy with you, Maxine!

Sincerely,

Christine

6   Naming, Learning, and Social Imagination

> To teach in the American school today is to undertake a profoundly human as well as a professional responsibility.[145]

Dear Maxine,

What I love about you, Maxine, is that it has never been enough for you to think philosophically. You *do* philosophy, and you have done it within the field of education.[146] Your existential concern for the "single one" and her self-creation extends to every human being in the educational encounter. Most philosophers of education are concerned with the learner and learning in the encounter, and in this, you also have a perspective (though your central concern is the teacher for the sake of the learner). Learning itself, you offer,

> is a conscious search for some kind of coherence, some kind of sense … The activities that compose learning not only engage us in our own quests for answers and for meanings; they also serve to initiate us into the communities of scholarship and (if our perspectives widen sufficiently) into the human community, in its largest and richest sense.[147]

There it is! Naming … as learning! In the search for coherence. In the introduction to discourse communities. Learning is a Naming process when learning orients the student to his own Becoming.

> The point is that learning must be a process of discovery and recovery in response to worthwhile questions rising out of conscious life in concrete situations. And learning must be in some manner emancipator, in the

> sense that it equips individuals to understand the history of the knowledge structures they are encountering, the paradigms in use in the sciences, and the relation of all of these to human interests and particular moments of human time ... If learning focuses upon lived life, it should enable persons to recognize lacks in the situations through which they move. Recognizing lack or deficiency (infringements on personality, exclusion, or neglect), they may learn how to repair and transcend. Much depends on how their life situations are understood, on the degree to which they can avoid taking what is for granted, on what they are willing to risk.[148]

And of course, you address curriculum and pedagogy, potent ingredients in the educational encounter.

> Curriculum ought to provide a series of occasions for individuals to articulate the themes of their existence and to reflect on those themes until they know themselves to be in the world and can name what has been up to then obscure.[149]

You argue that the "text" of curriculum and the interpretive activities surrounding that text are essential for Naming. "If curriculum is regarded as an undertaking involving continuous interpretation and a conscious search for meanings, there are many connections between the 'grasping' of a text and the gaining of perspectives by means of the disciplines."[150] Historical texts, for example, become "an initiation into the history to which we all belong ... the effort to grasp the self-formative process may become grounded in an ongoing interrogation of the social world we and our fellow human beings have constructed over time."[151] What these texts and acts of interpretation accomplish is a participation that allows self-perception. The text foregrounds a problem that the student may find personally relevant against his background consciousness or landscape, offering an opportunity to perceive his own meaning-making process and possibly reconstitute the meaning of his experiences.[152] You provide the experience of Karl in Kafka's *Amerika* as an example of such a process:

> At this point, however, once the specific problem has been determined to be thematically relevant for him, it can be detached from the motivational context out of which it derived. The mesh-work of related perplexities remains, however, as an outer horizon, waiting to be explored

or questioned when necessary. The thematically relevant element can then be made interesting in its own right and worth questioning. In the foreground, as it were, the focus of concern, it can be defined against the background of the total situation. The situation is not in any sense obliterated or forgotten. It is *there*, at the fringe of Karl's attention while the focal problem is being solved; it is to an extent "bracketed out." With this bracketing out and this foreground focusing, Karl may be for the first time in a condition of wide-awakeness, ready to pay active attention to what has become so questionable and so troubling, ready to take the kind of action which will move him ahead into a future as it gives him perspective on his past.[153]

Providing structures of knowledge that presents itself to the consciousness as possibility, requires that the student himself be engaged in generating the structures and lend the curriculum his life. In other words, committed action is required of him.

There is, however, a pedagogical problem. Few students come to the curriculum with a wide-awake consciousness. Maxine, you describe young people who "withdraw from the challenge of learning and growing. They are the sort who must be urged into the disquietude, the sense of crisis in which existential awareness begins."[154] You reminds us that they too are part of a social culture in which,

> Everywhere, guidelines are deteriorating; fewer and fewer people feel themselves to be answerable to clearly defined norms ... because of proliferation of bureaucracies and corporate structures, individuals find it harder and harder to take initiative. They guide themselves by vaguely perceived expectations; they allow themselves to be programmed by organizations and official schedules or forms ... For far too many individuals in modern society, there is a feeling of being dominated and that feelings of powerlessness are almost inescapable.[155]

Thus, the pedagogical challenge "is, in part, to remind people of these things, to arouse them to some degree of committed rationality."[156] You write,

> It is because of the apparent normality, the given-ness of young people's everyday lives, that intentional actions ought to be undertaken to bring things within the scope of students' attention, to make situations more palpable and visible ... Without being "onto something" young people

> feel little pressure, little challenge. There are no mountains they particularly want to climb, so there are few obstacles with which they feel they need to engage ...[157]

Students need help to "see," to go beyond, to find reasons to ask difficult questions and to engage in naming/learning. They need a kind of futuring and spark of curiosity only accessible by the individual's imagination.

Your response to the pedagogical problem is, of course, through aesthetic encounters in education that are "bound to disturb"[158] and alight imagination.

> Imagination [is] that particular cognitive capacity that is too often ignored in educational talk and yet is so fundamental to learning, to being in the world ... Imagination [allows] us to move into the "as-if"—to move beyond the actual into invented worlds, to do so within our experience. To enter a created world, an invented world, is to find new perspectives opening on our lived worlds, the often taken-for-granted realities of everyday.[159]

You recommend the arts, literature, and opportunities for multiple perspectives to tap into students' curiosity and imaginations.

> For those authentically concerned about the "birth of meaning," about breaking through the surfaces, about teaching others to "read" their own worlds, art forms must be conceived of as ever-present possibility ... (The) arts will help open the situations that require interpretation, will help disrupt the walls that obscure the spaces, the spheres of freedom to which educators might someday attend ... With situations opening, (then) students may become empowered to engage in some sort of praxis, engaged enough to name the obstacles in the way of their shared becoming.[160]

Maxine, I have come to see that most of what you write concerning children/students is for an audience of teachers. And you do so to portray the shared goal of the educational encounter: both students and teacher are human beings endeavoring to engage in their own Becoming. Time and again, you insist that the educational experiences described above, which might enable learners to transcend and commit to their own Becoming, can only be created and nurtured by teachers who attend to their own Becoming. The requirements for these experiences then are two-fold: 1) these experiences must be the goal of the teacher's work and 2) the teacher herself must be "in search of his own freedom" in order to arouse the same search in young people.[161] Both requirements, you assert, depend upon the nature of our personal commitment, our fundamental project—our means of creating ourselves.[162] This is so very different from my earlier epistemological conceptions for educational encounters which left me with a sense that I should know or should grow into already if I didn't!

From a concrete, practice perspective in the educational encounter, when you write for teachers, you attempt both to inspire our imaginations and to help us to Name potential obstacles in our lived-teaching-world. You note "contemporary schooling resigns teachers and students to functionaries" and offers "no space for dialogue, no use of the arts for disrupting the status quo.[163] The status quo for teachers is particularly debilitating for existential work in public schools due to the hierarchy of authority, routinized curricula and experiences, and inauthentic interactions with learners, who seem more and more to be products rather than subjectivities. You understand, Maxine, that teachers,

> fearful, perhaps irritated or skeptical, will be likely to accede. Their acquiescence may have nothing at all to do with their convictions ... They simply see no alternatives. The reality they have constructed and take for granted allows for neither autonomy nor disagreement. The constructs they have inherited do not include a view of teachers as equal participants. That, they are prone to say, is the way it is.[164]

Such a perspective renders teachers artless and weary. "They have neither the time, nor energy, nor inclination to urge their students to critical reflection."[165] And this, for you, is simply unacceptable, not only for the sake of the students but for the sake of the teachers' own freedom and Becoming.

You invoke our aspirations as well, by asking us to recognize our role in our students' humanization, both in terms of students' freedom as well as their ethical existence, and then to take action, by Naming, to that end.

> I am convinced that if teachers today are to initiate young people into an ethical existence, they themselves must attend more fully than they normally have to their own lives and its requirements; they have to break with the mechanical life, to overcome their own submergence in the habitual, even in what they conceive to be the virtuous, and ask the "why" with which learning and moral reasoning begin.[166]

Thus, Naming as praxis is a central component in the life and work of teachers as well. You spent much of your career and scholarship calling out the questions and imagination of teachers. You encourage us to be "personally engaged with [our] subject matter and with the world around."[167] We must be "alert to the models and paradigms affecting our vision so that [we] can break through the screens of seductive abstractions when we confront the individuals in our classrooms—and take the risk of intervening in their lives."[168] You insist we come not only to love the questions,[169] but also "to be made aware of how (we) personally confront the unnerving questions present in the lives of every teacher, every parent: What shall we teach them? How can we guide them? What hope can we offer them? How can we tell them what to do?"[170]

Threaded throughout your work is a gentle prodding, a reminder to teachers of the subjectivities of our students and the possibilities of our intersubjective, dialogic engagements with our students when spaces are opened in communities of trust. In this, you suggest the ethical relation within this ontological commitment.

> Knowing we are "other" with respect to [the student], we can nonetheless work for encounters with him for the sake of his authenticity and our own ... We may succeed in entering an "I-Thou" relationship; we may dare to engage in dialogue with him and open ourselves to him as he opens himself to us. But we recognize if we do this, that we are opening the way to tensions and anxieties, the disquietude that is so essential to growth ... Tranquility will not pervade such an atmosphere; the members of the class will not be put at ease. But neither will they be dealt with as objects, cases, specimens. Engaged as subjectivities as well as minds, they may discover the possibility of being with others and at the same time being themselves. They may learn one is not doomed to be a thing in an objective, public domain, so long as one ventures out of coolness and separateness –so long as one rebels through questioning and forming, and insists on the right to grow.[171]

I believe your conclusion might be that such encounters, birthed by the praxis of their teachers, empower students "to engage in some sort of praxis, engaged enough to name the obstacles in the way of their shared becoming."[172]

• • •

Ah, Maxine. Your work is really quite beautiful. I have been so struck, as you can tell, with Naming within your philosophy and its power to cut to the quick of the ethical gaps of an epistemological framework for teaching and teacher learning. It has engendered a reprioritization of my philosophy so that ways of knowing are relevant in so far as they open possibilities for ways of Being.

Equally compelling has been the possibility of a Naming praxis to help me to live and teach in ways that may align more closely with my ethical intuitions.

For this reason, Maxine, I was drawn to a study within Curriculum Studies in which I might explore Naming as praxis within teachers' lives. As I've noted, you address this in your work and you provoke our taking responsibility for our Becoming as teachers. I believe your writing and speaking bloomed from your own Naming praxis and imagination within your everyday world of teaching and Being. In this book, I assume an autobiographical project in which I Name the disquietude of tension in my life, most specifically related to my early teaching experiences. I wonder what intentional Naming will afford in terms of new ways of seeing the experiences of new teachers, new ways of seeing my own practice and ethical commitments, and new possibilities for Being teachers today. I hope that my own process might also provide a way for me to walk alongside fellow teachers, as you have done, as they develop their own Naming praxis.

I consider this study a leap into my own process, and as I move forward, I hope to do so before an audience of teachers. In the coming letters, I write to educator-colleagues and converse with them as you have done for years in your Lincoln Center talks. I endeavor to embody the humility and disciplined engagement you exemplified, searching for language and interpretation to Name and Imagine our mutual Becomings.

Sincerely,

Christine

Notes

1. Maxine Greene, *The Dialectic of Freedom*, 14.
2. William Pinar, ed., *The Passionate Mind of Maxine*, 1. Maxine's response when asked, "Who are you?"
3. Robert Lake, ed., *Dear Maxine: Letters from the Unfinished Conversation*. I began this work prior to Maxine Greene's passing. Due to the personal nature of my engagement with her text, I felt personally connected to her, all the more so reading the intimate connection many have expressed through letters addressed to her over the years.
4. Thomas Merton, *The Sign of Jonas*, 11. Throughout this document, I intend to use theological or religious-like sources and language. I assert the value of understanding curriculum as a theological text as documented by William Pinar, William Reynolds, Patrick Slattery, and Peter Taubman in *Understanding Curriculum*, 606–660. Scholars who represent these discourses such as James McDonald, Dwayne Huebner, David Purpel, and Marilyn Llewellyn, argue that spiritual or religious language counters the technical, skill-based framing of practice and the "obsessive criticism of the status quo" of educational scholarship. In doing

so, it foregrounds the moral, ethical, and aesthetic dimensions of education, refocusing our attention to consciousness and the human situations existing between people in educational relations. These are central concerns of mine and of Maxine Greene, and thus I find this language enriches the complications and possibilities within this work. See Bibliography for full citations of these discourses.

5 I wish to convey my understanding that *Naming* is a contested concept. While generally it is agreed that Naming represents the centrality of language to a person's ability to make or bestow meaning and in education can be seen as a concept in literacy development, my use of Naming stems from a critical orientation. This perspective suggests that the ability to Name implies human agency in the human being's quest for freedom. My study further differentiates Greene's existential and phenomenological notion of Naming, which, unlike pure critical theorists, sees the search for freedom as an existential one with social consequences rather than a purely political one.

6 Madeleine L'Engle, *Walking on Water: Reflections on Faith and Art*, 10.

7 L'Engle, 16.

8 Critical thinking emerged in the early 1960s from the work of Robert Ennis, who defined it as "reasonable reflective thinking that is focused on deciding what to believe or do," and claimed it consisted of particular thinking skills. Harvey Siegel insisted that critical thinking is tied to principles upon which reasoning might be founded. John McPeck argued that this kind of thinking must be domain and content specific for its richest uses, and Barbara Thayer-Bacon hoped that critical thinking might also engender self-awareness. Critical thinking in the last forty years has become an educational ideal, Richard Paul (1993) asserts, which "extends far beyond the conception of critical thinking as a course of study, and even beyond critical thinking seen as a set of skills and dispositions. As an educational ideal, critical thinking is an image of the ends of education: students who are rational and autonomous, who can apply critical thinking in their courses of study and in their lives as members of a social and political community." See this discussion in William Pinar, William Reynolds, Patrick Slattery, and Peter Taubman, eds., *Understanding Curriculum*, 773. It is this notion of the educational ideal which imbued my posture that teachers themselves had to be critical thinkers.

9 Alan Block succinctly captures the frustration: "Though we teachers continue to complain vigorously, we remain subjugated. We too often refuse to make payment. Ultimately, we complain because we feel powerless; we forget what it is we have to offer as payment. We complain because complaint is action without cost. We are not free and we remain enslaved. But I think we have to learn to pay for our tickets." Alan Block, *Ethics and Teaching*, 6.

10 Or NCLB, the 2001 Act of Congress which reauthorized the Elementary and Secondary Education Act.

11 Parker Palmer, *The Promise of Paradox*, 2.

12 Palmer, xxxvi.

13 Greene, *The Dialectic of Freedom*, 5.

14 "Being" or "Becoming" as I use them in this study bear the mark of an existential, phenomenological philosophy. I describe this in greater detail through an exploration of Greene's philosophy in subsequent letters. I also find it useful to think about Being or Becoming, in relationship to education, as *educational growth*. As John Dewey and then James Henderson explain, this "growth" is not measured by how much more content or how many more skills a student has acquired. Rather, Dewey asks "does this form of growth create conditions for further growth, or does it set up conditions that shut off the person who has grown in this particular direction from the occasions, stimulus, and opportunities for continuing growth in new directions? What is the effect of growth in a special direction upon the attitudes and habits which alone open up avenues for development in other lines?" John Dewey, *Experience*

and Education, 36. Also, see James G. Henderson and colleagues, *Reconceptualizing Curriculum Development*, 6.
15 L'Engle, 15–16.
16 Garman, *On Becoming a Dialogic Classroom*; Sidorkin, *Beyond Discourse*; Pinar, *The Synoptic Text Today*; John Dewey, *Democracy and Education*; Michael Gunzenhauser, "From Empathy to Creative Intersubjectivity"; Palmer, "A New Professional."
17 Maxine Greene, *Existential Encounters for Teachers*, 4.
18 Greene, 4.
19 Maxine Greene, "Curriculum and consciousness" best conceptually addresses my meaning here.
20 Greene, *Existential Encounters for Teachers*, 7.
21 Three volumes of tribute and scholarship have been written and collected by educators and others in reference to Greene's work. Robert Lake, ed., *Dear Maxine*; William Ayers and Janet Miller, eds., *A Light in Dark Times*; William Pinar, ed., *The Passionate Mind of Maxine Greene*.
22 Greene, *Dialetic of Freedom*, 14.
23 Greene, 5.
24 Patti Lather, *Getting Lost*, 13.
25 Epistemology, broadly, is the study of theories of knowledge: what counts as knowledge, what is the criteria for validation, who gets to claim what knowledge is of most worth, for example. An epistemological stance toward teaching, then, might focus on what teachers need to know, why they need to know it, who gets to decide what knowledge counts and from where such knowledge might be derived. Nel Noddings suggests, and I agree, that teachers need to be concerned with epistemology. "First teachers need to make decisions about the status of the material they teach: is it true? Does it matter whether it is true? Second, teachers need to evaluate the "knowledge" that comes to them from educational research. Third, teachers must decide whether knowledge long reserved for a few students should or can be made accessible to all." Nel Noddings, *Philosophy of Education*, 122–123. My point here is not to ignore or dismiss epistemology but to situate it within an ontological stance toward teaching.
26 Richard Paul, "Ethics without indoctrination." Critical thinking scholars suggest that ethics is tied to moral reasoning and that moral reasoning might be defined within a taxonomy of moral reasoning skills. Further, some categorize ethics as a particular kind of thinking. "One ethical insight all humans need to acquire is that ethics is frequently confused with other divergent modes of thought that often leads to a failure to act ethically (while assuming oneself to be acting ethically). Skilled ethical thinkers routinely distinguish ethics from domains such as social conventions (conventional thinking), religion (theological thinking), and the law (legal thinking)." Linda Elder and Richard Paul, "Ethical Reasoning in Education."
27 The Department of Instruction and Learning at the University of Pittsburgh is organized by content discipline. Pre-service teachers are instructed primarily within these domains, taking methods and content courses according to their specialization. Doctoral students in this department typically specialize by content domain, but this course "The Study of Teaching" attempted to cross disciplines through instruction of this epistemological approach to teaching. The course was designed for prospective professors of teacher education.
28 Lee Shulman, an educational psychologist, first expressed that teachers' knowledge might best be categorized into three domains: subject matter content knowledge, pedagogical content knowledge, and curricular knowledge. Lee Shulman, "Those Who Understand: Knowledge Growth in Teaching," 4–14.
29 Deborah Ball and Francesca Forzani, "The Work of Teaching and the Challenge for Teacher Education," 497. See also, Deborah Ball and David Cohen, "Developing practice, developing

practitioners. And see also, Deborah Ball, Mark Thames, and Geoffrey Phelps, "Content knowledge for teaching," 389–407.
30 Ball and Forzani, 498.
31 These realms are organized into content knowledge (common content knowledge, horizon knowledge, and specialized content knowledge) and pedagogical content knowledge (knowledge of students, knowledge of teaching, knowledge of content and curriculum), according to Deborah Ball, "What do math teachers need to know?"
32 James Hiebert, et.al., "Preparing teachers to learn from teaching," 47–61.
33 Ralph Putman and Hilda Borko, "What do new views of knowledge and thinking have to say about research on teacher learning?" 4–15.
34 Clea Fernandez, et.al., "A US-Japanese Lesson Study Collaboration Reveals Critical Lenses for Examining Practice," 171–185.
35 For other scholarship in this vein, see: Sharon Feiman-Nemser, "From preparation to practice," 1013–1055. See also Pam Grossman, et.al., "Teaching practice," 2055–2100. And Frank Murray, *The Teacher Educator's Handbook: Building a Knowledge Base for the Preparation of Teachers*.
36 Ball and Foranzi, 508. The ethics here seem to be tied to a sense of professionalism as well as to a sense of urgency "in the context of deep concern about poor and uneven learning in our nation's schools."
37 William Pinar introduces the concept of complicated conversations. "Informed by theory in the humanities, arts, and interpretive social sciences, curriculum theory is the scholarly effort to understand the curriculum, conceived here as 'complicated conversation.'"

As for curriculum itself ... "Through study of the school subjects, individual human subjects come to form in society, at particular historical moments, with specific and changing cultural significance. Because the curriculum is that complicated conversation between teachers and students over the past and its meaning for the present as well as what both portend for the future, curriculum theory is focused on *educational experience*. Through the study of academic knowledge, we articulate our experience in the world so that we may understand what is at stake in what we read and say in schools and in other educational settings. The curriculum is our key conveyance *into* the world." William Pinar, *What is Curriculum Theory?*, 1–2.

My curricular conversations were perhaps thin due to the narrow introduction to education provided to me through teacher prep courses and professional development.
38 "The purpose of Social Foundations study is to draw upon [the] humanities and social science disciplines to develop students' interpretive, normative, and critical perspectives on education, both inside and outside of schools." Council for Social Foundations of Education. A major concern of the field are issues of social justice related to education.

The central question in the field of Curriculum Studies is *what knowledge is of most worth?* It is "animated by ethics, history and politics. As such, it is an ongoing question, as the immediacy of the historical moment, the particularity of place, and the singularity of one's own individuality become articulated through the subject matter ... one studies and teaches." Pinar, *What is Curriculum Theory?*, xv.
39 William Ayers considers Shulman's list of teacher knowledge and acknowledges these "attempts to ... form a basis for the argument that teaching has become a more fully developed profession." However, they imply "that teacher knowledge is highly rational and technical— or that it ought to aspire to be so—rather than being multidimensional and intersubjective" William Ayers and William Schubert, eds, *Teacher lore*, 149.
40 Parker Palmer, "A New Professional: The Aims of Education Revisited," He writes, "The new professional needs to know how to name and claim feelings, neither denying nor being dominated by them; discern whether and how they reflect reality; ask if they have consequences for action; and if so, explore them for clues to strategies for social action."

41 On this account of incorporating more than the rational mind, see also John Dewey, *Human Nature and Conduct*, 136–137. "More 'passions' not fewer, is the answer ... Reason ... signifies the happy cooperation of a multitude of dispositions ... The man who would intelligently cultivate intelligence will widen, not narrow, his life of strong impulses while aiming at their happy coincidence."

42 To me this meant that they endeavored to know their subject well in addition to the latest pedagogical knowledge and skill that were purported to be significant. They made choices about their instruction accordingly.

43 Noreen Garman, *Teaching a Moral Craft?* and in conversation with me over the last ten years. As Noreen explains this imperative, you can see how I was not unique in my ponderings: "One question I ask my classes (seasoned public school educators) to ponder and discuss about a mindset for teaching: 'The common narratives about teaching tend to reflect teaching as a science-like profession, and, occasionally, as art. However, it's important, also, to think about teaching as a moral craft. Why is it, then, that we are challenged to think of teaching as a moral craft?' I'm always surprised at how difficult it is for educators to find language about moral imperatives related to teaching."

44 Some of these discourses can be found in the following: Michael Apple, *Teachers and Texts*; Henry Giroux, *Teachers as Intellectuals;* Jean Anyon, "Social Class and the Hidden Curriculum of Work"; Joel Spring, *Deculturalization and the struggle for equity;* Philip W. Jackson, *Life in Classrooms*.

45 This sentiment pervades American culture supported by a liberal political tradition which suggests that if an individual has political liberty, that she is free to make of her life what she chooses. This tradition does not contextualize the individual within her historical, socioeconomic, or cultural circumstances. See the following as an example of how entrenched this idea is, as well as the typical critique it attracts: Carmen Rios, "Debunking the 'Pull Yourself Up by Your Bootstraps' Myth."

46 The following are a sampling of their work, which have each been beneficial to my study. Linda Darling-Hammond, "Effective teaching as a civil right; Linda Darling-Hammond and John Bransford, *Preparing Teachers for a Changing World*; Lisa Delpit, *Other People's Children: Cultural Conflict in the Classroom;* Lisa Delpit, "Lessons from Teachers"; Lisa Delpit, "Will it educate the sheep?"

47 William Pinar, "The Problem with Curriculum and Pedagogy," 120.

48 Michael Gunzenhauser demonstrates in his study of the effects of high stakes accountability in A+ public schools that the testing climate intensified knowledge accumulation as an educational priority. He found that "excessive focus on knowledge works against the cultivation of selves capable of thinking and exploring possibilities." Gunzenhauser, *The Active/Ethical Professional*, 155.

49 "Study is the site of education ... While one's truths—academic knowledge grounded in lived, that is, subjective and social experience—cannot be taught, McClintock (see 1971, 169) underscores they can be acquired through the struggle of study, for which every individual has the capacity, but not necessarily the will (or the circumstances, I might add)." Pinar, *The Problem with Curriculum and Instruction*, 119. In his exploration of study, Pinar builds upon an earlier work on the concept of "study": Robert McClintock, "Toward a Place for Study in a World of Instruction," 161–205. Pinar also draws from the contemporary scholarship of Alan Block, for example: Alan Block, *Talmud, Curriculum, and the Practical*.

50 John Dewey, *Experience and Education*, 1933.

51 I am not, of course, the first to settle the aims of education on the growth or Being of humans. Some of these include: Dewey, *How We Think*; Ted T. Aoki, "What is it to be educated?" Maxine Greene, *Landscapes of Learning;* James Henderson, *Reconceptualizing Curriculum Development*.

52 William Ayers. *Teaching Toward Freedom*, 9.
53 Dewey, "Ethics of Democracy." See also, Robert Westbrook, *John Dewey and American Democracy*.
54 Dewey, *Democracy and Education*.
55 Dewey, "Ethics of Democracy," 22.
56 Dewey, "Outlines of a Critical Theory of Ethics" Dewey wrote that a primary external factor is the other individual members of one's society; thus liberty is contingent upon members' attitudes toward others' right to pursue freedom as well as toward the pursuit itself.
57 Dewey wrote of negative and positive freedom in "Ethics of Democracy." Freedom merely from social restraint (negative freedom) is empty if individuals do not have the personal resources to pursue the realization of self. Without the power over his own accomplishment (positive freedom), individuals are left rootless, captive to the ideas, directions and suggestions of others. Individuals must have the freedom to determine, deliberate, and invent in order to engage his capacities with his environment toward the achievement of his well-being.
Greene, in *Dialectic,* illustrated the complexities of freedom as a dialectic: freedom from and freedom to. She situated Becoming in freedom, noting that individuals need freedom from obstacles that create inertia, but individuals also require freedom to Become what they will become. As individuals engage in their own Becoming they must engage the internal/external dialectic as well. This dialectic is contrasted with notions of one or the other: freedom means "leave me alone" or freedom means "I can do whatever I want to without regard for the possible effects on others."
58 At the University of Pittsburgh, the Social Foundations of Education course was a prerequisite for undergraduates planning to pursue a certification or master's degree in teaching. I taught a section of this course, and the teaching fellowship also included participation in a study group with other teaching fellows of this course. While we collaborated in our planning, this group was also a space for deep reflective study
59 Jerome Bruner, *On Knowing*, 117.
60 Noreen Garman, "On Becoming a Dialogic Classroom." Garman specifically addresses students' will through a list of capacities, which students are asked to engage in as a member of the dialogic community. These include, for example, "the willingness to: … consider issues of social justice; to value multiple perspectives; to engage in the shared learning of the class members; to risk; to strive for warranted positions; to struggle for balanced participation; to care about the health of the group; to push intellectual reasoning to insightful and theoretical levels; to become an active member in a community; to appreciate the complexities of a postmodern world."
61 See note 25 above. Also, Joel Spring, *The American School 1642–2004*.
62 Gunzenhauser, "Creative Intersubjectivity," 70–71.
63 Sharon Todd, *Learning from the Other*, 15. This notion is also supported in the work of Ted T. Aoki. "An educated person … guards against disembodied forms of knowing, thinking and doing that reduce self and others to things, but also strives for embodied thoughtfulness that makes possible living as human beings" (Ted T. Aoki, "Themes of Teaching Curriculum," 114).
64 Maxine Greene, "Towards beginning," in *The Passionate Mind of Maxine Greene*, ed. Wm Pinar, 253.
65 Sidorkin, *Beyond Discourse*. See also, Mikhail Bakhtin, *The Dialogic Imagination*.
66 Michel Foucault, *Discipline and Punish* and *The History of Sexuality*.
67 Michalinos Zembylas, "Interrogating 'Teacher Identity,'" 112. See also, Gunzenhauser, "Normalizing the Educated Subject, 39.
68 Gunzenhauser, "Care of the self in a context of accountability," 2230.
69 Gunzenhauser, "Resistance as a component of educator professionalism," 29.

70 "We must make allowance for the complex and unstable process whereby discourse can be both an instrument and an effect of power, but also a hindrance, a stumbling block, a point of resistance and a starting point for an opposing strategy." Foucault, *History of Sexuality*, 101.
71 Foucault is among post-structuralists who pronounced the Subject dead. In this he suggested the individual is not autonomous but is instead produced or constituted discursively through power relations. "Discipline 'makes' individuals; it is the specific technique of a power that regards individuals as both objects and as instruments of its exercise." Foucault, *Discipline and Punish*, 170. "Discourse transmits and produces power; it reinforces it, but also undermines and exposes it, renders it fragile and makes it possible to thwart it." Foucault, *History of Sexuality*, 101.
72 Adrienne Rich, "Diving into the wreck."
73 Mary Belenky, et.al., *Womens' Ways of Knowing*.
74 Some of those discourses are represented here: Carol Gilligan, *In a Different Voice*; bell hooks, *Talking Back*; Jane Duran, *Worlds of Knowing*; Patricia Collins, *Black Feminist Thought*. Sandra Harding, *Science and Social Inequality*. Nancy Hartsock, "The Feminist Standpoint."
75 Nel Noddings, *Philosophy of Education*.
76 Paulo Freire, *Pedagogy of the Oppressed*, 99.
77 Freire, 88.
78 Freire, 88–89.
79 Freire, 109.
80 Mary Daly, *Beyond God the Father*, 8. "Women have had the power of naming stolen from us. We have not been free to use our own power to name ourselves, the world, or God."
81 Dewey's confidence in a scientific method seemed to ignore that individuals may not chose to use it. Noddings, *Philosophy of Education*, 67. Also, as James Henderson argues in *The Path Less Taken.*, Dewey's communitarian emphasis may subsume the individual, whereas Greene's work centers the existential individual and posits her as socially constructed and constructing.
82 L'Engle, *A Circle of Quiet*, 32.
83 L'Engle, *Walking on Water*, 35.
84 Situated within the research tradition of phenomenology (see note 87 below), interpretation is movement toward understanding. "The phenomenological task is to live so that language becomes visible, becomes … a "lens" (Pinar et al., 446). The nature of my understanding is hermeneutic, and I must acknowledge that when I speak of the meaning of Greene's work, my own meaning, as the interpreter, enters in as well. Michael Crotty, *The Foundations of Social Research*, 102.
85 Greene, *Existential Encounters*, 8.
86 Greene, 7–8.
87 "Phenomenology is a disciplined, rigorous effort to understand experience profoundly and authentically. For phenomenologists, experience and its conceptualization are distinguishable modalities. First is experience; language and thought follow." Pinar et al., *Understanding Curriculum*, 404–405. Van Manen, as explored within this text on 407, characterizes phenomenological research as investigating lived experience, reflecting on one's taken-for-granted view of things in order to practice thoughtfulness about what it means to be alive. A key quality of phenomenology is that it does not produce knowledge for its own sake, rather knowledge production is meant to disclose what it means to be human. "To work phenomenologically, is to dwell with language in ways so that the problems of the everyday world become different problems, and the classroom becomes a different reality." Pinar et al., 422.
88 Greene, *Existential Encounters*, 12.
89 Greene, *Landscapes of Learning*, 17.
90 Greene, *Existential Encounters*, 155.
91 Described by Virginia Wolfe as the "cotton wool of daily life" in Greene, *Dialectic*, 2.

92 Greene, *Dialectic*, 54.
93 Greene, 12.
94 Greene, 12.
95 For further descriptive and critical reading of the contemporary problematics of schooling and their impact on teachers, see Peter Taubman, *Teaching by Numbers* and Gunzenhauser, *Active/Ethical Professional*, for example.
96 Greene, *Existential Encounters for Teachers*, 16,
97 Greene, *Landscapes of Learning*, 38.
98 Maxine Greene, *Teacher as Stranger*, 80.
99 Greene, *Landscapes of Learning*, 38.
100 Greene, 80.
101 Greene, 34–35.
102 Badass Teachers Association (BATS) is an online organization of over 56,000 teachers and their supporters, which began June 2014. As an activist organization, it derived its purpose from the following rationale: "At a time when high stakes testing and attacks on teacher autonomy have become official policy of both major parties, supported by the wealthiest people in the nation, and cheered on by the media, teachers may have reached a tipping point regarding the campaign of demonization directed against them, and the micromanagement of their classroom lives, especially because leaders of teachers unions—who have accepted funds from groups like the Gates Foundation who support test driven teacher evaluation—have not fought back effectively against these efforts." The group's vision reads: "This is for every teacher who refuses to be blamed for the failure of our society to erase poverty and inequality, and refused to accept assessments, tests and evaluations imposed by those who have contempt for real teaching and learning." http://www.badassteacher.org
103 Greene, *Dialectic of Freedom*, 4.
104 Greene, *Landscapes*, 163.
105 Greene, 162.
106 Greene as told to Janet Miller, "Epilogue—'Coming together to Act on the Possibility of Repair': Conversations with Maxine Greene," in Robert Lake, ed. *Dear Maxine*, 159–160.
107 Greene, *Dialectic*, 2.
108 Greene, 2.
109 Greene, 2.
110 Greene, 4.
111 Maxine Greene, "Prologue to Art, Social Imagination and Action,"
112 Greene, *Dialectic,* 9.
113 I believe the emphasis on imagination is due to Maxine's own focus on the elaboration of Imagination throughout her work. I do not mean to suggest that scholars have missed this aspect of her work. Others have written about Maxine's use of critical interpretation, but I have not found others who explicitly address this as "naming," which highlights the aspect of interpretation through language and as praxis. See, for example, James Henderson, *The Path Less Taken,* and Robert Lake notes this aspect of Greene's work and calls it "critical imagination" in *A Curriculum of Imagination in an Era of Standardization.*
114 Greene, *Dialectic*, 7.
115 "What is common to all varied notions of situated freedom is that they see free activity as grounded in the acceptance of our defining situation. The struggle to be free—against limitations, oppression, distortions of inner and outer origin—is powered by an affirmation of this defining situation as ours." Charles Taylor in Greene, *Dialectic*, 20.
116 Greene, 6.

117 Greene, 8.
118 Greene, 9.
119 Greene, 9.
120 Greene, 55.
121 Greene, 15.
122 Greene, 104.
123 Greene, 101.
124 Miller, Epilogue in *Dear Maxine*, 160.
125 Miller, 161.
126 Greene, *Dialectic*, 58.
127 Greene, 58.
128 Greene, 99.
129 Greene, 83.
130 Maxine Greene, "Language, Literature, and the Release of Meaning, 124.
131 Greene, "Curriculum and Consciousness," 147.
132 Greene, *Dialectic*, 60.
133 "I would emphasize as well the capacity imagination gives us to move into the 'as-if'—to move beyond the actual into invented worlds, to do so within our experience ... Things appear differently; they appear in the light of possibility." Maxine Greene, "We Who Are Teachers Know That Imagination Has This Multiple Power, 82.
134 Greene, *Dialectic*, 78.
135 Greene, 95.
136 Greene, 21.
137 Greene, 21
138 Greene, *Teacher as Stranger*.
139 Maxine Greene, "Blue Guitars and the Search for Curriculum," 110.
140 Greene, 112.
141 Greene, *Dialectic*, 86.
142 Greene, 56.
143 Greene, 99.
144 I use naming "praxis" to respond to Maxine's dialectic mediation. This Frierian notion of praxis calls forth the rich interplay, the dialogue, of theory and practice as possibility for educators to encounter and engage their own Becomings as well as the opportunities for shared projects of freedom within educational experiences. This dialogue disrupts the dichotomy of the past-ness of theory (in educator training) and the present-ness of practice, while engaging in the hope of the future. Multiple perspectives emerge regarding experience through discourses represented within theory, permitting space for imagination toward educational and social action through the interpretation of experience.
145 Greene, *Existential Encounters for Teachers*, 1.
146 Greene, *Teacher as Stranger*, 6–7. In this section, Greene draws on Arendt, Sartre, and other philosophers to contemplate "doing philosophy." She contrasts knowing what philosophers have thought in the past to a way of approaching knowledge. Philosophy might be a way of "framing distinct sorts of questions having to do with what is presupposed, perceived, intuited, believed, and known ... a way of contemplating ... what is taken to be worthy of commitment." To do philosophy is a way of becoming "highly conscious of the phenomenon and events in the world as it presents itself to consciousness."
147 Greene, *Landscapes of Learning*, 3.
148 Greene, 19.
149 Greene, *Dialectic*, 18.

150 Greene, "Blue Guitars," 114.
151 Greene, *Landscapes*, 23.
152 Greene, "Blue Guitars," 115.
153 Greene, "Curriculum and Consciousness," 145
154 Greene, *Existential Encounters*, 9.
155 Greene, *Landscapes of Learning*, 43.
156 Greene, 22.
157 Greene, *Dialectic*, 121, 124.
158 Greene, *Landscapes of Learning*, 38.
159 Greene, *Variations on a Blue Guitar*, 81–82.
160 Greene, *Dialectic*, 131, 133.
161 Greene, 14.
162 Greene, *Existential Encounters*, 155.
163 Greene, *Dialectic*, 12–13.
164 Greene, *Landscapes of Learning*, 44.
165 Greene, 38.
166 Greene, 46.
167 Greene, 48.
168 Greene, *Teacher as Stranger*, 80.
169 Greene, *Dialectic*, 134.
170 Greene, *Landscapes of Learning*, 47.
171 Greene, *Existential Encounters*, 160–161.
172 Greene, *Dialectic*, 133.

CHAPTER 2

Letters to My Colleague

> [It is] exhilarating to be alive in a time of awakening consciousness, and also confusing, disorienting, and painful ... Sleepwalkers are coming awake and for the first time this awakening has a collective reality. It is no longer such a lonely thing to open one's eyes.
> ADRIENNE RICH (1971, 35)

∴

1 Toward a Method of Inquiry for a Teacher

We who are teachers must be freed to consult what we truly know, and freed to select the projects by means of which we define ourselves. When we are compelled or lured to remain passive receivers of discrete parts of a curriculum, say, obliged to speak in a manner others determine and to follow some extrinsic logic, we become disempowered.[1]

Dear Kathy,

I am writing to you today in an attempt to explain what the heck I'm doing with this study. I think a letter to you will buoy my confidence and also give me an opportunity to really flesh out with another teacher how our teacher understandings have come to be seen as legitimate knowledge.

You are, of course, my dearest friend, who has seen me become who I am, but you are also an intellectual and a fellow teacher. I watched you, over the years, thoughtfully and humbly develop content, pedagogy, even artistry to create challenging and dynamic educational experiences for your students. I have great respect for how you think about teaching and also how you orient yourself to the possibilities of serving and growing within your community—be it classroom, school, neighborhood, or city. Always your strong mind considers the context and particular characteristics of your encounters. Always your full heart drives your consideration.

As I write this thing, I often think of you. I wonder and hope that what I am doing might be useful to someone like you in your work and life. I often think of teachers, of intellectual, reflective care-oriented human beings, as if we are in conversation. I listen to you and hope what I say might be a support to your pursuit of a well-lived, and I think you might add, helpful life.

You and I know others who have attempted a doctorate, most of whom we respect and most of whom have told us to stay away from such an "opportunity." (And yet my idealism has me in this predicament despite the warnings!) We also know education. We know the kinds of things that pass for research. It's "data-driven." It's "science-y" in a really narrow way. It is this kind of shared knowledge that prompts me to write to you. Because, as you know my dear, I am not science-y and I have not approached my doctoral work conventionally. And, as you also know, this terrifies me. I have difficulty even explaining and describing the nature of my study. When people find out what I'm doing, I want to put a banana in their mouth and run away. Don't ask me to tell you what my study is about!! In fairness, I realize that others in my position may feel this way. But my fear is primarily driven from a place of uncertainty and insecurity: Can I reveal and defend my way of knowing to the world? Will anyone care about or need the work that I have found so gratifying?

I cannot foresee the future, of course. But my way of knowing? Yes, I can reveal it. I can speak it. In fact, it is defensible! (Haven't I come a long way to even suggest this?!) With this letter to you—my intimate and my colleague, I hope to create a safe enough space for myself to step out into what feels like significant vulnerability. I am not doing this the way I am supposed to do it. Is it still intellectually respectable? Does it smell reputable enough, strong enough to be a credible study? Is it legitimate? To write an interpretive, narrative, autobiographical and epistolary piece is to say "I am Christine. A teacher. This is how I make sense of the world." It is to say "I cannot do it someone else's way anymore." At once, I claim myself and also allow a version of myself—the one who strives to be good and will compromise herself to be okay with you and you and you—to sit in the backseat for a while.

My goodness, I do need a good friend right now.

Writing to you also gives me permission to really tell you what I'm doing and share this awakening and satisfying experience with you. How I come to create meaning, with this study, I believe, is well warranted by scholarship that has come before me. If I can communicate to you the logic of how a study like mine can be justified, then I may be close to the possibility of sharing this understanding effectively with more teachers. You see, ultimately, I hope this study encourages other teachers to envision how they might claim their own ways of knowing and Being in the world. It seems to me that following through with our moral and ethical commitments has a lot to do with how authentic—how close to ourselves, how honest with ourselves—we permit ourselves to be.

To begin, allow me first to summarize the study itself—my elevator speech, if you will. I am identifying and studying Naming, within the existential and phenomenological work of Maxine Greene, as a praxis for teachers. I am wondering if Naming is a useful philosophical orientation for teachers so that we can counter the data-and-expert-driven, student-as-product, teacher-as-mechanized-cog-yet-solely-accountable narrative about education and open space for ourselves to engage in educational encounters as human beings. Can a Naming praxis encourage our own Becoming? Can a Naming praxis help us more closely align our teaching with our ethics? I make my inquiry by writing my experiences autobiographically and critically interpreting them in dialogue (a Naming itself) with other teachers, with cultural voices and with discourses of scholarship. Further, conducting this study "upon myself," I enact a Naming praxis and may therefore determine whether I find myself able to imagine alternate possibilities for Being and whether I am more closely aligned with my ethical sensibilities. In my portrayal, then, I provide an aesthetic experience for my fellow teachers to Name and Imagine their own praxis or orientation toward teaching as human beings.

• • •

Where are the numbers? Where are the interviews? Where is the neutrality and objectivity necessary for scientific work in an autobiographical project? Where is the triangulation for validity? How is it reliable? What are you testing? How can this be legitimate, rigorous scientific research?! These questions come to mind—and are so numerous—because as teachers we are inundated with measurement and data that is supposed to objectively define whether or not human beings are "learning." We are told that measurement indicates whether or not tweaking and adjusting the simple equation: teacher + right method + content = student learning/strong economy/international prestige for the USA. Isolate the variable, accumulate data and dispassionately analyze it. The assumption here is that this equation amounts to good education.[2] So many of us know that this simply isn't the case.[3] Learning isn't just about whether kids know the right answer to content questions. We, as educators, crave ways to explain and describe what happens in our classroom, what seems to happen when a child grows, and what we have to think about to create a space where that might happen. The kind of "research" that gets funding and publicity doesn't match what we know or how we know what we know. This kind of research excludes teachers and assumes we are the problem, a problem that needs to be attacked, adjusted, and solved.

Well, research extends beyond this paradigm of "rational" objectivity.[4] Research, as disciplined inquiry for the sake of coming to know or making sense of the world, can also take into account the messiness of the human beings involved in education.[5] It can claim that the "capacity of human beings to make meaning of life events and to exercise a sense of agency in their lives is not considered a confounding variable to be controlled through research procedures."[6] This is the stance of the interpretivist research tradition in an entirely different paradigm.[7] It assumes that humans make meaning and that meaning is embedded in the action they take as they live.[8] This is actually quite similar to Dewey's idea of the reconstruction of an experience.[9] The experience does not shape us, rather the meaning and significance we make of it does. What shapes us is the story we tell ourselves about what we encountered.[10] Thus, an interpretive study pays attention to the human action and queries about the deeper meanings that have been constructed within as a result of that action. Such a study attends to the interpretive or discourse communities that have helped the human make meaning.[11] What existing stories help to define the meaning or create new meaning? How has this human being interpreted experience to make sense of it for her Being in the world?

This research tradition is helpful for me as I consider how I make meaning, how I interpret my experiences and then made decisions about my life. I come to understand and choose who I am "on the boundary of my Self and the outside world."[12] There is a dialectic that I engage in dialogically. In other words, I have to use language and have conversations to hear and tell these stories that offer interpretations of my experience to help shape my meaning-making.[13] Being human, engaging in my own Becoming, exercising my choice—these are dependent upon my dialogic engagement in the world.[14] How free I am to choose who I am Becoming is dependent upon the nature of my engagement and the interpretations with which I am engaged. If I approach my Becoming passively, as a matter of course, then the strongest interpretation, discourse community, or narrative may define the limits of my existence. If I am open to, even expectant for multiple discourses and I have conversations and deliberations with them, I allow for the possibility of alternate ways of Being. The richer the interpretation, the greater resources my imagination may have to draw upon for my agency in the world, or to conceive of going beyond my current state.[15] You could say that I AM the discourses or interpretations. They constitute me. The me as a teacher, the me as a woman, the me as a mom— each of these Selves is constituted discursively.[16]

A quick and narrow example. I have offended a friend of mine. My first resource is to understand the situation through my opinion in my own mind. Was what I did bad enough to be offensive? Is this friend easily offended? These questions (and their answers) are shaped by stories I've used to make sense of what "bad" means, what constitutes "offensive," whether being easily offended is something to pay attention to in a friendship. These might come from my parents or from *Sesame Street* or from discourses about ethics. And each of *those* items are conceived through interpretations of other human beings. Right there, I have three layers of interpretations: (1) what appears to be my gut reaction and (2) the interpretations that shaped my immediate reaction and (3) the stories that shaped those interpretations! I could reach for multiple perspectives, like my friend's or our mutual friends. They would then have quick and deeper layer interpretations that, when shared, might also inform my understanding of our situation. These might flip my own interpretation on its head, or make strange what otherwise appears to be a given.[17] I then have an opportunity, conversing with these perspectives, to determine what kind of friend I am and what kind of friendship I want. In this way, my understanding (through multiple interpretations) informs my Being and future Being in the world, in my relationships. But I could also just trust my immediate reaction. My experience of Becoming then would be limited to the stories that are so ingrained and taken-for-granted, that I don't even have to think about how I want to BE or act in this situation.

If we recognize that when it comes to relationships, we see or understand only partially due to how we are situated in the world, I would think we might want (at least a few) sufficiently rich perspectives, so that we have a greater chance to see and Be in ways that allow us to do the least harm to one another.[18] If I am going to pay attention to interpretation instead of going it "lone wolf," then I need some humility. And I need a sense of belonging to something greater than myself. Probing my experience with multiple interpretations seems to create a space for me to attend to my relationships. In this sense, interpretative inquiry might foreground the ethical possibilities as well as the human being acting in the world and her dialogic relations.

Thanks for being in this with me!

Christine

2 (Re)Claiming Interpretation: Currere

And the Word became flesh, and dwelt among us.[19]

Autobiography is an architecture of self, a self we create and embody as we read, write, speak and listen. The self becomes flesh, in the world. Even when authentic and learned, it is a self we cannot be confident we know, because it is always in motion and in time, defined in part by where it is now, when it is not, what it is not. The self who welcomes the dawn is a self constantly expanding to incorporate what it fears and resists as well as what it desires.[20]

Dear Kathy,

I think that we teachers need to be assured that how we come to meaning and understanding is legitimate in terms of creating education. We know what we know is "true" on some level but no one listens and we doubt ourselves anyway. So here I am again with you to demonstrate the fact and the reasoning for how and why our ways of knowing can be trusted and valued. In my last letter, I left off with considering the ethical implications for multi-dimensional thinking.

Access to multiple interpretations is a significant issue in terms of staying connected to our human need to keep growing, our ways of making sense of our world and experiences, and our ethical commitments to each other and our communities. And access to interpretations has been a problem for teachers. Historically, political, cultural, academic, and professional narratives marginalize teachers, their experience and interpretation, as well as their ethical commitments. We are scapegoats or technical advisors. Many of these discourses narrowly define and thus confine teachers' Becoming. Today, in American education, teachers often are not even permitted to speak about what they encounter, let alone how they make sense of it.[21] Maxine Greene summarizes this troubling situation well:

> People who lack access to language of power, who are inarticulate even about their lived lives, are unlikely to "surmount the boundaries in which all customary views are confined, and to reach a more open territory." Yes, becoming literate is also a matter of transcending the given, of entering a field of possibilities. We are moved to do that however, only when we become aware of rifts, gaps in what we think of as reality. We have to be articulate enough and be able to exert ourselves to name what we see around us—the hunger, the passivity, the homelessness, the "silences."[22]

Limited access to language and interpretation is unsurprising in a feminized profession, where the people in the professional role as well as their knowledge have historically been marginalized.[23] Thus, it made sense for me, as a woman and a teacher, to grapple with feminist and Curriculum Studies' forms of inquiry that attend to this issue of access to language and interpretation.[24] In the early seventies, feminists turned to autobiography, comprised of lived, situated experience and relationships, to legitimize their interpretations and counter the dominant, traditionally male, more abstract and rational (read: sans emotion) stories about the world and women's lives. Feminist poet, Adrienne Rich, initiated and inspired women to theorize autobiographically in her essay "When We Dead Awaken." While Rich hesitates to use herself as an illustration, she convincingly lays out an argument of the necessity of such an autobiographical project not only to herself, but for women, the women's movement, and society. In an Ibsen reference, Rich writes that she engages in "woman's slow struggling awakening to the use to which her life has been put."[25] Her purpose is to foreground the assumptions (the stories and interpretations) that define the possibilities of women's existence in order that women may begin to know themselves. She commends to her listeners an understanding of revision as "Re-vision, the act of looking back, of seeing with fresh eyes, of entering an old text from a new direction."[26] And in doing so, she frames the issue troubling her as an act of survival to counter the self-destructive trend for women in a male-dominated society. Autobiography, thus, permits me to interpret my experiences and investigate my interpretations; I am therefore free to make choices about my Being in the world based upon how I make sense of it.

History also demonstrates the transformative potential of Rich's autobiographical move early in the feminist movement to establish "women's ways of knowing" as legitimate and useful to research queries. Feminist researchers resisted the notion that only abstract or testable information counts as knowledge, and they emphasized concrete, lived experience as rich resources for understanding.[27] In addition, human relationships also became a source of knowledge as some studied specifically how women come to know the world.[28] Autobiography as a legitimate warranting of one's knowing and Being is in its nascent stage when Rich speaks at the MLA conference in 1971, but in the years following, it becomes a primary method of inquiry in the feminist movement[29] and provides the basis for investigation of feminist epistemology.[30] Subsequently, feminist epistemology becomes a way of knowing to investigate phenomena in human Being, sociologically, philosophically, and even scientifically.[31]

At about the same time, curriculum scholars began to reconceptualize the field of Curriculum Studies, shifting its focus from developmental psychology frameworks for curricular design to inquiry rooted in the humanities around the nature of the experience of educational encounters.[32] They gave autobiographical inquiry a prominent place in the field. Scholars had begun to account for knowledge and knowledge production in schooling as fraught with issues of social justice.[33] While the question, "whose knowledge is of most worth?" remains an important political critique of official knowledge and a significant inquiry in the field of Curriculum Studies, interpretative inquiry around ways of knowing shed light on injustice done to students' possibilities for learning and Being.[34] When students' ways of knowing are marginalized, for political or pedagogical purposes, students' freedom and Being are limited.[35] Thus, teachers' study of their own knowing and Being is significant work toward ethical practice. Who teachers are, how they are constituted, the possibilities for their ethical being in relation to children—these considerations contribute to the kinds of educational experiences in which children might engage. In this way, teachers' self-excavation has transformative implications for social construction. Pinar and other curriculum theorists reasoned that like the feminist movement from the particular to the social, individual autobiographical work of educators may manifest larger social issues.[36] He states:

> There may exist fundamental structures or processes that are observably quite different when manifested in individual personality but are the same when studied at the level of their roots. These might be basic structures or processes of the educative process in the humanities.[37]

Currere, a form of autobiography, emerged as a unique method of inquiry and theorizing within the field of Curriculum Studies.[38] It is the living and encountering of curriculum, defined by the reconceptualists as the materials, conditions, and institutional structures that comprise one's educational journey.[39] Currere "seeks to understand the contribution academic studies makes to one's understanding of his or her life (and vice versa) and how both are imbricated in society, politics, and culture."[40] It is what one does with the curriculum, how one experiences it, "the active reconstruction of his passage through its social, intellectual, physical structures."[41] In this sense, "the autobiographical process is not an act of 'consciousness, pure and simple' as it must refer to 'objects outside itself to … events, and to … other lives'; it must participate in the 'shifting, changing unrealities of mundane life': it is never atemporal."[42] We have the opportunity to envision and negotiate the tension of difference, the dialectic (internal/external, individual/community) that is the subtext of all educational narratives.

Currere might then be an "attempt to reveal the ways that histories both collective and individual and hope suffuse our moments, and to study them through telling our stories of educational experience."[43] In our story-telling of our educational experiences, Currere asks that we consider past, present and future. It involves four phases.[44] The phases are not conceived linearly, but in a cycle of self-reflectivity. They are: regressive, progressive, analytic, and synthetic. The regressive phase begins with the description of one's educational past. What is *there* in one's consciousness. One "returns to the past, to capture it as it was, and as it hovers over the present."[45] In the progressive phase, one imagines what might be possible in the future, including "expressions of who one is not now, of material felt to be missing, sought after, aspired to. It is discerning how who one is might hide what one might become."[46] The analytic phase creates distance from one's past, present, and future, in which to freely "bracket the educational aspects of our taken for granted world [so as to] loosen one's usual holds on thinking that reflect cultural conditioning and results in vaguely instrumental and sharply other-directed thinking .... [This] requires loosened identification with contents, hence a perspective not equivalent to them."[47] The final phase, the synthetic, "totalizes the fragments of educational experience and places this integrated understanding of individual experience into the larger political and cultural web, explaining the dialectical relations between the two."[48]

Rooted in existential phenomenology, psychoanalytic and feminist theory, Currere illuminates the possibility of reclaiming interpretation and agency. Elucidation of one's journey and probable concomitant, cultivation and awareness of one's existential freedom all lie, in a sense, in a broader social context. One's existential freedom is necessarily and importantly colored by one's practical and political freedom ... this kind of analysis is useful only as it widens our understanding of the nature of the pilgrimage.[49]

Currere and feminist autobiography confirm that my experience and my meaning-making are worthwhile "subjects" for exploration, necessary even for my ethical concerns as well as for this specific project of explicating Greene's Naming. These methods of inquiry help me get to an authentic place, as close to my Self as possible as a teacher. In this space, I may confront my Self and my responses and interpretations of lived experiences. I have the opportunity to question, critique and reinterpret my Being in the world so that I have access to greater freedom, to more choices about who I might Become.[50] To do so within my teaching work, I believe, has possibilities and consequences for the other human beings with whom I am connected. That gives me a lot of hope and some degree of relief.

Whether this method functions as the appropriate inquiry stance for this study, however clearly it responded to the problem of access to interpretation, is unresolved. More on this dilemma in coming correspondence.

Thanks for walking beside me through this,

Christine

3   Engaging Teachers in Inquiry: Teacher Lore

> The wilderness has many aspects, of course; the demons have many faces. What is happening makes me wish, more and more desperately, for authentic dialogue among educators. It is time our own voices are heard with greater clarity, the voices of those who engage with the young in their concreteness and particularity.[51]

Dear Kathy,

As a teacher-inquirer, my aim for study is how teachers make meaning, make it together, and make it public to support the most ethical, just conditions for the education of children. Currere and autobiography, while un-solipsistic in their active and intentional inclusion of multiple perspectives, still seem somewhat removed from the conversations I want to have with other teachers about Naming and within a dialogic Naming praxis that is this study. It is important to me to write with my teacher voice for an audience of teachers. And it's not that there isn't precedent for teacher memoir. Of course we are familiar with teacher memoirs like Mike Rose's *Lives on the Boundary*, which through autobiographical account elucidated reflective practice within concrete and lived experiences. But, you know me, I do not have the hubris to imagine that my memoirs are significant at my age. More significantly, I have been so accustomed to the idea that teacher knowledge is not "officially sanctioned."[52] We are rarely invited to participate in the creation of knowledge about our own work because we are viewed as static and mechanical technicians embodying "someone else's sense of our classroom life."[53] Research conducted on teaching and learning has long oriented itself toward objectification of teachers, "in much the same way that ethologists study baboons," rarely incorporating teachers' understanding of curriculum.[54] Harsh, I know, but this contrast of inquiry orientations, of watching/studying teachers versus recognizing that teachers create curriculum, whether that creation is sanctioned or not, is powerful. Powerful enough to make me tremble when I consider how to honor the quiet voice in the deepest recesses of my intuition insisting that teachers have something to add to the understanding of "education." Beyond contribution, given access to our own meaning-making, perhaps we might be more authentic and engage with children in ways that don't trouble our ethical sensibilities quite so often.

My mentor pointed me to Teacher Lore as a possible framework of inquiry for this study, and I have to say that I was immediately intrigued. "To capture the discoveries of teachers, their insights 'in the making,' is a central mission of Teacher Lore. To enable these missions to be shared with other teachers is its further mission."[55] Yes! Right up my alley, honoring teachers, suspecting there is so much *there* to understand! Scholars such as William Schubert, William Ayers, and their colleagues and students at the University of Illinois at Chicago were frustrated by the lack of teacher participation in the understanding and creation of curriculum. They wondered what wisdom was being lost.[56] You see, these scholars who conceptualized Teacher Lore sought to prioritize praxis, "which assumes a continuous critical reflection that joins and mediates theory and practice."[57] An emphasis on praxis upholds a Deweyan and pragmatic tenet that truth values of a proposition be determined in the consequences of its use. Dewey claimed that knowledge gained through the head, heart and hands of the educator, "render the performance of the educational function more enlightened, more humane, more truly educational than it was before."[58] This claim upholds the idea that what teachers have learned from their experience is what lies beneath the educational environment they create. Thus, educational theorizing can actually be conceived as praxis itself! Schubert suggests, "the lived experiences of teachers as well as the idea that teachers are themselves creators of knowledge and theory that can illuminate an understanding of curriculum, teaching and the educative process."[59] The focus is on the teacher-as-agent within this educational web.

So let me briefly describe how these scholars understood "Teacher Lore." They derive the term *lore* from anthropological studies pertaining to the broad array of knowledge and learning acquired through the experience of a group,[60] but their emphasis is on the lore of teachers, and they "characterize teacher lore as the study of the knowledge, ideas, perspectives, and understanding of teachers."[61] Teachers relate their knowledge most often, however, through the stories they share about their practice. I am delighted by the premise that teachers capture experience and understanding together as a unique community! And, Kathy, when I encountered Teacher Lore, you came to mind. How often you express gratitude for your colleagues, how much you believe you learned from them about teaching, even about how to BE in the world. I think it's useful to provide a vivid image which mirrors your belief in the power of a community of trusted colleagues. Janet Miller provides a rich telling and reflection of this in her autobiographical essay in the seminal teacher lore text.[62] She describes the third period gatherings of several teachers, including herself, during the "free period" they shared, and the stories told to one another based upon their daily, practical experience. Bear with me, as I want to share her description in some volume here for a fuller picture of this teacher-phenomenon.

> Our conversations were ongoing, usually concentrating on particular students' antics or on questions of method and content ... Our talk was seamless, fragmented only to those who did not share the synchronous rhythms of ringing bells, rotating students, and shuffling papers and

texts ... We shared similar concerns, questions and frustrations about the ephemeral nature of our work as high school teachers.[63]

I valued those communal explorations with my colleagues, those conversations ... I had not only a sense of common grappling with those experiences but also a sense of knowing that could only be easily communicated among those who worried and wondered each day about the often seemingly capricious processes of teaching and learning. That knowing did not reflect a certainty about the approaches and techniques to which our work as teachers was often reduced by others who watched us through the windows of our classrooms or evaluated us through the student achievement scores published in the town newspapers. Rather that sense of knowing signified an awareness of the variety of our own and our students' experiences, backgrounds, and understandings that influenced, in complex and often hidden ways, the constantly evolving nature and forms of our interactions.[64]

Ours was a form of inquiry spurred by our daily encounters with colleagues, administrators, parents, and students, and framed by the ringing of bells and the testing of students' understanding or at least memorizations of the "snippets" from our disciplines that we had presented in our classes ... Our kind of talk about teaching, because of its apparent meandering and wondering nature, seemed virtually impossible to categorize, to replicated, to control, or even to share with those who did not teach.[65]

Thus, as my colleagues and I huddled together in our morning oasis, our questions and our common as well as unique experiences of the classroom coalesced as forms of knowledge about teaching that could be easily communicated only to one another. We shared our evolving knowledges not through sets of goals and objectives or measurable means or standardized checklists of our behaviors, but rather through the stories that we told to one another.[66]

In this sense, Teacher Lore is an attempt to capture what already occurs between and among teachers. A sharing of knowledge acquired, within experience, through stories. An opportunity to reflect on one's practice through the sharing of those stories. An extension of the oasis created when teachers gather together and share the stories of their experience in teaching.

The term "lore" thus captures the intuitive, the informal, the spontaneous and subjective undersides of what, in recent years, have been codified as planned, predictable, controllable, and objective elements of "effective" teaching. Lore is what we know to be similar in our teaching experiences, even as we tell our stories in order to point to the differences among us. And, over time, the telling of our stories allows us to hear our own changing and evolving understandings of ourselves as teachers.[67]

This was the kind of research that seemed to match my philosophical tendencies. Teacher Lore drew first from the pragmatic philosophy of Dewey, but I found much contemporary philosophy echoed those tenets. The scholars who conceptualized Teacher Lore as inquiry saw teachers not as objects but as human beings, who "seek to create meaning and purpose through interaction with and reflection on the contexts of their experiences."[68] And the premise of the meaning-making is a Deweyan notion of the individual interacting with a troubling situation that demanded critical reflection, interpretation, and action inevitably leading to social (re)envisioning as well.[69] In other words, the premise of Teacher Lore inquiry begins with attention to the teachers *Being* and *Becoming* through critical interpretation of their experiences. Further, Teacher Lore leans on an ethical premise that assumes human goodness and compassionate interaction between human beings. Teaching then could be conceived as a relational, moral craft.[70] The logic of Teacher Lore is visible in the everyday dilemmas—ripe for individual reasoning—and incorporates the logic of Deweyan deliberation through democratic interaction. Teacher Lore is a call for a logic that moves beyond archaic dualistic debates and is instead grounded in the practical tasks of dialogic communities.[71] This same democratic faith informs the theological underpinnings of Teacher Lore. The "curricular" questions, what knowledge and experiences are most worthwhile to pursue are the basis for asking what is the good life, how can I lead a good life, what is a good society, and how can I contribute to it. These questions are so fundamental that their intense pursuit is religious in character."[72] How often I have sensed that the work of teaching, that the experience of education is sacred in its poignant humanness? Finally, the aesthetic dimension of Teacher Lore comes from a Deweyan notion that we can come into expressive knowing through our aesthetic awareness in the patterns and images of everyday life. In this way, Teacher Lore sees teachers as the aesthetic interpreters.[73]

It turns out we have a lot of cheerleaders—scholars struggling to include teachers in meaning-making about the world of education. Through Teacher Lore, these scholars attempt to "capture the disparate literature, giving it a rationale and language as well as a bridge to the more formal idea of research on teaching."[74] They address first a theoretical framework for this inquiry, although these scholars resist a rigid framework in the interest of providing adequate space for teachers to tell their stories as authentically as possible.

They fear a strong theoretical framework might stifle deeper inquiry by separating learning from spontaneity, limiting the reflection of the practitioner in the course of action.

Nevertheless, as scholars, they cautiously offer discourses and discourse traditions into which Teacher Lore might be situated.[75] First, they locate the emergence of Teacher Lore in two specific discourse communities: Curriculum Studies and Supervision.[76] Second, as a methodology, Teacher Lore can be situated within the qualitative research tradition of Curriculum Studies. The field draws on "a wide array of research traditions, approaches, methods and techniques," but the "main focus is on an in-depth exploration of the diversity and complexity of experience of individuals groups families, tribes, communities, and societies that are often at controversy, underrepresented, or misrepresented in the official narrative."[77] In fact, Teacher Lore responds to critics who demean teachers' decision-making processes, citing an apparent lack of theoretical foundation. The methodology itself serves to "respect teacher voices and recognize that building teaching theory is personal rather than academic, practical rather than distant."[78]

In addition to these roots of Teacher Lore, this method of inquiry resides in an overarching tradition of teacher research, specifically drawing on teachers' knowledge, some of which was developed in a similar vein resistant to objectifying teachers.[79] I am going to briefly list strands of teacher research to strengthen our sense that our stories can and should be told. Our perspective, experience and knowledge *count* as research. The following traditions are illustrative of work in progress along this line: first-person teacher accounts offer—"a glimpse of the knowledge and values of the theory within these teacher-authors"[80]; phenomenological renderings—such as van Manen's *The Tone of Teaching*[81]; action research—conceives of teaching as intellectual experimental work[82]; teacher-as-researcher—pairs teachers with university researchers for collaborative inquiry[83]; reflective practitioner—respects teachers as people who reflect in action[84]; educational criticism—posits that people who do the rich complex work of education must be connoisseurs of what they observe, describe, and interpret[85]; personal-practical knowledge of teachers—values the thinking processes of teachers[86]; and autobiographical and biographical accounts.[87] Teacher Lore scholars espouse these accounts as the best sources for understanding teachers: "[our work] fits within these streams or traditions, sometimes overlapping several of them, drawing insights from many, and hopefully contributing to each in some fashion."[88]

Methodologically, Teacher Lore is an interpretive inquiry into teachers' praxis. It attempts to answer questions such as: What beliefs, values, and images guide this teacher's work? What teaching philosophies are embedded in her practice? What are the insights this teacher has acquired through her practice? What has this teacher learned from experience in her work? Teacher Lore also serves as teacher reflection. But it attends to these questions in response to Robert Coles' call for narrative, story, autobiography, memoir, fiction, oral history, documentary film, painting, and poetry in inquiry in order to respond to the contradictions, diversities, and complexities of human experience.[89] The narrative and interpretive traditions cause Teacher Lore researchers to seek "truth-likeness" as opposed to objective truth, which is not context sensitive.[90]

Further, Teacher Lore highlights the dialogic nature of praxis as it serves to substantiate the reflective sharing of stories and knowledge that already exists. Miller writes that she and her colleagues did not have a way to frame their third period conversations that would reveal them to be fruitful as "forms of curriculum creation or research or teachers' knowledges."[91] For her the word "lore" is significant as it "captures the intentions and knowledge of wondering, involved, caring teachers."[92]

> What the concept of teacher lore now provides for me, then, is a framework or scaffolding upon which to build understandings of myself as an active creator of knowledges about teaching, curriculum, and research. The notion of teacher lore confirms and affirms the necessity of dialogue among teachers as a way of creating and revising our knowledges about teaching and learning.[93]

Thus, the inquiry of teacher lore not only provides understandings for research on teachers, teaching, and curriculum, it may also serve the growth of the teachers themselves.

Representation of Teacher Lore, however, potentially becomes a tricky business. While the lore may begin with the teacher's story and possibly even the teacher's interpretation of the story, the final "product," so to speak, usually passes through the researcher. Therefore, it seems important to proceed with caution as a researcher with this methodology. Miller has concern about the relationship between teacher and researcher. She worries

> about the possible impositional nature of this relationship if teachers' research is still set within the contexts of others' research on those processes ... I worry about the impositional possibilities of the research relationship if the direction as well as the evolving interpretations of the particular research focus are not constructed as a form of praxis (Lather, 1986) and are not enacted as reciprocal, negotiated, and constantly evolving understandings.[94]

In response to her concerns, to avoid "baboon study," Miller encourages those involved with Teacher Lore and its interpretation to reflect as the teachers do and mine their own assumptions about teaching and research and to recognize changes that might have occurred as a result of their interactions with those involved with their research. Schubert, Ayers and the authors of the book's essays concur and they each include autobiographical context for the work. They write,

> Teacher lore can be presented through teachers' own words, and through the interpretations provided by experienced teacher/researchers who interview and observe teachers. Each of us who contributed to this book is an experienced teacher. Therefore, at one level, we reveal our own stories and at the same time we report on and interpret stories of other teachers who have influenced our perspectives on teaching.[95]

Schubert notes the role of the interpreter as one of the important findings of the Teacher Lore Project.[96]

Even though my study does not explicitly include other teachers' stories, I raise this issue of the ethical complications of engaging with someone else's stories. First, for me, it exemplifies how critical is my own autobiographical mining if I want to be involved with teachers' growth in ethical ways. Second, how careful these Teacher Lore scholars have been verifies the significance of teachers' knowledge in and of itself. Finally, the exemplar within Teacher Lore is teachers' experience and knowledge layered with multiple interpretations, indicating the possible significance of a dialogic and deliberative stance toward teachers' growth in Being.[97]

I am sure it is clear, Kathy, that the promise of Teacher Lore is undeniable for me. It allows us to understand more clearly, with greater nuance, the work of teaching,[98] illuminates that which we cannot see in the daily grind of teaching work, encourages the contribution of every teacher to the broader understanding of teaching by honoring the work of the individual teacher, empowers teachers to imagine socially transformative and potentially emancipatory experiences,[99] and enables teachers' agency in making sense of their work.[100] It disrupts normative understandings of teachers and teaching,[101] and counters contemporary notions of school reform:

> The dominant metaphor of the rich and powerful posits schools as businesses, teachers as workers, students as products and commodities, and it leads rather simply to thinking that school closings and privatizing the public space are natural events, relentless standardized test-and-punish regimes sensible, zero-tolerance a reasonable proxy for justice—this is

what the true-believers call "reform" ... The gravitational pull of this narrative is so great that everyone finds themselves re-voicing the deceptive goals and the phony frames. This is the power of narrative and points to the necessity of counter-narrative.[102]

My own rationale for my study was further strengthened, especially by Bill Ayers' interpretation of the contemporary educational atmosphere and his call for counter-narratives. Surely, teachers like me and you are well-suited to thoughtfully tell these counter-interpretations of American education. Teacher Lore provides a solid foundation in which to stand to engage in disciplined, interpretive inquiry about my experience and work. My stories, richly embedded with multiple interpretations provided through discourses communities and other teachers, told overtly to teachers may also contribute to other teachers' praxis. I become a voice with which to engage dialogically about teachers' own practice and Being as a teacher. Janet Miller expresses this potential well, and I'll end this letter with her thoughts:

> I wish that early in my teaching career or in my preparatory studies, I had been introduced to such a way of thinking about my own teaching ... divergent visions of what it means to be a professional teacher ... I might not have struggled so much with my own sense of disjuncture and fragmentation within prescribed versions of "good" or in today's terms "effective" teaching ... I regret that I had no formal, or in a sense, validated "divergent visions" from which to draw as I began to teach ... (And later, as a teacher, with others) we all might have been able to see those daily encounters as a form of inquiry that honored our own changing and developing understandings of our work as teachers, had we the conceptual frames and rich descriptions that the examples of teacher lore here presented provide.[103]

Wouldn't it have been something to start our professional life in this mode, poised and open to the Lore of our colleagues?

Creating Lore with you,

Christine

4 Logics of a Naming Study

> I had to either consider myself a failed woman and a failed poet, or to try to find some synthesis by which to understand what was happening

to me. What frightened me most was the sense of drift, of being pulled along on a current which called itself my destiny, but in which I seemed to be losing touch with whoever I had been.[104]

There is the effort to invent a situation in which there can be spaces for doing, spaces for attending, spaces for becoming. And spaces for action.[105]

Dear Kathy,

To this point, we've discussed some rich possibilities for justifying teachers' knowledge and experience, but now let's return to my little study. How might I study an existential and phenomenological concept of Naming in the context of my experience and understandings as a teacher?

I determined that an interpretive research tradition would serve me well, and I soon discovered that it would do so exceptionally in an intimate dissertation study. Noreen Garman and her colleague Maria Piantanida thoroughly addressed the interpretive dissertation within significant scholarship, and I found it mirrored my intentions and orientation.[106] Working from an interpretivist perspective means that I claim that the meaning of human action is inherent in that action, and these scholars believe that this perspective allows me, within a small education study, to unearth the meaning inherent in classroom action.[107] Further, I myself become the instrument of research, rather than say an "experimental design" within a traditional post-positivist research tradition. That means I need to hold myself "alive and open to hear what Being may speak," which "requires nimbleness, a fine-honed sensitivity in order to let oneself be the vehicle of whatever vision may emerge, a degree of attention, and an active listening."[108] Knowledge then is considered (inter)subjective because context (socio-historical-political-gendered-ethnic, etc.) really matters. This is where the dialogic comes in again, and it is assumed in this interpretive study that "dialogue is central for defining the core of one's practice."[109]

It makes sense then that the interpretive study would manifest a deliberative and tentative character. Deliberation eschews certainty and simple answers in favor of grappling with diverse sources and ideas to come to thoughtful, wise action.[110] Discursive deliberation is not a comfortable orientation. It assumes that the researcher will be "working on the edge of one's knowledge and skill," which "implies entering new conceptual territory, pushing beyond the comfort zone of one's assumptions, challenging one's understanding of self, others, and the nature of one's field of study."[111]

My task for this study, I learned, is to move from the situational to the conceptual. The first-person position indicates the source of interpretation. And this self-study is formed and challenged by

A balance between the way in which private experience can provide insight and solution for public issues and troubles and the way in which public theory can provide insight and solution for private trial. [This] forms the nexus of self-study and simultaneously presents the central challenge to those who would work in this emerging area.[112]

These scholars suggest that rather than articulating the method (procedures and techniques) involved in making these conceptual leaps, the interpretivist focuses on a logic of justification. In other words, what are the logical issues and justifications that inform my stance? I am to look to my philosophical orientations as well as to a specific research genre in terms of its language and conventions to construct my warrants for my inquiry. Of critical importance is the "extent to which my 'procedures' fit with the knowledge generating assumptions embedded in the genre claimed for the study."[113] The interpretivist must go beyond description and answer "why."

Therefore, I must claim a form of inquiry, so as to clarify my logic of justification for this study. I believe a blended inquiry of the autobiographical method of Currere and Teacher Lore is possible and imperative to my study. The tenets of Teacher Lore, as well as examples by its theorists Schubert and Miller especially, permit me to theorize autobiographically. In fact, the conclusions of Teacher Lore scholars seemed to suggest this as an ethical imperative before I consider involvement with other teachers. Teacher Lore offers a big umbrella for inquiry around teachers' knowledge. While Schubert extensively claims Deweyan pragmatic foundations for Teacher Lore, the emphasis of the inquiry on interpretative modes of knowing allows for various epistemological traditions that prioritize teachers' Becoming. In this way, the psychoanalytic roots of Currere, for example, would be welcome as well as the existential ones.

The boundaries and horizons of Currere provide a disciplined approach to my personal narrative. You will see in my narratives all four of the "phases" of Currere, not necessarily presented linearly; rather, my writing within and across the phases further encourages multiple interpretations. My theorizing begins with concrete, lived experience but is not limited by the dimensions of my interpretation within or just after that experience. I am to investigate my self-formation in relation to my "education" writ large. Currere also pushes me to engage with broader social and cultural contexts and implications within the four phases. Inevitably, these multiple perspectives permit me to pursue richer possibilities for my freedom in Becoming. But to write autobiographically in this way within Teacher Lore also substantiates my knowledge as public, intended for understanding amongst teachers, while demonstrating the possibilities of teachers' knowledge to broader educational issues. A study within an intimate study confined to discursive deliberation further demands careful attention to language and interpretation for the express purpose of challenging and potentially transforming my way of Being in the world.

A study in which these inquiries fold into one another is in fact a demonstration of a teacher's praxis with an emphasis on her human Becoming. Up to this point, I have referred to my desired outcome from praxis: that a teacher is more authentically connected to herself and therefore more free to choose ethical possibilities for her encounters with students. My reading of Piantanida and Garman aligns this act of discursive deliberation with Greene's Naming. By intentional critical engagement in our fundamental project of teaching, a concrete and practice-based space, we create the possibility for alternate ways of Being. They argue, "Of critical importance is the idea of challenging our self-understanding because in practice-based research, professionals are calling into question what they think they already know. Expert practitioners, working at the leading edge of their own knowledge and skill, presumably have developed theoretical sensitivity through knowledge of 'best practices' and nuances of classroom life."[114] With some awe, Garman and Piantanida, describe these expert practitioners:

> [And yet], they are still willing to call that knowledge into question for themselves. In doing so they open themselves to confusion and uncertainty, creating the possibility of transforming their way of being educational practitioners. Such transformations, when they happen represent a reforging of one's ontological stance. With a different stance, new perspectives, new insights, and new understandings might be gained—the type of wisdom that Flyvberg (2001) and Schwandt (2001) associate with phronesis.[115]

Using this blended inquiry—Teacher Lore and Currere, I am able to enact Naming as I explore its explication and potential to my own Becoming as a teacher. Further, as I do so within conversations with teachers, I make public understandings and interpretations thus far relegated to my own mind and my own classroom. Without further ado, then, let's get into the nitty-gritty of the logics of justification and what I've done here in this study.

A significant feature of interpretive research is "text." Drawing from post-structuralists, interpretive inquiry claims that everything—life experiences, events, relationships, activities, practices, cultural artifacts, and so forth—is a text. Thus, the possibilities of directly encountering and knowing "the reality of human experience" are encounters with text.[116] Text therefore stands in the place of "data." It is the representation of situation and meaning, potentially fruitful for deeper insight into complex human affairs. Piantanida and Garman organize text into four types of text: *raw, experiential, discursive,* and *theoretic.*

The *raw* text is every text assembled, or information gathered, in the process of studying the phenomenon in question. For me, this included Maxine Greene's work, discourses in feminist theory, Social Foundations of Education and Curriculum Study, inquiry-based discourses on autobiography, narrative, memory, and Teacher Lore, jotted notes of memories of my teaching experiences, literature and art and philosophy and essays. Anything I studied to better understand Naming. I used my journals, my favorite poetry, and my go-to sites of cultural and political critique. My conversations at school, with you, with colleagues at Curriculum Studies conferences were all raw text as they supported my exploration of the questions: what am I really trying to understand and what types/sources of information can support this? Here is one area I can address a mainstay of "science-y" research: rigor. Traditionally, rigor can be demonstrated by attention to generalizable patterns and delineating the line between cause and effect related to an external encounter. My goal in this interpretive study is not generalizable patterns but differences. Rather, the rigorous quality of the investigation at this juncture occurs in how I, as the researcher, resonate with the *raw* texts over extended time. In this time, "alternative interpretations are formulated, interpretations are compared and contrasted. [They are] visited and revisited to see if different aspects of the text become more salient as other aspects seemed."[117]

The *experiential* text involves a creative and profoundly interpretive process to portray the problematics of a phenomenon. The real task of the experiential text is to construct an inviting context with which to portray the phenomenon and theorize within. While a scientific approach would reduce data to summaries, the experiential text must be sufficiently nuanced and textured so as to reveal possibilities for interpretive exploration and meaning-making. The *experiential* text represents the choices I make to highlight various meanings, decisions about details, and faithfulness to genre in order to reveal a layer of meaning that may have significance in relation to the phenomenon under study. These *experiential* texts are fictive in the sense that their representations are limited by the boundaries of my situatedness as the interpreter. My aim with these texts is verisimilitude, a vitality that feels "true" to my reader and thereby contributes to the believability and credibility of my study.[118] Verisimilitude also demonstrates rigor. It is the outcome of resonating with the raw texts. In a sense, I mediate between and among narratives and discourses to challenge myself and my reader to question normative assumptions, simplistic interpretations, and prescriptive solutions that "feel true."

> A well-crafted experiential account ... by evoking [such] questions, sets the stage for theoretic text which will offer concepts—a heuristic map—that help others to discern what was important in the experience and what might constitute wise action.[119]

But before we can get to the theoretical, we must engage discursively, so let's discuss the *discursive* text of a study like mine. As I begin working with the experiential texts, I enter a recursive process with discourses. The dialogic engagement here is quite apparent. Discourses represent a way of thinking and talking about a phenomenon agreed upon within a community.[120] Post-structuralists suggest that the discourse is specifically "our social relatedness as inscribed in and expressed through language."[121] It is also the institutional system for the production of knowledge. At this point, my diligence in seeking out multiple perspectives, especially within these scholarly discourses, represents the move in a more scientific paradigm to be precise and replicate my experimental procedures. My dialogic engagement with discourses enlarges the conversations that were *raw* texts. I am now conversing with communities of scholarship and demonstrating how these substantiated ways of understanding phenomenon warrant my *experiential* and ultimately *theoretic* texts. My interpretations are potentially richer with *discursive* text as I engage in the public space of intellectual dialogue, which these discourses represent. I can both legitimize my theorizing while also guarding against an autobiographical proclivity to narcissism. The *discursive* text helps to create a heuristic to other agreements reached by communities of scholars regarding aspects of self, others, and human affairs.[122] Coherence among interpretations, within the heuristic, is my standard, rather than a strict correspondence to "reality," which science-y people require.

⋯

Before I move on to discuss what the *theoretic* text represents, I am going to pause here, Kathy, to describe my particular process of working with and through *raw, experiential,* and *discursive* texts for this study. If the specific work of the study is not made apparent, then my theoretic text will feel like I'm reaching for pie in the sky. My conceptual leap to the theoretic text necessitates a clear picture of my work.

The decision to conduct interpretive inquiry emerged from *raw* textual study of research discourses. I situate this study in the interpretive research tradition, specifically "the way of hermeneutics."[123] As I've mentioned, this is a tradition supported by discourses in Curriculum Studies.[124] In this philosophical tradition,[125] understanding is not a procedure or a solution to a particular problem. Instead, understanding is interpretation; it is "engaging in a dialogic encounter (with text or human action) ..., where meaning is negotiated mutually in the act of interpretation; it is not simply discovered."[126] Gadamer's historical hermeneutics suggests the interpreter must be front and center in her research.[127] The historical traditions of the interpreter are a "living force that enters into all understanding ..., conditioning our interpretations ..., thus understanding requires engagement of one's biases."[128] You can see how the interpretive tradition embodies my philosophical stance.

It was not a simple decision to write an autobiographical study.[129] You may have noticed, given the multi-letter exploration I detailed to you! I knew that I wanted to illuminate the concept of Naming in Greene's work, but as I mentioned, I was afraid, to do so with my own experiences. Thus, my *raw* text study initially included a lot of genre reading. While I considered other qualitative methods, in the end, I really felt like I needed to experience the kind of self-excavation those in Curriculum Studies suggested would bring to light normative assumptions about the how and why of one's teaching work. This was especially necessary if I found it significant to a Naming praxis and wanted to demonstrate it (or help other teachers understand and do it themselves!) I then read around the personal essay and narrative genres as well as the autobiographical work in feminist studies and the method of Currere.[130] I ruminated with these and Teacher Lore through writing, grappling with their possibilities in light of my concerns.

I did have to confront the idea that memories could be reliable sources of information upon which to build a study! Thus, in my *raw* text study, I read extensively in cognitive philosophy discourses as well as in narrative discourses. Just this week I came upon an article in *The Atlantic* which echoed the interpretation in my experiential text.

> Though perhaps the facts of someone's life, presented end to end, wouldn't much resemble a narrative to the outside observer, the way people choose to tell the stories of their lives, to others and—crucially—to themselves, almost always does have a narrative arc. In telling the story of how you became who you are, and of who you're on your way to becoming, the story itself becomes a part of who you are.[131]

To be clear, as an autobiographical piece, the study relies upon what cognitive scientists call autobiographical knowledge, defined as the reflection upon memory episodes. Cognitive scientists and philosophers also support the idea that reconstructing autobiographical knowledge is an integral part of the way in which we create identity and maintain a continuity of self while looking toward the future.[132] They have found a primary function of autobiographical knowledge "appears to include making sense of the past so to have a coherent view of the self with which to direct future behavior."[133] This warrants my use of memory experiences, autobiographical knowledge, as a text to study teacher's self-creation or Becoming.

Autobiographical knowledge quite commonly embodies a narrative mode. Curriculum Studies discourses ground narrative research within the interpretive tradition by the work of such scholars as Jerome Bruner.[134] Narrative modes of knowing center around the broad, inclusive question of the meaning of experience; whereas the paradigmatic mode centers on the epistemological question of how to know the truth. The narrative mode "establishes truth-likeness or verisimilitude."[135] Moreover, this mode, as others within the interpretive tradition, strives for coherence, rather than correspondence, in order to provide a "vivid picture and the meanings about the experience under study."[136]

This further strengthened my inclination to work in story in the autobiographical mode. I believe I have made quite plain my reasoning for choices in terms of what I selected of this *raw* text to contribute to crafting my experiential texts. But quickly I want to illustrate that within my field, Curriculum Studies, this type work has yielded significant meaning in terms of understanding curriculum more broadly and critically[137]; of challenging ahistorical, essentialized notions of selves[138]; of negotiating the tension between the personal and the public.[139] Stories such as these "are a means for interpreting or reinterpreting events by constructing a causal pattern which integrates that which is known about an event as well as that which is conjectural but relevant to interpretation."[140] Specifically, for this project of Naming, I focus on memory episodes (autobiographical episodes) which bear the mark of pain, discomfort or tension (more on how I came to that decision in a moment). McMahon eloquently articulates my aim.

> All of my stories, be they mildly or "wildly" fictive, are born of difficulty; as Pinar says, "whatever difficulty exists, there is a story behind it, often 'whole, bright, deep with understanding'" (1981, 173–88). I write because I am trying to reach a place of understanding. I am working out a teaching problem that presents itself to me in a way I cannot ignore or define. Something has created a dissonance within me, but I am not sure enough to label what it is exactly because it seems complicated or because it presents itself to me as uncomplicated. Either way, I do not want to rush to terminology that does not reflect the layers of meaning I suspect lie

beneath the interactions of the classroom. I want to write my way into understanding what it is I feel and think about the situation. I write my literary narratives because, in doing so, I come face to face with the nature of my unrest.[141]

When I created the *raw* text from my memories, I jotted descriptions of the ones that bore some angst in my remembering. This was important to me because Greene considered discomfort or disquietude a kind of red flag requiring Naming. These feelings or emotional responses to my experiences needed exploration through critical interpretation because they may indicate an obstacle to my existential need for freedom in Becoming. So I mined my memories. It wasn't hard. These teaching experiences had gnawed at my soul for years. I ended up selecting those tensions that still strongly resonate with me today, those that I still see around me and still bother me. Those which have offered me little resolution or peace.

The challenge was then to craft an *experiential* text of these memories. I had to pay attention to the details of the narrative genre in order to create verisimilitude around the disquietude. I zeroed in on moments, thoughts that represented tensions, disquietude, frustration, confusion, certainty or uncertainty. I wrote to foreground these feelings. I had to identify the details that brought potential meaning to the tension I experienced. It had to feel consequential and worth exploring by you, Kathy. The narrative genre insisted on my considerations of time and place, which are essential to its structure. The character details needed to feel "real" as well. Along the way, to attend to my narrative responsibility, I asked a fellow teacher, who is also a creative writer and editor to read for narrative quality, voice, and verisimilitude. I continued to write and revise with her suggestions in mind.

An important part of this was to try to compose these vignettes as if I was reflecting upon it almost immediately after it occurred. I wanted to capture what I thought was happening then. If I could do this, then I could open avenues of interpretive exploration regarding possible normative assumptions I carried with me. I paid attention to voice, my voice, as it sounded to me then (though it was difficult not to project judgement from the present on that voice and thinking).[142] I also addressed, in my narrative telling, how the experience and my reconstruction of it at the time oriented me toward future experiences. What "position" or decision was adopted to move forward?

I made two more significant decisions when crafting my memories as experiential texts. At some point in this process, I discussed with my teaching fellows study group how much shame surrounded these episodes. I struggled to see myself in any way other than in the narrow light that I hadn't know what to do in this circumstance. I had somehow failed the system, myself, and the child. We discussed the possibility that chronological sequencing of these stories could reduce the conclusions to a linear narrative that "I was young and foolish and now I'm older and wiser and I know better." In fact, they suggested, when I described other encounters with children as a teacher and other teaching scenarios, it seemed to them that I was also a wonderful teacher. I realized that I had essentialized myself. I had smoothed over the alterity of my own Self in favor of a one-dimensional version who just couldn't seem to get it right. I considered how I might portray both the "wonderful" teacher and the "conflicted" teacher. To this end, I included in the narratives the professional judgement, pedagogical thinking, and curricular deliberations which I embodied and felt proud of myself for having done so. I included the perceived consequences that led me to shame or to pride, usually found in the children's responses to my work with them.

Conversation with those same teachers in the study group, who happened to be burgeoning scholars as well, also bore fruit in terms of my decision to include personal experiences that may seem unrelated to my teaching. They reminded me that Maxine discouraged the personal-professional dichotomy. It was true. Naming had entered my life even before I met Maxine and knew what it was! The grappling with Naming in my situated and contextual selves (teacher, mother, woman, wife, daughter, scholar, and friend) potentially demonstrates the power of a Naming praxis if we envision each context as a project of our Becoming.

Having written the memory vignettes as *experiential* text, I returned to them as texts to study. I combed through the pieces looking for language of tension, certainty or uncertainty, frustration, or the sense of something missing. I ascribed a word or phrase to describe the nature of concept in tension: power, authority, professional responsibility, compliance, victim, students, ethics, good student = good teacher. Throughout, I engaged in discursive deliberation, creating my *discursive* text. I played with what these words represented. I found issues of power (professional responsibility, authority, compliance); issues directly related to ethics; issues related to aims of education; issues related to students. I used words from the narratives but eventually I began to tag themes with some language from the discourses as well. I immersed myself in the narratives several times. I went through pieces again and looked for what was in conflict. Surprisingly, I began to see that the conflict occurred within a situation related to students ... and I was always left alone with the feelings of disquietude, uncertainty, or bewilderment.

One of the *raw* texts that continued to resonate with me was Parker Palmer's discourse on paradox.[143] It proved a useful heuristic for bringing to light the texture and nuances of the phenomenon. Further, I hoped that as an interpretation it would enrich my understanding of Naming as I moved into the *theoretic* text. So, with my next task, using the language of paradox, I described the nature of the tension in each situation involving the specific connection to the student that left me with those feelings. I juxtaposed the pull of a normative assumption with the red-flagged feeling triggered by student response. I created tension diagram statements for each specific situation. Some examples include: I could feel the tug of professional responsibility for order simultaneously with my frustration and embarrassment when my students in Harlem who would not comply when I did what I was supposed to do as their teacher; I was overcome by a powerful pressure to get in line with my institutional team's wisdom regarding Marty and also baffled by a feeling Marty had been harmed by that decision, that something wasn't right, something was missing. Those statements of paradox supported my engagement with the discourses in the experiential text meant to portray how I might Name those teaching experiences and come to ontological freedom as a teacher Being. The paradox made my troubling circumstances visible and tangible in language and juxtaposition, and I began to taste some freedom. I had something to study in context, rather than fixed knowledge to apply regardless of circumstances. A promise of alternatives lingered as a result of such a study.

In terms of the *raw* text of discursive scholarship, I responded most predominately with historical discourses. They represented seminal historical texts from the 19th, 20th and 21st centuries. They represented historiography of the dominant groups in education (white, male administrators and scholars) as well as critical theorists, feminists, and curriculum theorists. I layered the *discursive, experiential* text with multiple interpretations to conjure multiple possibilities for Naming what may have stood in my way of ethically relating to children and myself. In doing so, however, I noted that, in the difference and nuance, a strong assumed or expected identity of myself as an American Teacher emerged. Despite the difference in discursive explanations across time and the situatedness of the interpretive community, they consistently reinforced an archetype. At this point, I framed this *experiential* text with the *raw* textual discourse of Foucault I had studied. While I knew I couldn't do a definitive "genealogy" study of the American Teacher, this Foucauldian concept certainly contributed to my interpretation and the possibility for theoretic meaning-making.[144]

The *theoretic* text represents my conceptual leap, from context to meaning. If I have done my job to this point, Kathy, I should have bridged the concrete encounter, elucidating key details through interactive interpretation to "imbue the account with verisimilitude so that a conceptual issue might be examined."[145] In the *theoretic* text, I make meaning of the *experiential* and *discursive* text, and I put them into perspective. This is when I am permitted to exercise my authorial right to put forward my understanding of the phenomenon.[146] I am not suggesting that I have discovered the conclusive meaning. But the work of the study should warrant my theoretic contribution to scholarship.[147] In this way, my truth claims, or conceptual explanations, emerge out of complicated conversations.[148] I do not wish to enumerate the raw discursive texts that support my theoretic text as this is the work of my final letter.

You and other teachers can judge for yourself whether this study is legitimate. The criteria for a study such as mine is straight forward. Here are some of the questions which represent a high standard of quality. Does it hang together in a structurally sound manner? Is it intellectually honest and authentic, ringing true in terms of the quality of the discursive text? Is it rigorous in the quality of thought that went into the inquiry and in its connection to the aforementioned questions of integrity and quality? Is it useful and relevant to a professional, scholarly audience? Is the study communicated in such a way as to feel meaningful? Is it powerful, provocative, evocation and moving?[149]

Ultimately, my aesthetic portrayal of the study contributes to the rhetorical quality of the study. In terms of my portrayal, I wrote letters, incorporating the epistolary genre, to emphasize my desire to be in conversation with teachers, to extend the dialogic possibilities for the reader and for myself as I wrote.[150] The epistolary genre also makes public private interpretation; affecting change beyond myself is my hope after all. I wanted to make visible my student (at Greene's feet), colleague, mentor, daughter, and scholar Selves transparent in these letters as well. The inclusion of literature and art was my attempt to represent the imaginative possibilities Maxine so fervently asserted when we engage dialogically with them. Every quote, excerpt, and picture functioned as an impetus for Naming or Imagining in my life. Perhaps their indirect manner creates an opportunity for your deeper interpretation of my work. Perhaps they make possible richer interpretation of the idea of Naming toward teachers' Becoming. Hopefully, my aesthetic decisions invited you into dialogic engagement with something that felt worthwhile in its meaningful possibilities for your own Becoming as a teacher. Perhaps ethical and wise action feel within reach?

Thanks so much for being on the other end, Kathy. While I've certainly listened in the past to move into the dialogue represented in these letters, I can't wait to hear how and what you think about all of this. Let's talk soon, my friend.

Yours,

Christine

Notes

1 Greene, *Variations on a Blue Guitar*, 126.
2 See Ellen Lagemann in *An Elusive Science* who describes the confinement of education research to positivist and post-positivist knowledge assumptions. The earliest educational research came to be defined by three principles as claimed by Edward Thorndike, preeminent and early education researcher. First, learning as stimuli, responses, and the connections between them came to be so narrowly defined by the thrust of behaviorism in educational psychology. Second, those components of learning could be quantified and, in this way, research became excessively quantified to the extent that course work in education research were "for all intent and purposes" manuals of statistics. Finally, due to Thorndike's fixation with genetic determinism, psychometrics and test development, testing and tracking became the primary preoccupation of education.
3 See the following blogs as examples of educators attempting to counter this premise and articulate education otherwise. Peggy Robertson, *Peg with Pen*; Steven Singer, *Gadfly on the Wall*; Anne Tenaglia, *Teacher's Lessons Learned*; Anthony Cody, *Living in Dialogue*.
4 "Scientific research has begun to be recognized as one among several of its species of knowledge generating." Elliot Eisner, "The promise and perils of alternative forms of data representation," 4–10.
5 "In our work with autobiographical texts of educational experience, Pinar and I have substituted hermeneutics for the positivism of the social sciences that still dominate curriculum research. As we concur with Richard Rorty's claim that hermeneutics has displaced epistemology by providing another politic for scholarship that refuses the dichotomization of subject and object, we invite endless problems of interpretation, not as impostors at the banquet planned for the truth but, indeed, as the guests of honor." Madeline Grumet, *Bitter Milk: Women and Teaching*, 60.
6 Maria Piantanida and Noreen Garman, *The Qualitative Dissertation*, 50.
7 "Interpretivism emerged in contradistinction to positivism in attempts to understand and explain human and social reality. As Thomas Schwandt put it (1994, p. 125), 'interpretivism was conceived in reaction to the effort to develop a natural science of the social. Its foil was largely logical empiricist methodology and the bid to apply that framework to human inquiry.' A positivist approach would follow the methods of the natural sciences and, by way of allegedly value-free, detached observation, seek to identify universal features of humanhood, society and history that offer explanation and hence control and predictability. The interpretivist approach, to the contrary, looks for culturally derived and historically situated interpretations of the social life-world." Michael Crotty, *The Foundations of Social Research*, 66–67.
8 "Interpretive researchers are concerned with the personal and social meaning that human beings construct beneath all the observable behaviors ... The "loose" qualitative counterparts (of scientific, quantitative folks) are concerned chiefly with the content of the story: is it credible? Does it contribute to the larger sense-making conversation?" William Ayers, "Keeping Them Variously," 151.
9 In *Democracy and Education*, Dewey defines education as "that reorganization or reconstruction of experience which adds to the meaning of experiences, and which increases ability to direct the course of subsequent experience" (89).
10 Paul Ricoeur, *Hermeneutics and the Human Sciences*.
11 Stanley Fish, *Is There a Text in this Class?* See also Noreen Garman, "Imagining an Interpretive Dissertation."

12 Garman, "Imagining an Interpretive Dissertation," 4.
13 "For the interpretivist, the world is constructed by each knower/observer according to both subjected and intersubjective dialogical exchanges." Garman, "Imagining," 2.
14 Alexander Sidorkin, *Beyond Discourse*.
15 Bronwyn Davies suggests agency is never freedom from discursive constitution of self, but the capacity to recognize that constitution and to resist, subvert, and change the discourses themselves through which one is being constituted ... it is through the intellectual freedom to recognize and critique multiple readings that one can resist being positioned by (more powerful) others. In "The Concept of Agency: A Feminist Post-Structuralist Analysis," 42–53. See also William Pinar, "Currere: Toward Reconceptualization."
16 While the existentialist is concerned with "the single one," that individual need not be taken as an essentialized, one-dimensional Being. Pinar in "Autobiography: A Revolutionary Act" explains this clearly, "The self is undeniably plural. While it is so that the self is an interactional self, the self is also capable of singularity and solitariness, a 'room of one's own.' Being in relation to others does not deny singularity. Besides being in profoundly formative relationship with others, one is oneself a shifting configuration of introjected as well as self-dissociated fragments of (past) others, in kaleidoscopic reconfigurations located in place and across time, structured in gendered, racialized ways, 38.
17 "To take a stranger's vantage point on everyday reality is to look inquiringly and wonderingly on the world in which one lives." Greene, *Teacher as Stranger*, 267.
18 "The figure is never fully illuminated. Light moves through time as well as space, and so clear seeing is burdened with all the limitations of human consciousness, always situated in spatial perspectives and temporal phases." Grumet, *Bitter Milk*, 60–61.
19 John 1:14, *Holy Bible: New American Standard Bible*. (LaHabra, CA: The Lockman Foundation, 1995).
20 Pinar, *Autobiography, Politics and Sexuality*.
21 See, for example: "Section 6.10.7.11 of the NMAC deals with staff responsibilities regarding testing, and it includes a list of 'prohibitive practices'—things that staff are forbidden to do. At the end of the list, that it shall be prohibitive practice for the staff member to 'disparage or diminish the significance, importance or use of the standardized tests.'" Peter Greene, "NM: Defending the Test."
22 Greene, *Releasing the Imagination*, 111. See also Grumet, "The Politics of Personal Knowledge," 69. Grumet describes storytelling as a negotiation of power as seen in discourse traditions in ethnography and anthropology. That narrative is the cultural symbolization of the life of a community; thus the implication is that access to that narrative grants power to contribute to shaping the life of that community.
23 I detail teaching as a feminized profession in the proceeding section, *Letters to New Teachers*. For further study, see seminal work such as Grumet, *Bitter Milk*, and Jo Anne Pagano, *Exiles and Communities*.
24 Pinar suggests that for women and African Americans who are "already on the margins, when testifying to subjective experience the dominant regime fails to recognize, self-writing may help form a mobilized, coherent self in solidarity with (subjugated) others," in "Autobiography," 51.
25 Rich, 34.
26 Rich, 35
27 Sandra Harding and Merrill B. Hintikka, eds., *Discovering Reality*.
28 Belenky et al., *Women's Ways of Knowing*.
29 Florence Howe, *Women and the Power to Change*; Nancy Hartsock, "The Feminist Standpoint; Linda Nicholson, *The Second Wave*; Shari Benstock, "The Female Self Engendered"; Linda

Anderson, "Autobiography"; Tess Cosslett, Lury, Celia, and Penny Summerfield, *Feminism and Autobiography*; Janet Miller, *Sounds of Silence Breaking*.

30 Sandra Harding, "Feminism, Science, and the Anti-Enlightenment Critiques; Patricia Collins, *Black Feminist Thought*; Jane Duran, *Toward a Feminist Epistemology*; Londa Schiebinger, "The exclusion of women and the structure of knowledge."

31 Elizabeth Spelman, "Aristotle and the Politicization of the Soul; Alessandra Tanesini, *An Introduction to Feminist Epistemologies* (Malden, MA: Blackwell Publishers, 1999); Jane Duran, *Worlds of Knowing*; Sandra Harding, *Science and Social Inequality*. Patti Lather, *Getting Lost*.

32 Pinar et al., *Understanding Curriculum*, 187, 211–212. See also Pinar, *Curriculum Theorizing* (Berkley, CA: McCutchen Publishing, 1975). An example of early theorizing in the conceptualist mode is Pinar and Grumet, *Toward a Poor Curriculum*.

33 For example: Michael Apple, *Official Knowledge*; Michael Apple, *The State and Politics of Knowledge*; Gloria Ladson-Billings, *The Dreamkeepers*.

34 Pinar, *The Synoptic Text Today*.

35 Dewey, *Experience and Education*; Greene, *The Dialectic of Freedom*; Pinar, *The Synoptic Text*.

36 Demonstrated within Pinar and Grumet, *Toward a Poor Curriculum* as well as Janet Miller's *Sounds of Silence Breaking* and Peter Taubman, "Canonical Sins."

37 Pinar, "Autobiography," 47. He refers also to Dewey who wrote in *The Public and Its Problems*, "In general, behavior in intellectual matters has moved from the public to the private realm ... Under such circumstances, autobiography represents an important strategy of cultural politics and the reconstruction of the public sphere," 267.

38 Pinar, "Currere: Toward Reconceptualization."

39 This is James Macdonald's thought incorporated by Pinar in *Curriculum Theorizing*. Pinar also defines curriculum as a Latin root/infinitive, which suggests the investigation of the nature of the individual experience of the public: of artifacts, actors, operations, of the educational journey or pilgrimage.

40 Pinar, *What is Curriculum Theory?*, 45.

41 Grumet, *Toward a Poor Curriculum*, 111.

42 Pinar, *Synoptic Text*, 53.

43 Grumet, "Restitution and Reconstruction of Educational Experience." See also Greene in "Curriculum and Consciousness," who similarly suggests that the one Becoming, "using his imagination must move within his own consciousness and break with the common sense world he normally takes for granted ... The reader must go beyond what he has been. In his search for meaning, he moves outward into diverse realms of experience [to] recreate and regenerate in terms of his own consciousness the materials of the curriculum," 255–257.

44 Pinar, "The Method of Currere."

45 Pinar, *What is Curriculum Theory?*, 36. "Uncovering this self which feels 'congruent, integrated, right' ... The person I was conditioned and brought up to be. It is the discursive practice of truth-telling, of confession ... To oneself one comes to practice the autobiographics of self-shattering, revelation, confession and reconfiguration. Self-excavation precedes the self-understanding, which precedes self-mobilization."

46 Pinar, 36.

47 This requires a phenomenological methodology to look at things as they are/were.

48 Pinar, *What is Curriculum Theory?*, 38.

49 Pinar and Grumet, *Toward a Poor Curriculum*.

50 Janet Miller argues that teacher autobiographies must be more than unproblematic teacher stories. Rather, they need to "explore and theorize social, historical, or cultural contexts and influences, including language and discourse ..." She encourages teacher autobiographies to avoid "traditional framings [that] usually have encouraged teachers to resolve discrepancies

... and simply reinforce static, predetermined and resolved versions of ourselves and work. Rather Miller contends that teacher autobiographies must then encounter 'contradictions, gaps, views from the margin, views from the center ... a field of multiplicities' that require rearrangement and reconsiderations of self. Further, instead of adding to compilations of "teacher stories," teacher autobiographies should take us somewhere we couldn't otherwise get to"; Miller, "Autobiography and the Necessary Incompleteness of Teachers' Stories," 145–159.

51 Greene, *Releasing the Imagination*, 170.
52 Janet Miller, "Teachers Spaces," 15.
53 Miller, 15.
54 William Ayers and William Schubert, "Teacher Lore: Learning about Teaching from Teachers," 107. See also Schubert, "Teacher Lore: A Basis for Understanding Praxis," 211. Schubert found this to be the case in the third edition of the Handbook of Research on Teaching (Wittrock, 1986) and found very little concerning "the need to take seriously the guiding precepts that teachers derive from experience," Of the volume's 1,037 pages, only 10 referred to "teachers' implicit theories of teaching and learning ... Too many researchers on teaching do not grant sufficient credibility to the theories and knowledge that teachers develop from experience. Through teacher lore, we want to offer such credibility."
55 Ayers and Schubert, "Teacher Lore," 116.
56 Ayers and Schubert's interest turned and returned to contrast the power of experiential, practical knowledge with the lack of teacher participation in most sanctified research on teaching. They wondered: "Where are the voices of teachers? What knowledge and experiences do teachers consider most worthwhile? Why do great classroom teachers typically retire into obscurity, without being asked what they learned? What wisdom is being missed, what lessons lost?" "Teacher Lore," 107.
57 Schubert, "Teacher Lore: A Basis for Understanding Praxis," 214.
58 John Dewey, *The Sources of a Science of Education*, 76–77.
59 Dewy, 77.
60 Schubert and Ayers, *Teacher Lore*.
61 Schubert "Teacher Lore: A Basis for Understanding Praxis," 207.
62 Janet Miller, "Teachers' Spaces."
63 Miller, "Teachers' Spaces," 11.
64 Miller, 11.
65 Miller, 12.
66 Miller, 12.
67 Miller, 14.
68 Ayers and Schubert, "Teacher Lore," 107.
69 While this is an epistemological argument, it also highlights the political philosophy undergirding Teacher Lore. Schubert asserts that Dewey recognized the web of politics, economics, society, and individual liberty; and his concern for equity were echoed by Freire, Apple, Giroux, and Boulding. Schubert in *Stories Lives Tell*, 218.
70 Schubert, in "Teacher Lore: A Basis for Understanding Praxis." This concept is rooted in Deweyan explications of values and human goodness. Nel Noddings expresses this relational moral dimension in this same book.
71 Ayers and Schubert, "Teacher Lore."
72 Schubert, "Teacher Lore: A Basis for Understanding Praxis," 219.
73 Schubert, 219. See also Elliot Eisner, *The Educational Imagination*.
74 Noreen Garman in Schubert and Ayers, *Teacher Lore*, back cover review.
75 Schubert and Ayers, *Teacher Lore*.
76 Curriculum studies provides a view of curriculum, in which it "unfolds in the democratic probing of genuine human interests and concerns of teachers and students, and its value is

found in the extent to which it helps participants create and draw upon knowledge that gives meaning and direction to their experience." From this, Teacher Lore becomes vital as it captures the experiential insights of those participants as well as the teachers' theories of action in practice. In terms of supervision, Schubert cites from the literature both the growing use of democratic collaboration and the development of the idea of "empowerment that accrues when 'outside experts' realize the need to share authority with 'inside experts,' those who can relate their daily practice to a particular set of circumstances." Teacher Lore brings to light teachers' understandings of their circumstances. Schubert, "Teacher Lore: A Neglected Basis for Understanding Curriculum and Supervision," 282–285.

77 Ming Fang He, "Qualitative Research," 703–704.
78 Pamela U. Brown, "Teacher Lore Research," 863.
79 Gretchen Schwartz, *Teacher Lore*. Schwartz and colleagues published a Fastback for Phi Delta Kappan in which she contributed to the theoretical underpinnings of teacher lore. Theoretically, she adds and leans on, specifically, Bruner's argument for narrative as the way in which "people construct knowledge of much of their world" (p. 12); more generally, she asserts the argument of constructivist learning theory that human beings construct their own knowledge, and "teacher lore is one way to personalize learning and help teachers discover their specific needs." (p. 13).
80 Schubert in *Stories Lives Tell*, 212.
81 Ayers and Schubert, "Teacher Lore," 106.
82 Researchers in this vein include, for example: Alice Miel, *Cooperative Procedures in Learning*; Ann Lieberman, "The Meaning of Scholarly Activity and the Building of Community."
83 Lawrence Stenhouse, *Curriculum Research and Development in Action*.
84 Donald Schon initiated this widely adopted notion both for research purposes as well as in terms of the conception of teachers' identities.
85 Eisner, *The Educational Imagination*.
86 Michael Connelly and D. Jean Clandinin, "Narrative Inquiry."
87 Pinar and Grumet, *Toward a Poor Curriculum*, for example, and Richard Butt, "Arguments for Using Biography in Understanding Teacher Thinking."
88 Some of these strands from Schubert and Ayers, ed. *Teacher Lore*, viii.
89 He, 706.
90 Robert Blake and Brett Elizabeth, eds., *Becoming a Teacher*.
91 Miller, "Teaching Spaces," 15.
92 Miller, 14.
93 Miller, 14.
94 Miller, 17.
95 Miller, 9.
96 Schubert in Witherall and Noddings, ed. *Stories Lives Tell*, 222.
97 Miller in *Creating Spaces and Finding Voices* beautifully articulates her work in collaboration with teachers to demonstrate the social nature of autobiographical research.
98 "Unfortunately teachers' stories are hard to find. They are generally dismissed even by teachers, even by the storytellers themselves, as personal and unimportant. They are in the main uncollected and unexamined, and they become then irrelevant as a source of knowledge about teaching. Teacher lore is largely a lost treasure, and the natural history of teaching is subsequently diminished." Ayers in Schubert and Ayers, ed. *Teacher Lore*, 150.
99 "We want to create spaces in which we might come together not only to analyze these situations and relationships but also to work together to change and transform that which we find to be oppressive or inequitable or silencing for any of us within our educational communities ... We have begun to understand empowerment as an active process in which we must engage on a daily basis." Miller, "Teachers' Spaces," 21.

100 "Teacher lore disrupts static and mechanical conceptions of teachers' work, posting our own questions in order to make our own and not some others' sense of our classroom life." Miller, 15.
101 "Teacher lore disrupts versions of teacher knowledge that posit teachers only as technicians, compliant transmitters and managers of ideals and structures of knowledge into which they have had little officially sanctioned participation." Miller, 15.
102 Ayers in Blake and Blake, ed. *Becoming a Teacher*, 21.
103 Miller, "Teachers' Spaces," 15.
104 Rich, *When We Dead Awaken*, 42–43.
105 Greene, *Variations on a Blue Guitar*, 127.
106 Noreen Garman and Maria Piantanida, eds., *The Authority to Imagine*. Maria Piantanida and Noreen Garman, *The Qualitative Dissertation*.
107 Piantanida and Garman, *Qualitative Dissertation*.
108 Rollo May, *The Courage to Create*, ref. in Piantanida and Garman, 80–81.
109 Garman and Piantanida, *Authority to Imagine*, 4.
110 Piantanida and Garman suggest those diverse sources include practice-based and research-based discourses.
111 Piantanida and Garman, 67.
112 Piantanida and Garman.
113 Piantanida and Garman, *Qualitative Dissertation*, 81. See also, "self-conscious method" in Brent Kilbourn, "Fictional Theses."
114 Piantanida and Garman, 66.
115 Piantanida and Garman.
116 Piantanida and Garman, 87.
117 Piantanida and Garman, *Qualitative Dissertation*, 113.
118 Garman and Piantanida in *Authority to Imagine* describe verisimilitude as the place where "reader and author meet to share the reality under study," 109. See also Jerome Bruner, "Narrative and Paradigmatic Modes of Thought."
119 Piantanida and Garman, 112.
120 Stanley Fish in "Is there a text in this class?" explains that an interpretive community embodies a particular way of "reading" the world. We might think of discourse as the formal representation of an interpretative community. The discourse carries with it a particular way of thinking and responding with regard to a subject under study. The language and vocabulary of the discourse communicate the values, assumptions, beliefs, and opinions of the interpretative community. These discourses are represented by scholars within a field of study while particular genres of research are considered logical extensions of the interpretive lens of the community.
121 Piantanida and Garman, 87.
122 Piantanida and Garman, in *Qualitative Dissertation*, explain a heuristic as a "conceptual representation of a phenomenon that conveys the complexity of the phenomenon in a way that makes it more accessible for discourses, deliberation, and inquiry. In the scientific tradition, hypotheses are one form of heuristic. In the arts and humanities, heuristics might take the form of visual or verbal images or metaphors," 57.
123 Michael Crotty, *Foundations of Social Research*; Ricoeur, *Hermeneutics*.
124 Garman and Piantanida, *Authority*; Piantanida and Garman, *Qualitative Dissertation*. See also Pinar et al., "Understanding Curriculum as a Phenomenological Text" in *Understanding Curriculum*.
125 Norman Denzin and Yvonna Lincoln, eds., *The Handbook of Qualitative Research* (Thousand Oaks, CA: Sage Publications, 2000).
126 Schwandt, "Three Epistemological Stances for Qualitative Inquiry."

127 Crotty, *Foundations of Social Research*.
128 Schwandt, 194.
129 While this mode of inquiry is now over 40 years old, I would argue that many teachers, steeped as I have described in a normative post-positivist education culture, may have a difficult time with this decision.
130 Exemplars which represent grappling with research discourses similar to my own include: on the personal essay, see Maria Piantanida, "Speculations on the Personal Essay as a Mode of Inquiry," and Marjorie Logsdon, "Writing Essays: Minding the Personal and the Theoretic"; on narrative inquiry see Patricia McMahon, "Narrative Yearnings: Reflecting in Time through the Art of Fictive Story."
131 Julie Beck, "Life's Stories." Her research included discourses in narrative psychology represented by Dan McAdams at Northwestern University, Jonathan Adler at Olin College of Engineering, and Monisha Pasupathi at the University of Utah.
132 John Sutton, "Memory," in *The Stanford Encyclopedia of Philosophy*; Helen Williams, Martin Conway, and Gillian Cohen, "Autobiographical memory," in *Memory in the Real World*.
133 Susan Bluck, Nicole Alea, Tilmann Habermas, David Rubin, "A Tale of Three Functions: The Self-Reported Uses of Autobiographical Memory, *Social Cognition* 23, no. 1 (2005), 91–117.
134 Jerome Bruner, *Acts of Meaning* (Cambridge, MA: Harvard University Press, 1990).
135 Bruner, "Narrative and Paradigmatic Modes," 97.
136 Piantanida and Garman, *Qualitative Dissertation*, 113.
137 Pinar and Grumet, *Toward a Poor Curriculum*.
138 Miller, *Sounds of Silence Breaking*.
139 Grumet, *Bitter Milk*.
140 John Robinson and Linda Hawpe, "Narrative Thinking as a Heuristic Process," in *Narrative Psychology: The Storied Nature of Human Conduct*, ed. TR Sarbin (New York: Praeger, 1986).
141 McMahon, "Narrative Yearnings," 186.
142 Janet Miller, in *Creating Spaces and Finding Voices*, helped me here as she problematizes the notion of a fixed voice which is always able to articulate itself and embodies identity singularly. Instead, she posits multiple voices which demand collaboration or relation to be "found" and heard. Certainly, for me, the ability to distinguish between a voice embodying my early teacher Self and the voice I have presently came through intersubjective engagement with my study group as well as with the multiple voices represented by discourses.
143 Parker Palmer, *To Know as We Are Known*. Palmer, *A Hidden Wholeness*. Palmer, *The Promise of Paradox*.
144 For an explanation of my use of this concept see note 24 in "Letters to New Teachers." This notion is explained and exemplified by Michel Foucault in *Discipline and Punish* and *History of Sexuality*.
145 Piantanida and Garman, *Qualitative Dissertation*, 109.
146 Garman and Piantanida, *Authority to Imagine*, 12. They write of the work entailed in claiming the authority to imagine, to theorize. This calls to mind feminist discourses around the notion of claiming authority which refer to authority as a rhetorical effect. Like Garman and Piantanida, these discourses do not situate authority in an object or position. Rather, it might be claimed through the visible work of language and rhetoric substantiated pragmatically in lived experience. These discourses are represented in Dale Bauer, "Authority," in *Feminist Pedagogy*.
147 Eisner in Piantanida and Garman, *Qualitative Dissertation*, asserts that qualitative inquiry is ultimately a matter of persuasion, of seeing things in a way that satisfies or is useful for the purpose we embrace. We take evidence from multiple sources. We are persuaded by its "weight," by the coherence of case, by the cogency of interpretation. In the end what counts is a matter of judgement.

148 "[Complicated conversation] is conversation with oneself (as a 'private' person) and with others threaded through academic knowledge, an ongoing project of self-understanding in which one becomes mobilized for engagement with the world. Conceived as complicated conversation, the curriculum is an ongoing effort at communication with others that portends the social reconstruction of the public sphere." Pinar, *What is Curriculum Theory?*, 47.
149 Piantanida and Garman, *Qualitative Dissertation* categorize the criteria in this way: integrity, verity, rigor, utility, vitality, and aesthetics, 193–197.
150 There is precedent within Curriculum Studies to portray the legacy of her work in personal letters to Maxine Greene. See Lake, *Dear Maxine*. The letters are both a tribute and an extension of her work, intended to "encourage others to take on the challenge of looking beyond our individual lives and build community," Second, this genre allows for a certain intimacy with my readers, hopefully other teachers/educators, and thus provides an accessibility to the theory which I believe is important for practitioners. "Letters are written with a recipient in mind and therefore create the context for shared epistemologies and relational aspects of understanding." Sonia Nieto, *Dear Maxine,* xi. See also Robert Lake, "Letters as Windows into a Life of Praxis."

CHAPTER 3

Letters to New Teachers

> It may be that education can only take place when we can be the friends of one another's minds. Surely there will be much to discover if we put our stories next to [one another's].
> MAXINE GREENE (*Stories Lives Tell*, 1991, XI)

∴

Dear Ruth and Joy,

I just finished tidying up after you left tonight. As I tossed the tea bags and rinsed the cups, I could not ignore my full heart and racing mind. You brilliant women, in the infancy of your teaching careers, invigorated me with your vitality and thought expressed through your frustrating and exhilarating stories working with children in schools. I am so thankful we grabbed a moment in our very busy lives to sit around my fire and finally talk about how you are experiencing teaching fresh out of challenging undergraduate programs in other fields. I'm humbled and honored that you are asking me questions and listening intently to my teaching stories, searching for some wisdom amongst them.

I shoveled ashes over the fire and considered how rarely we as teachers have the opportunity to fan our own flames of passion and inquiry and wisdom, permitting our fires to catch with one another. A bit corny perhaps, but I feel so alive after our gathering. I'm imagining in metaphor!

And I have an idea. Because you asked, because you seek connection with me in our shared teaching projects, because teaching for you is about Being the kind of human being you hope to be, and because we are incredibly busy, I wondered if you would permit me to write to you. I thought I would put in letters my stories, my journey of Becoming who I am, and some insights that might be useful to you. What do you think?

I'd like to start by sending you some narratives I've written of my early days in teaching, a bit of the good with the bad. Then I'll relate to you the way I've grappled with them over the years to come to interpretations that have freed rather than confined me as a teacher and a human being. Sound OK? If we ever get a chance to sit down, I would love for us to extend the letters into our conversations, as I know you both: you will be bursting with your own stories and insights! I love that about you!

Thank you for your humility tonight, for including me—in my "ancient-ness"—in a vibrant conversation about life and teaching!

Basking in the joy of our time together,

Christine

1   Teaching Vignettes

1.1   *Choosing to Become a Teacher*
Following three years of intensive study of history through my university's honors tutorial program, I was no longer merely passionate about history. I had ambitions to do important scholarly work as a historian. Without much guidance, I whipped through five or six graduate school applications to prestigious doctoral programs in history. As almost an afterthought, or maybe I couldn't resist the multi-generational pull to become an educator, I applied to the Master's program in Social Studies at Teachers College, Columbia University. In addition, I found a federally-funded scholarship which supported graduate study in history for teachers committed to teaching the Constitution at the secondary level. In the course of completing these last two applications, I encountered the question "Why do you want to be a teacher?"

I paused. I closed my eyes and considered my experience in education. I recalled my first history teacher, my mother (you remember, of course, that my parents started a school when I was in third grade?). At the front of our classroom or in the front of our car, my mother's passion for all things historical ignited something in me at an early age. I learned to honor the past every time we stopped the car because there was another brown historical marker commemorating some past person or event. We would climb out of the car at other times and my mother would stir my curiosity as she pointed out the topography and wondered aloud at the kind of life one might carve out if a person found herself here without other human beings. I found inspiration upon her introduction to the biography section in the library and I encountered one fascinating human after another: people who accomplished great things or overcame awesome odds. Time and place became relevant when I heard her, exasperated, bickering aloud in the kitchen to her imaginary pioneer woman friend,

"You may have had a lot on your plate going where no one had gone before; feeding and clothing your family from scratch; never getting a nice, hot bath.

But you didn't have the technology that makes my life so breathtakingly fast; and you didn't have children to run to swimming, gymnastics, and piano and somehow feed them a nutritious dinner; and you didn't get your master's degree while teaching full time, playing cabbie to these adolescents! I say we call a truce. No comparison!"

History, people of the past, these were resources to draw upon for understanding while striving toward a well-lived life.

As my Social Studies teacher through middle school, my mother established and managed an educational experience on which I draw to this day. She wove into her curriculum National History Day, a history program/competition for students in grades 6–12. Every year, the program provided a theme, such as "Revolution, Reaction and Reform in History." We students selected a topic in history which we believed fit the theme. My mother always encouraged us to choose local topics; then we could use the resources of the Western Reserve Historical Society, the Cuyahoga County Archives or the Cleveland Public Library for our primary source research. She then organized her instruction around the skills we might need to thoughtfully research, synthesize, and analyze our topics. For five months, we approached our projects as historians, learning how to take notes, learning how to read primary and secondary sources, learning how to use an archives, learning how to organize notes into themes and keep an annotated bibliography, and learning to synthesize our notes into understanding and frame our research around a thesis rooted in the theme. For culmination of the practice and application of these skills, we could decide to present our work in a paper, museum display, audio-visual piece, or stage performance. Each of these presentation categories had their own standards of excellence which helped us to learn how to communicate our argument cogently and effectively. District, state, and national competitions allowed us to hone and revise, clarifying and solidifying our work for stiffer competition. Three years of this experience taught me to value disciplined thinking and filled me with confidence as an adolescent. I was doing the work of a real historian! It was hard work, the work of courage and perseverance. But oh did it feel good to share my work and proudly answer questions about a topic only I knew so well.

And then there was Mr. Tottenham, the ex-Merchant Marine, who taught my tenth grade European history course. He was British but he didn't exactly speak the Queen's English. His lectures, chocked full of anecdotes of the antics of royalty, were peppered with the language of his first career. Elizabeth, he would say, didn't give a rat's tit if Parliament agreed. She would have her way and show them who was queen! In story after story, animated in language and a fervent pacing from the black board to our faces, Mr. Tottenham created characters with motives and feelings, agency in their world. The textbook's timeline made sense because he showed us the people and intrigue pulsing through time, their actions and reactions marking that time in memorable events. As entertaining (and shocking!) as his instruction may have been, Mr. Tottenham expected cogent, thoughtful essays. In preparing for his essay exams, I discovered that history could also be framed by analytical themes. Mr. Tottenham charged into the past uncovering human nature with ferocity and demanding critical and thoughtful attention to the way in which human agency caused history to unfold.

In college, I studied with professors individually, one per semester as a requirement and benefit of my university's honors program. We studied a topic of my choosing within their expertise. Two of these professors, Dr. Jellison and Dr. Martin, fed my passion for the study of the social and political role of the family, particularly the mother, in American history but expected me to learn history as a discipline. Dr. Jellison would not allow me to read merely for facts to assemble evidence for my thesis. We examined and judged sources, weighing how the ways in which the authors framed history might determine the facts I would find in each source. Dr. Martin emphasized historical context as I studied the social expectations and stories of immigrant families in American history.

"Big picture, Christy!" He bellowed enthusiastically across his small desk to me. "You can tell the story with the details of this family's life, but it's not the whole story! They are in those particular conditions due to larger forces as well! Rewrite this with the context in mind. It will be great! I can't wait to read it!"

For my honors thesis, Dr. Jellison gave me permission to tackle what in her mind was an enormous topic: a comparison of the Puritan Goodwife, the Republican Mother, and the True Woman. Deftly, she guided me to and through resources, asked me questions that led to my rethinking how I framed the project as a comparison, and by her subtle but undeniable intellectual support, I reimagined the paper not merely as a comparison but as a social evolution, critically examining that evolution in light of the experience of the woman in each era. The completed project surprised and satisfied us both. Neither of us considered the possibility which emerged as my conclusions. We were both really proud of my work.

These were just my history teachers! I had a language arts teacher in elementary school who instructed us to write new stories and essays almost every week. We learned to diagram sentences for every part of speech, even gerunds! (I remember that was quite a feat!) My French teacher, who taught me as an upper classman, kept me honest as I tried to take advantage of junior/senior privileges. She checked up on my reasons for sub-par work, calling my parents, making me look her in the eye until I squirmed and vowed to do my best the next time. Early in ninth grade at the height of my adolescent naiveté, my biology teacher observed some boys and I in the hallway. After class the next day, he pulled me aside and advised me to keep my wits about me when boys gathered and I was alone—advice that has helped me with safety decisions ever since! Of all of my teachers, I could name only one or two who negatively affected my well-being. Most garnered my respect through their expertise, integrity, high expectations, or attention to my personal character development.

I emerged from this meditation on my education as if waking up to a calling. I had to teach! I'd been given so much! I had amazing teachers and knew what it was to be in educational cultures that helped me to grow academically and as a person. Why do I want to be a teacher? I responded to that application: Because when so many riches have been deposited into me, I have to give back! I owed it to my teachers, to my parents, to carry on what they had put into me. How could I be anything else?!

In a moment, I knew I wouldn't be a historian, at least not in the traditional sense. But history would be the means by which I would reach children and help them to think about who they wanted to be in the world.

My completed applications bore fruit. Teachers College at Columbia University accepted me for enrollment the following summer, and I received the fellowship as well. Years of hard work, of aiming high and learning to follow through to reach my goals seemed to pay off. I was headed to TC, once home to Dewey, and I was set to embark on a career of enriching and changing lives.

•••

That June, I made my way through the underground maze of hallways between graduate student housing and Grace Dodge Hall, the main classroom building at TC. Smells of mildew and old paper, the scent of scholarship and history, accompanied me as I eagerly anticipated my first course, Social Studies Methods. With my background, my history with history education, I felt a deep sense of belonging. I AM a history teacher. And today is my beginning.

I soon discovered that I was by far the youngest student in my class with the least amount of teaching experience. Teachers in their thirties and forties were returning to school for advanced degrees. Those closer to my age had at least experience as substitute teachers or as instructors in summer and after school programs. But actually, this didn't faze me. I knew what good education and good teaching looked like. I was called to this profession, and I was passionate about history. I also had an education in education being around my parents for so many years. I knew Dewey and Adler and Plato, though admittedly, I hadn't read any of them yet. I felt, nevertheless, pretty confident in my background and in my abilities as a learner. I just had to tackle what they put in front of me.

Three weeks into this six-week course, the instructor required us to teach a lesson to the class on any Social Studies topic. The assignment challenged me initially. Any topic? And what would I do with that topic? I flipped through a textbook from back to front, and just as I was losing hope, inspiration struck at the Declaration of Independence. I could teach them how to read the Declaration of Independence for the principles of America democracy! Invigorated with historical passion and charged with a sense of duty, I created a lesson plan that consisted of my asking the students what I thought were Socratic questions in the hope of creating a Socratic discussion. I intended to lead the class to the principles through my questions. Inspired, my heart beat rapidly with exuberance. I couldn't wait until class the following day.

I sat through one teacher performing a rap and asking us to deconstruct the rap in small groups and make comparisons to a slave spiritual, and then I participated in a text study during which my group responded to document-based questions similar to an AP exam. I evaluated my peers as having done a good job, impressive even, but again, I felt confident in my own plan.

Energy still coursing through me, I distributed copies of the Declaration of Independence and asked them all to read the preamble. Then, I asked a question, really quite loudly, it seemed. And the room remained silent. No one responded. Silence greeted my follow-up question as well. I was dumb-struck. A veteran teacher sitting near the front of the room leaned toward me and wondered if I was really asking a different question. I realized that my question did not make sense to them. They didn't understand what I wanted from them!

My palms grew moist. My energy level remained high but now it centered in the pit of my stomach and blood seemed to drain from my brain. I stood at the head of the conference table, facing my peers, without a clue how to proceed. Grabbing my lesson plan from the table, I turned to the blackboard behind me. My fingers couldn't quite hold the chalk, but I clung to this instruction tool, shaking with determination. I wrote another question on the board. The words were almost illegible. I stopped mid-sentence, frantic. I turned slightly to the right, to my instructor and silently pleaded for help. She nodded and encouraged me to take my time. I stepped to the front of the table and again assumed a position of authority.

"Okay, um, let's try this ..." I flipped through my plans and notes. "Umm." I pushed papers to this side and that. "Ahh ..."

Bent over the rough wooden table, my carefully arranged long hair tumbling to shield my face, I exhaled one sob, releasing my exuberant, confident, passionate energy. Deflated, I quickly wiped the tear that leaked from my left eye and raised my head to my peers.

"I don't know what to do." I straightened up and backed away from my presumed authority, defeated.

My instructor came forward and explained that my failed attempt would be useful as a learning experience for the class. She dismissed me.

To return to my seat, I had to squeeze behind the other students or step over their feet, so try as some might, they couldn't avoid me. Some whispered comfort and others shifted with discomfort as I passed. Numbly, I took my seat and heard, as if through Broadway traffic at Lincoln Center, my peers deconstruct my lesson and point out each failing and flaw.

What happened? How could it have happened? I've seen this kind of lesson, this idea of questions and discussions, and the goal of teaching skill and content to develop citizenship ... I'd seen it all done before! I know what this is supposed to look like, and yet no one was engaged by my energetic provocation to thinking critically. Maybe, I just didn't prepare hard enough. I would have to work harder next time. I know what I'm doing. I just didn't do it well. That must be it, but it was unacceptable. I pushed the failure down and moved forward. I would do better in the next task.

1.2 *Becoming a Teacher (in Harlem)*

Ira, a graying hippy and member of the intelligentsia (it appeared), spoke rapturously about a different kind of progressive "inner city" school. The ten of us in my Social Studies Methods course at Teachers College, Columbia University (TC) had gathered in a basement room of the institution and listened to Ira discuss the work he and other teachers at an alternative public high school in Harlem were doing. It was a radical approach to traditional schooling, built on progressive thought, which had found great success in the last decade. My ambition to teach well and in educationally sound ways rose to meet his call for student teachers. I HAD to teach there. I HAD to go where I was needed, to a poor, urban neighborhood of minorities in a school led by critical thinkers. I met him after class with my response and he eagerly embraced my offer, asking me to visit the school with two other interested student-teachers.

Of my introduction to the school itself, I remember most vividly the conversation I shared with Jack, one of two ninth and tenth grade Humanities teachers. We had spent a little time with a younger female teacher who taught seventh and eighth grade Humanities, but she struck me as overly ambitious, like she had something to prove. I could not imagine us connecting in a way in which we respected each other's ideas. I wasn't sure I could learn from her because of her inexperience but also because it felt like the flow of our relationship would be ideas and knowledge deposited from her and into me. I think I was worried that I would be confined by her. My pride caused me to react viscerally and negatively when I considered working with her.

Jack, however, with rumpled polo shirt partly tucked into faded brown corduroys, spoke to me with ease behind his scruffy beard. He seemed to welcome my passion for American history, the basis for the annual curricular theme "What Justice Means to Me," and he beamed when I spouted my favorite passages from *To Kill a Mockingbird*, a central text of the course. Jack told me the students called him, and all of their teachers, by their first name. He laughed gently at my surprise and off-handedly mentioned the goal of breaking down traditional barriers to learning for these particular students. The informality of first names fostered relationships among equals, he told me, as if only speaking out an assumption he presumed we shared. I bristled at how he embraced this sign of disrespect with such nonchalance, yet he, the curriculum, and the school intrigued me. When I learned that of the three student-teacher candidates, Jack chose me to help him teach two classes of sixteen students, I was surprised and honored. It seemed like a badge of approval for an experienced educator to include me in this project, which TC so clearly found exceptional and worthy of its support.

• • •

Living in New York City was exciting and lonely, and traveling into East Harlem to carry out my student teaching responsibilities intensified both feelings. Early in the year, before the cold sent me on the M22 bus, I walked across the island from my little room in graduate student housing on W. 123rd and Amsterdam down to 110th St. to cross at the north end of Central Park. There was a terrific hot bagel cart there, so I had a fresh sesame to warm my hands in the brisk fall air as I traversed the park, trees and green and cyclists to my right, stone and glass in Art Deco rising from my left. I walked with a greater sense of ease as the year passed and the city became more familiar, but I could never quite shake the discomfort that gurgled in the pit of my stomach when I stepped out of the park and into the streets of East Harlem. I had a full block east and three blocks south to walk before I was safely in the building. Sometimes consciously, sometimes not, my pace quickened onto 5th Avenue and I tried not to see or to pretend I didn't care that everyone else on the street was some shade of brown to my white. I was becoming a worldly-wise woman after all. These things didn't matter to me. I belonged here in Harlem, working hard to help people. And yet, I did walk pretty fast, and I did breathe easier once I had been cleared to enter the building by the security guard at school.

Once in the door, I navigated several corridors and two sets of stairs to my classroom. The hallways were bustling with lively 7th–12th grade students, who called to one another and laughed loudly but rarely with anger or aggression.

Hallways and bathrooms were bright and free of graffiti. Except for the security guard at the door, who asked me my name until she knew me, and the children who bore little resemblance to friends, family, or neighbors in my life, I never felt like I was in an "inner city school."

•••

In the first week of my first semester of student teaching, Jack and I took the classes down to the school library to select books for their personal reading. It was a large space, the equivalent of two classrooms, with a long wall of north facing windows which greeted us with bright sunlight as we entered, illuminating and introducing me to the school's voluminous treasure of books. Shelves filled with books lined the four walls of the space and jutted out toward the center of the room every six to eight feet. Gently used round tables and chairs were tucked within the spaces between shelves. The students fanned out when we entered the room, as if they had been there before and knew where to go for their favorite genres.

A few students walked a bit aimlessly, unsure of themselves. The part-time librarian was not there that day, so I approached Ruby, a fourteen-year-old girl who could best be described in one simple word: sweet. Seriously sweet. Ruby was Dominican, I think, but her skin was olive rather than the darker shade of some of her Dominican peers, her eyes a stunning blue. Her full, thick sandy hair was always pulled away from her cherubic cheeks with a headband, a different color every day. Ruby's petite stature carried her gentle kindness well. She was well-loved and respected, giving pause to friends when they noticed she might disapprove of their behavior. Of course, I loved her right away and responded immediately to her reach for connection. When she needed a book recommendation, I did not want to let her down. And, frankly, this was my first "assignment"; I confess that I felt I had something to prove.

It didn't feel like a difficult assignment. I have loved to read since elementary school. At the time, when people asked if I loved to read, I told them I was "voracious." I like the sound of that word and what it might tell people about me: a lover of literature, a connoisseur, an intellectual. Reading held a place of honor in my family. And we didn't read just anything. My dad stocked his study shelves with non-fiction, vintage sets of Winston Churchill's *History of England*, *Wilson Quarterlies* and biographies, while my mom's library began on the surface of her nightstand with recent Newberry Award winners; memoirs of missionary women, copies of *Pride and Prejudice* and the like flowed down into stacks on the floor; and early Newberry's intended for review before an upcoming unit cascaded out from a stuffed Cleveland Public Library tote bag.

(she taught reading as well as history at their school). I'd be lying if I told you that this is all they read, but reading was nourishment and as such the bulk of our family's reading diet was "meaty." Early in my Summer Reading Club days at our local library, my mother—reading teacher extraordinaire—taught me the difference between "candy" books and great literature. She pointed to the work of specific authors, Madeleine L'Engle's *A Wind in the Door* and Katherine Patterson's *Bridge to Terabithia* outstanding, worthy literature; Judy Blume's work, good; Francine Pascal's *Sweet Valley High* series, definitively candy.

Beyond that, I learned to distinguish great literature by how it might affect my person. For this, I observed my family. My mother descended from a line of scholars and theologians for whom reading was an intellectual activity—being well-read a sign of a good upbringing because it meant one had a sure foundation and steady path forward toward growth in a life well-lived. On my father's side, there was always at least one large print book open on my Grammy's kitchen table. Her father was a book binder, who read every single book he bound, from fiction to engineering textbooks. Grammy's pattern and the lore about my great-grandfather communicated a responsibility to me about reading and being a human being. My father descended from blue collar immigrants, but in his adult life, he actively studied the lives of great men and women in an aspirational intent to become more than what he was raised to be. I had so much respect for him, for both sides of my family. In them, I witnessed an intentional quality to the selection of books and literature in my home. Concepts like the "Western Canon" and Great Books were not unfamiliar to me as a young person, as they were used as guides in literature selection, helping to separate the wheat from the chaff.

I understood my assignment for Ruby to be one that was thick with meaning. The book I selected for her needed to be great literature in order to both feed her intellectually and be worthy of her time. I went straight for *Jane Eyre*. She had just finished a Jodi Piccoult novel, so I estimated that Ruby was a strong reader, albeit misguided spending her time in a "candy" book. But *Jane Eyre* was a classic, and I loved it as a teenager. Perfect selection! I was silently triumphant, but beaming at Ruby as I turned from the shelves with the book in my hand.

Ruby's eyes brightened at my attention and she earnestly listened to me describe the plot to her. My enthusiasm seemed contagious. She stretched for the book, flipped to the first page and sank into a chair as if she believed she'd need the seat once she got lost in the book's world.

Jack's wide-eyed response to my selection came with a light-hearted laugh, "Wow. You're hard core." This puzzled me. I thought that as her teacher, and as the intellectual that he was—working on a graduate degree in philosophy from Columbia—Jack would recognize the merits of my selection. But I was just a little bit proud, too. Yes, maybe I was hard core. It's important to aim high.

The following week, when we headed to the library again, Ruby carried the book down with her. I hadn't seen her with it all week but assumed she'd taken it home to read.

"Are you finished already?!" I wondered.

Ruby's rosy cheeks brightened. "No."

"Well, what part are you reading now?" I asked, skimming the most dramatic scenes in my memory, wondering which ones we might be able to discuss.

Her blush deepened to crimson, and Ruby opened the book to the middle of the first chapter. I glanced at the dense, Gothic description of the setting. "Oh, just keep going. It gets good!" I encouraged her. She nodded slowly and smiled kindly at me, but her eyes gave me pause. Several weeks passed and I overheard her comparing notes on Wally Lamb's *She's Come Undone* with Jack. Her eyes danced and the volume of her voice rose above its typical calm tenor. When Jack returned to our desks at the front, our eyes met and he said, "She really got into that book!"

"So she finished *Jane Eyre* finally?" I asked. He shook his head in response. She never read it. My heart fell in disappointment. Why didn't she like it? How could she not finish it?

• • •

Nate lived with his grandmother. His mother was in jail; for what, I'm not sure. Her absence came to me in whispered undertones, a colleague's head bent toward mine as children milled and wrote and traded barbs around us. We spied Nate and exchanged knowing glances. Nate's father ... well, I don't know where his father was. He came up in conversation vaguely and infrequently. Nate's teachers took his father's absence for granted. But, there was nothing unclear about Nate's residence. Decidedly, Nate lived with his grandmother. Perhaps his grandfather sheltered him as well. His grandmother, however, lived in Nate's presence at school.

All of the children at this school arrived at the prompting of some adult in their lives. It was not a neighborhood school, which traditionally schooled children in the local vicinity because they were legally obliged to enroll. Instead, it was an alternative school in East Harlem, established within the public school system but outside of the restrictions and obligations of institutional rules and policy. And to participate in the education of this school, a child needed an advocate in their life who could exercise their right to remove the child from the neighborhood school by filling out the necessary paperwork, speaking to the right people, finding an alternative school, and enrolling their child (with more paperwork).

So in Nate's presence, we did indeed see his grandmother. The existence of caring adults in the lives of these children spoke through their attendance here. I could never say these children were to be pitied because they didn't have family who cared about them. In fact, that narrative was quickly put to rest in my mind when I understood this condition of the children's enrollment in this school.

Nate possessed a grand aura. We all laughed when Nate laughed, and we reflected upon our own beliefs when Nate opined. He regaled us with tales, a broad smile across a soft round face, a booming heralding voice recalling adventures. Nate's body, two years older than most of his peers, enfleshed his personality perfectly. I am not a petite woman; in fact, as an adolescent, my pediatrician lovingly referred to me as "perfectly proportioned for strength." Still, I was diminished when confronted by his physicality. I had to look upwards to make eye contact, and that was after craning my neck and rocking back onto my heels. When Nate's humor turned to wisecracks and creative excuses to ignore his school work, my pointer finger was hard at work in admonition while his grin stretched through his thick, round shoulders extending far beyond my own. I could hug him if he wasn't so infuriating and, frankly, scary.

In the midst of an in-class writing assignment on "What justice means to me in *Their Eyes Were Watching God*," I noticed Nate stretching with a huge, full-bodied, and vocal yawn, resting once his hands supported the back of his head. A blank notebook decorated the table in front of him. "Nate, get started," I called to him from a table across the way where I was sitting with Manya, coaxing an opinion from her to start her essay. He hunched over the notebook with his pencil poised to write. But it never moved. Within a few minutes, Nate was up wandering around the room, poking classmates as he passed by. He eventually landed at the pencil sharpener where he very, very slowly cranked the gadget. Nate glanced over his shoulder, grinning, and caught the eye of Shanda. Shanda giggled, as he knew she would. She shared Nate's sense of humor, and I struggled to help her focus on school work in the same ways I did with Nate. Once Nate had her attention, he shook his booty in rhythm with the cranking motion, speeding it up and slowing it down to a beat in his head. Shanda's giggle turned into a guffaw and vigorous elbow-jabbing to John sitting beside her. Soon her whole table bopped their heads and tittered and whispered in response to Nate. With an indulgent smile, I called in a deep, warning cadence to each of them: "Nate ...." And then, "Shanda ...." Shanda quieted with an endearing, "C'mon Christy, we just having some fun." Unspoken was the "you know we don't mean any harm." Shanda tended to reach for a connection to me even when she did something she knew I might not like.

Nate kept sharpening his pencil. Defiantly, it seemed. I marched across the room to his side. I heard a few ominous "ooos" from students, a soundtrack to confrontation. In a quiet, calm but firm tone, I asked Nate to take his seat. Still goofing around, Nate laughed, "I'm just sharpening my pencil." I spoke more firmly and insistently. "Nate, take your seat and get to work."

He turned to face me, just a foot away. Nate looked down at me, but square in the eyes. "I don't want to write." My sense of righteousness was outraged by his blatant lack of respect for me, his disobedience. And so, despite his looming presence and the nausea building in my gut, I raised my voice to make it full and wagged my pointed finger at his face, "Nate, I don't want to ask you again. Please sit down." His chest and shoulders swelled and I fought to maintain my power in his massive presence.

Our stand-off held briefly. Jack casually called from the back of the room, "Nate, come on. Grab your notebook and try the hallway." Immediately, Nate turned in response to him, complaining, "Aww, Jack …" and yet he walked to the table, retrieved his notebook and exited the room.

I tried not to miss a beat, bending to the table in front of me to inspect the progress of the students sitting there. As if unfazed, I engaged with each of them, read a few sentences, and answered questions along the lines of "Is this enough?" I worked my way through that table of students and out into the hallway. I could not let that stand-off define my relationship with Nate.

On either side of the hallway, a handful of students sat alone trying to compose their thoughts on paper. They were relatively quiet. Nate joined them, squished into a right-handed desk meant for a leaner body. His notebook open, he propped his elbow on the paper and rested his head in his hand as he stared at the paper, flicking it with his pencil. I turned out of the classroom and caught this image. This was not the picture of defiance. Nate seemed lost and tired.

When I approached him, I knelt at his desk. "Nate, can I help you?" He didn't look up, but he mumbled, "Christy, I don't have anything to say. I don't know what to write. This is dumb." His pencil tapped and tapped.

"Nate, I remember in our discussions that you had a lot to say about this book. What did you like about it?" I inquired.

"I don't know," Nate stonewalled.

"Really?! You were pretty darn loud about your opinion. What got you going?"

"I don't know. It just bothered me how much shit Janie took."

"Nate, write that down," I instructed. I wanted him to get something on the page.

"Write what?"

"It bothered me how much shit Janie took." I repeated that line several times as he slowly scrawled it. We proceeded to write line by line his responses to my guiding questions, as I pressed him to describe what he meant by "shit" and how Janie "took" it. The pencil lead crowded out the white space and, by the time class ended, Nate had written a page and a half back and front.

"Nate, look at what you accomplished," I made him look back over the pages. "You did that in 15 minutes! You just need to write another page, probably two more paragraphs, to finish!"

"Yeah, I guess. Oh yay, homework!" He began with a hidden grin but then quickly changed his demeanor back to jokester as he feigned disinterest and cluttered his stuff into a pile. I was proud of him. Of us. Of our work together. Of myself.

When I collected the essays the following day, Nate's essay had not progressed. I felt defeated and confused. I had gotten him off to such a good start. Why didn't he finish?

•••

Jack left me alone with the class of 16 about two thirds of the way through the year. I stood in front of the class and buoyantly announced our agenda, to hearty cheers ... a movie with our lesson today! A PBS special on Lincoln. The opening credits rolled, and we settled in. Sometime between narrations by famous actor X and another historian's backstory filler, I sensed a shift. The whispers began. I sat up straight in my chair and looked over at Nate and John with my stink eye. They quieted momentarily, but the shift was foundational. Voices around the room rose. The class tittered and chatted and cajoled. I leapt to the VCR and paused the movie. I turned and faced the class. In my most, "hey, we're on the same team but I mean business" voice, I bargained.

"Here's the deal, guys." (My university supervisor told me I used "here's the deal" too much. After her two observations, she had only two other pieces of advice, so "here's the deal" must have been a glaring and big teaching no-no. Shame and incredulity kept her words with me.) "We have half an hour left and then we can get into our next project. Hang in there. Pay attention!"

"C'mon, y'all! Shut up!" Manya, an imposing, vocal, and vibrant girl shouted in support.

The class quieted. Nate and John exchanged sly smiles. A few of the girls rolled their eyes at the boys. I pressed PLAY.

Within minutes, the whispers began again. Someone tossed a paper ball. Chairs squeaked as students moved in conversation. My stomach knotted and I stomped to the screen and raised my voice. "Look, I asked you to stop. Cut it out!" I trembled a little. Nate had begun to talk in a normal voice and now he turned his back to me and continued his conversation. Another table of students, boys and girls followed suit. I turned to pleading and, frankly, lying, to get them to respond to me in a way I wanted them to. I felt a kind of desperation. I couldn't figure out how to elicit cooperation. How to make them OBEY ME.

"Guys, we had a really cool activity planned but it's taking us so long to get through this video, we might not have time for it." I lied. There was no such cool activity planned. Time was dwindling and I had resorted to manipulation.

"Hey, shut up!" Cooperative students chimed in. "Come on, everybody, let's do what she wants." I could tell a few of them took pity on me.

A disgruntled and half-hearted hush fell over the room, and again, I pushed PLAY. When the volume rose, yet again, I was just baffled. What was wrong with me? Why couldn't I get them to respect me? Why wouldn't they listen? I asserted my authority again.

"Hey! Enough! I'm turning this off until you are quiet." I startled them into silence, but then Nate kind of chortled, looked at me, tilted his chair back and turned to his friends to resume his storytelling.

"I'm going to leave the room until you can get your act together." Grasping for another tactic, I walked into the hall and shut the door.

The chatter continued, so I charged back in, calmly pleaded, "Be quiet." I pushed PLAY.

For ten more minutes, a few students watched, others doodled, most whispered and giggled. I shot them all dirty looks. When the clock's second hand finally inched to the end of the period (no bells at this progressive school), I stood on my proverbial soap box and firmly told them to stay in their seats. They were not dismissed. I then laid on the thickest guilt trip I could conjure.

"I told you we had a really terrific surprise planned for you. I mean it was really great. But you couldn't keep it together. I'm so disappointed in you." I bent my head and shook it. My voice was sad and just a bit whiny, maybe on the brink of tears. My hope was to shame them into remorse and reestablish myself as the one to whom they were accountable.

As I dismissed the class, sweet Ruby reassured me with pity in her blue eyes. Manya told me, "It's OK. You did OK."

"Forget about them, Christy" another boy called out. Most students left the room, passing me in the doorway as if nothing traumatic had happened. Conversations continued, though a few pointedly looked away from me. Nate especially avoided my eyes, but his chin was out and shoulders back. He laughed with friends and shoved his way into the hall.

I tidied the room in a daze of shame and fury. What wasn't I getting? What was wrong with these kids? Argh ... I lied! I was manipulative!

As I packed my teaching bag, I packed away these feelings as well. I was embarrassed. And I didn't know how to handle the pain of not being able to handle them. I had to just figure this out and NEVER let it happen again!

•••

"You know, Christy, it took me an hour to get here on that damn bus?" Manya laughed and called to me from across the room, as the rest of her peers read *To Kill a Mockingbird* silently. Her vocal tone was as deep and rich as her brown skin.

"That's a long time, Manya. How 'bout you get back to reading?"

"Awww, you know I don't like to read. The sun is too bright in here. It hurts my eyes. You know what we gotta do, we gotta have you read to us." Facing the window, she shielded her eyes and batted her lashes.

I sighed. Manya always had an excuse. And I was a no-excuses kind of teacher. You do the assignment you are told to do. No questions asked. I believed that children often resisted what was good for them. School, this assignment, and the effort required to complete the assignment were all good for Manya. I needed to make her do the work for her own good. This was especially true, in my estimation, because Manya was pulled out for support services. It wasn't clear why she required the support; to me, she seemed slower when she did her work from time to time, but I didn't know her diagnosis. Manya was also vivacious, good-natured and, well, a stinker. She loved goofy chatter and play, always rounding out the fun with the heartiest of laughter. And yet, Manya was formidable. I respected the inner strength I sensed in her soul and bore on her strong frame. I wanted what was "good for her." I wanted to be good for her.

"Manya, I'll read to you on Friday. For now, get to work, girl." I smiled, but I spoke firmly, looked at her meaningfully and walked away. She was quiet but distracted. I caught her reading from time to time but the period ended and she didn't seem to have turned a page.

Concurrently, I was enrolled in a required course entitled "Accommodating the needs of diverse learners in the regular classroom." Honestly, I felt like this course contributed to the watering down of high expectations in American education. Don't get me wrong. It's not that I didn't believe children with learning disabilities didn't need support. Or that they didn't merit inclusion in the regular classroom. Rather, the flavor of the class seemed to draw from the soft, "mamby-pamby" sentiment of the worst in the progressive tradition of child-centered education. It seemed to emphasize honoring the whims of children who didn't know what was best for them. Despite my concern and irritations, I completed the assignments to the best of my ability, never voicing my criticism or asking questions. I just grumbled and got an A because that's what I knew how to do: respect the authority of the classroom, follow the rules, and do my best.

The following week, I received an assignment to describe an experience when I accommodated the needs of one student through a practical adjustment in the classroom. Needless to say, I could not think of one, but an opportunity arose when I heard the familiar …

"Christy, what kind of bagel did you get today? You know you love those raisin bagels. I don't eat those things. Too sweet." Manya chided me with a guffaw, ignoring the writing assignment I just instructed the class to begin.

"Oh, Manya. Get to work!" Shaking my head, I spoke gently but emphatically from the front of the room.

Manya complained, "It's too bright, Christy. How do you expect me to work with that sun comin' in here like that? You know my eyes can't take it."

I took one step toward exasperation when I remembered the assignment. I bent to the desk in front of me and retrieved my sunglasses from my purse. I carried them over to Manya.

"Here. Try these. They'll help with that bright sun." I extended the sunglasses to her.

Manya's eyes popped as she reached for them. "What? Really? I can wear these?"

"Yep." I grinned. "Now get to work!"

And you know what? She did! It was my turn to marvel. Were her complaints not about getting out of work? Was the sun really too bright? Or maybe she was trying to get out of the work. It was a cloudy day. I had no idea what diverted her focus and effort. Either way, look what happened when I listened to her and made an attempt to meet her spoken need! Something shifted between us, in her attitude and willingness and, frankly, in my own heart. I was mystified, but I noted this moment and tucked it away.

1.3 *Becoming a (Substitute) Teacher*

With a month or so under my belt as a substitute teacher—a plethora of worksheet completion overseen, quizzes administered and games of "Heads Up, Seven Up" dangled and played for good behavior—I headed into Chase Middle School with a bag of sub tricks that assured a pretty decent day for me. Chase may have been the neighborhood school serving the "other side of the tracks" in this racially diverse Chicago suburb of socioeconomic extremes; it may have been the "bad" middle school, but I just finished a year teaching in East Harlem, for goodness sakes! I was a graduate of TC who knew a thing or two about progressive education. I was a sub instead of a teacher in this district by choice. I wanted to enjoy my first year of marriage to an NCAA wrestler still competing in graduate school—perhaps travel to tournaments with him, spend after school hours learning to cook—and get the lay of the land professionally before I settled down, unleashing my ambition and service.

I remember a quintessential fall day. The air was crisper than cool as I strode up the path to the main entry. It was Halloween. The wind flicked my hair about my face, but it was fresh and mimicked the rush I seemed to get almost every time I'd approached school in the last year. I was excited to be a professional, an adult with a purpose and place.

I maneuvered through the buzzing hallways and found myself standing at the entrance of a classroom full of African-American students. I wasn't late. But there they were.

My heart caught in fear. Was it my heart? It was something deep. Primal.

But there I stood. There was the customary bright folder on the desk containing lesson plans, but as it was Halloween, the school scheduled a dance mid-day. The daily rhythm was adjusted, disturbed accordingly.

Perhaps there were plans. Maybe I organized the students into groups and instructed them to spread out to different areas of the room. I may have done this. There is so little of which I am certain that day except for the visceral feelings accompanying the events that followed.

Someone turned a radio on, quietly at first, the bass and a faint melody audible. The students were talking, their volume growing despite my stern requests for quiet work. They weren't talking about their work. They weren't even pretending to.

A boy cranked the radio from the back of the room. Someone started to dance.

"Would you please turn that down?" When no one acknowledged my request, I raised my voice, "Turn that down, please!"

Laughter.

From the other side of the room, chairs scraped as kids got out of their seats and walked toward the radio.

"Sit down! Go back to your seats!"

There was some laughter, but for the most part, no one was even looking at me.

I became frantic. I pushed past students huddled and lounging at the front of the room. I stumbled over a shoe, my sweater caught on the back of a chair, and I tripped several paces into the crowd around the radio. Mid-trip, I rose to steady myself and shoved into the back of a boy.

"Hey, watch it!" The gang of students started to guffaw at me. Some looked angry and aggressively echoed their friend, "Get off him!"

My throat caught and eyes widened at the insinuation that I could be "foe."

I pleaded, "Off!" and reached for the radio. A faceless student swept it from my grasp.

"Just please keep it down," I said and turned to the whole class. "Please be quiet."

The chatter became cacophony.

I couldn't catch anyone's eye. I couldn't charm or manipulate or threaten or engage anyone.

I panicked. The chaos of disobedience was more than I could bear. I couldn't speak for fear my sobs would signal total defeat and a successful mutiny.

I hurried across the room, certain that the behavior I encountered was dangerous to me and to the students. It had to be stopped. I pressed the intercom for help.

"Please, send someone to help me in this room," I called in indignant frustration.

The intercom crackled in response. As I waited for reinforcements, I shrunk into the corner between the door and the wall, distancing myself from the uncontrollable. My face was hot and tears leaked from eyes. What was happening here?!

I must have been relieved and sent to the office to get a hold of myself or get my next assignment because I can't remember who came to restore order and rescue me or how I came to be alone in a corner of the main office. Without eyes on me, a sob heaved in my chest and burst from my tongue. As I gasped in outrage, I trembled.

I heard movement behind me, and I straightened my back and wiped my eyes. When I turned to identify the movement, I saw a man walking into the vice principal's office and taking a seat behind the desk. The school secretary followed him in, and I watched them whisper and glance at me. When the secretary emerged, she held me in her gaze until she settled into her perch overlooking the entrance to the main office.

"Have you pulled yourself together? Are you ready to try again?"

Her condescending inquiry and tone stunned me. She, and by extension the man in authority, sees me as the problem?! My incredulity quickly receded into my utter embarrassment and shame. My face grew hot and I summoned my go-getter mask.

"Oh my goodness, I'm just fine. Where to next?" I looked her in the eye, beaming cheerful obedience through my gaze. She led me to the gym to chaperone the dance and as I walked, I scolded myself.

How did you let those kids get the better of you? Why couldn't you control them? Get it together! Make it happen!

I chaperoned the crap out of that dance, ingratiating myself to kids and playing the part of responsible colleague checking the bathroom stalls. I was certain that my shame was plastered all over their conversations. Everyone knew of my failure. I worked harder to prove that it would never happen again.

When the dance concluded, the crowd of students herded me through the gym door and back into the nip of fall. My head bent, I plodded against the wind to the curb, waiting for the buses to pass so I could cross the street to my car. Still lost in my failure and gazing toward my feet, I caught the flash of yellow as a bus accelerated slowly passed me. As I watched it move past me, my eyes were blinded by wet, hard, cold ... pellets ... liquid? I heard peals of laughter. The taunting, empty Styrofoam-cup-holding culprits hung out of the windows, some still pointing at me as the bus proceeded along its route and I wiped ice and soda from my eyes.

Since that moment, I have held in my heart righteous anger ... but also penitent acceptance of just punishment for my failure.

1.4 *Becoming the (Ideal) Teacher*

My parents enrolled me in the Cleveland Public School System when I approached kindergarten age. The system's stellar reputation in the sixties had taken a hit through busing and redistricting in the seventies, but many Clevelanders still felt the system held promise by the early eighties. My dad was one of them. My parents were happy with my kindergarten experience at my neighborhood elementary school, but they were quite dismayed by my social interactions in the first few weeks of first grade. In fact, my mother was horrified by the language little boys used when they spoke to me. My classmates, most likely mimicking older siblings, called me "hot stuff" and insinuated inappropriate activities we could do together at recess. By October, I found myself in a Lutheran elementary school, which my parents hoped would be a healthier and more protected environment for me. I lasted until the end of the year.

My father and mother viewed my formal education as a tool in my human development; they believed that with a challenging academic curriculum I would learn to set goals, persevere, and practice diligence, and that I would develop other character traits allowing me to build competence and a sense of self-worth. This little Lutheran school provided an environment where I could excel, but without much effort. In addition to citizenship awards, I won every academic prize the school had to offer. And so, second grade brought a second attempt at my neighborhood public school. The gifted program started in second grade; perhaps higher expectations and a richer curriculum might provide a healthy classroom environment and require me to engage my person more deeply into the educational experience.

The gifted program did not deliver as my parents had hoped, and so that year, they toiled with several friends to establish a new school that mirrored their values. By providing an academic curriculum tailored to the instructional level of each child, they hoped that these children might use their educational experience as a way to shape their character. Thus, by third grade, I was in a private school, taught by my mother and a few women from our neighborhood, and headed by my dad. I continued there until eighth grade. Following my parents' vision to use a challenging academic environment to help me grow as a person, I studied for entrance exams into the area's elite private schools. Again, the public options in Cleveland did not offer anything close to what my parents felt they needed in terms of an educational partner in raising me. I attended Hawken School, an institution founded in the spirit of Dewey and his fellow turn-of-the-century progressives.

While my experience at an elite high school was far outside my lower middle class family background, I took for granted that I might teach in a private school by the time I was looking for gainful employment after graduate school. Instead, my first teaching experiences were in Harlem and the inner suburban ring of Chicago—public schools—and I considered the idea that maybe these schools, accessible to all children, needed teachers committed to their education. I saw how my talents and experiences could be useful to children in public schools. My conscience awoke in the midst of these considerations. I began to wonder: to whom am I accountable? For whom and to what end do I work? With my background in American history, I had been drawn to a Deweyan notion of preparing our children to participate in and experience a democracy. What was more democratic than public schooling? Did these children not deserve a challenging and engaging educational experience to help shape their sensibilities and character toward a productive life among their fellow citizens in this democracy?

• • •

My inspirations were soon overshadowed by my desire to find work. My grandfather's former student teacher and good friend was the Lower School Head at a wealthy suburban independent school with an open position for middle school history. I applied for that position, and Paul, my grandfather's friend, placed my resume on top of the Middle School Head's desk. When I interviewed for the position, I taught a sixth grade lesson on latitude and longitude. The students read the textbook's description the night before, so I began by asking what they remembered from their reading of the text. Then we played with the words; I gave them pneumonic devices and actions to help with their recall and understanding.

"Latitude is flat-itude," I pronounced as I stretched my arm horizontally and parallel to the floor.

"Loooooooooongituuuuuuude," I exaggerated, simultaneously stretching one arm toward the floor and the other toward the ceiling.

The students mimicked me and we verged just shy of crazy-silly as we acted out these geographic terms for one another. We transitioned smoothly from the hilarity; the novelty of a new teacher enabled quick response time, perhaps.

With their atlases opened on their desks and working in pairs, the students followed my demonstration, placing their fingers on the X and Y axes at the degrees I called out, slowly following the lines until their fingers met at a city. The pace of this activity picked up as the students mastered the finger connections, so we moved on to another activity in which I hoped to address their competence with this new skill. We rearranged the desks and tables so that there were two aisles on either side of a row of desks facing the front, and I divided them into two teams. Atlases on the front desk, two 12-year-olds bounced from toe-to-toe anticipating my question as I called out a city or a location. The students raced to find the coordinates, exuberantly shouting their find and leaping triumphantly to the back of their lines—hardly waiting for my confirmation, so certain were they of their new skills.

The atmosphere was intense and joyful … electric. I could feel the awe and approval from the history department, three men over the age of 55, at the back of the room. The Middle School Head was equally enamored through the course of our interview when I spouted theory and how I saw it implemented in practice. Specifically, he was impressed with my facility with Howard Gardner's multiple intelligences theory, considering different abilities and capacities in middle school children.

I got the job. I felt affirmed and was practically bursting with pride. My ethical dilemma, scratching at my enthusiasm, rose to challenge my easy acceptance of the position, but as I discussed my discomfort with my uncle he suggested that perhaps I could learn to teach at this school. Having learned classroom management and how to teach Social Studies, maybe then I could find a job that would also require me to learn how to negotiate a more challenging environment. Sold! His advice was logical, even wise, I thought, so I dove into being a history teacher, my dream and avocation.

•••

But throughout my time at this school, the wealth and privilege of these children and their families troubled me. No, the children's entitlement and their parents' hubris could irritate me. What troubled me was whether or not my presence at this school was ethical, given the privilege. How could I make a difference? What difference was there to be made? I wondered if my colleagues felt the same. Many had taught at this school for the entirety of their careers, ten—fifteen—even twenty-five years. I asked them, and I asked my peers who joined the profession as recently as I had. Their responses and rationales for teaching in this environment, offering their service to these children, shared a common theme resembling an altruistic calling of sorts: "These children will be leaders in this country. We need to make sure they develop into thoughtful, generous, wise adults."

For most of my tenure at this school, I appropriated this logic because it fit within my philosophy of teaching for democracy. That is, I saw my work as preparing citizens to become critical thinkers, able to recognize multiple perspectives so that they could function to perpetuate American democracy. Function, for me, implied service and sharp thinking. When I fought battles over dress code or half-hearted efforts or insular condescension, sometimes I cringed at how small, how very, very small were the educational problems of the wealthy. But then I'd sigh and remind myself that these children needed help to grow up as healthy, competent, kind people—just as every other child did.

This thought was not merely convenient. Perhaps instilled by my parents in their decisions and conversations about my own education, I was drawn to the intersection of education, school, and the development of human beings. I believed in the empowering possibility of educational experiences to support the growth of an individual to live a full, rich, and meaningful life. I clung to this notion and found myself stumbling upon it through my pedagogy, student discipline, and my experience with colleagues and our administration.

• • •

In my first year, teaching eighth grade, I embraced my inner Jack Keating, passionate, outside-the-box, subject expert and lone, daring educator of *Dead Poet's Society* fame. I took the mantle from Mr. Tottenham, but instead of profanity-filled stories, I wooed my students into historical thinking, clear communication and hard work with Howard Gardener's multiple intelligences. I required them to outline texts to learn to read carefully and identify themes. We carefully walked through their outlines together. We memorized states and capitals. We read *Across Five Aprils* to enrich our study of the Civil War. We recited American poetry through the ages and embarked on large and small research projects to learn the historical method. I left the product of some of these projects open-ended, allowing the students to write a paper, perform a skit, or prepare a visual presentation. My class leapt at the chance to perform, and this became particularly apparent as we studied Native American history.

I isolated this thread of history as a unit to look at the Native American experience across time. For eight weeks—four weeks past the intended scope of the unit—we read portions of the textbook to set the stage for a new era and then the students broke out into groups to research and study the Native American perspective of that time, each project typically ending in a performance. The highlight of the unit was a class movie, totally student-driven, in which they acted out the parts of Cherokees and President Jackson through the Trail of Tears. The students came to class with the idea, inspired by Parker—our class documentarian, as all of his projects culminated in a video presentation (he is now a film-maker in Hollywood). Day after day for two weeks, they burst into my classroom with anticipation for their film work. We trampled through the wet leaves on the soccer field, cameras and scripts in tow. Classmates huddled together, weeping and trudging the trail. Jackson haughtily looked on with his advisors.

I stood in awe of their motivation, thrilled by their joy and experience of history. I boasted of their engagement, proud of them and of myself. Deep inside, there were flickering moments of wondering if I was a fraud. Were we merely playing? I dismissed this thought as my insecurity in the face of the students' delight. In fact, I reframed my curriculum from that point forward. The complexity of the notion of Manifest Destiny, its multiple perspectives, and far-reaching consequences was so evident to the students that I took that theme throughout the rest of American history. We weighed "American interests" against those people affected by those interests.

While I stumbled through teaching sixth and seventh grade, with their younger children and World Cultures curriculum, that year with my eighth grade students remains a hallmark in my mind of my own teaching and my own learning. I was feeling my way through, going with my gut, but adjusting my plans according to my students' needs and to align with the expectations of the curriculum. The only mar on that year was an incident of plagiarism.

A research paper was the eighth grade curricular staple. I tried to work research skills into the units preceding the research paper, which traditionally fell just after the mid-term, prior to Spring Break. Having never planned an entire year of curriculum, it was difficult for me to plan ahead and figure out how long it would take us, realistically, to make it through my plans. I often sacrificed skill-building for covering content. I had to get to the 1980s at least by the end of the year. By January, we were only just approaching the Civil War!

By the time we reached the research paper milestone in the year, we had practiced note-taking and recognizing relevant information by our weekly practice reading texts and creating outlines of our notes; and the students practiced organizing information around a thesis or theme through their mini-projects in every unit. The assignment itself, written at least a decade earlier, included a step-by-step approach to the research process; thus, I felt comfortable assuming the students had the tools they needed to complete the assignment (though, ever critical or ever primed to "grow and do better" I knew that I would have to focus more on the skill build-up to the assignment next year).

You can imagine my surprise, then, when two papers shifted from pubescent formality to absolute scholarship for three to four paragraphs every two pages. Plagiarism! I was astounded. I was offended! My sense of righteousness was almost outraged. The papers belonged to Jacob and Dustin, bright boys but not particularly high-achieving. I often commented on the lack of effort in their work, while praising their ideas. They were full of fun and quite engaging, even during academic tasks in our classroom. But I was not surprised that it was these two boys who plagiarized. They needed to be taught a "lesson," but my difficulty with confrontation and my need to be liked tempered my outrage. I went to the division head, arbitrator of student discipline and parental issues.

Mary had taught math for many years, and just that year, she assumed the position of Upper School head. Having been six months under her leadership, I felt she was fair, wise, and supportive of teachers. In her estimation, and in the opinion of a few other teachers and administrators she consulted, the boys needed a lesson that would leave a mark. Those involved in the conversation seemed to share my offense and disbelief that the boys thought they could get away with it. Who did they think they were?

Mary called their parents into the office, and we met with each boy and his parent separately. Dustin's dad, the CEO of an international, multi-million-dollar pharmaceutical laboratory, turned to his son upon hearing our indictment. The husky boy cowered, slowly leaking tears. His father's voice boomed, too loudly for the confines of the office. The man's reprimand expressed a kind of disappointment and scorn that suggested this incident only fed a narrative the man told himself about his son. Inwardly, I cringed. It was too hard. It was too much.

Jacob's mom was a thirty-something divorcee whose inherited wealth permitted ownership of a lake house and a ranch and a lifestyle which included pursuits of further education, hobbies, and philanthropy without traditional employment. Jen and I had become friendly throughout the course of our conversations about both of her children whom I taught. She respected both Mary and me. Jen met our report agreeably with measured concern. Under the surface, however, there was a levity I couldn't quite put my finger on.

A tiny feeling emerged when Mary informed me of the boys' punishment: three days' suspension, and it resurfaced a bit more strongly after the interactions with both parents. Was the punishment itself too much? Suddenly it occurred to me: did the boys even understand what plagiarism was?! That thought was almost too much to bear. I could not entertain it. I buried it and told myself that this was an important lesson for the boys. I stuck to my guns. When the boys returned to class, they were somewhat sullen. With the force of my personality and pedagogical resources, I willed them to engage and have a good time. They couldn't resist participating in the WWI trenches I had created with overturned tables, a video *All Quiet on the Western Front* playing loudly for ambiance, and crumpled paper for ammo. Our relationship was never the same. As they graduated and we said good-bye, I wondered if I'd violated something between us or if I just didn't like it when people didn't like me. Again, it was pretty painful to even consider. I bore anguish when I considered Jacob and Dustin.

• • •

Except for that hiccup, I soared as an eighth grade teacher in my own estimation; but oh, those sixth and seventh graders gave me a run for my money. I just couldn't seem to adjust to how young they were relative to the high school students with whom I began my career.

I also taught a class of seventh graders comprised of a good number of boys. Seventh graders, I learned, were an interesting bunch. The most challenging age in middle school. Hormones kicked in and freshly shaven young men played kickball alongside little boys their same age. Girls wore clothes too tight or too baggy, and touched their faces constantly, were confounded by things popping up on their bodies. Are these bumps good things or bad things?! Oh and the moods! Aggressive teasing, dramatic encounters, crying, embarrassment, and revenge. Seventh grade seemed an excellent soap opera from the outside, but to teach these children was to play Russian Roulette with one's dignity.

This class was consistently out of my control. I shouted. I cajoled. I pulled tried and true manipulations, incentivizing good behavior with fun activities and candy. One day the chaos reached a fever pitch, based on the gauge of my nerves. I raised my voice and ordered the students to quiet down and get to work. Three boys in the corner of the room, Milo, Nathan, and Preston could not pull themselves together, so angrily, I threw Nathan out of my classroom. I told him to wait in the hall. My heart tore a bit as I did that. Nathan and I had jovial relationship. He was endearing, though defensive at times. But out he went, a sacrifice to the gods of Classroom Management.

The room hushed for a time, until one of the boys, Milo exercised the plaintive call of self-righteous. The round, Greek, mama's boy tattled. "Mrs. Neider, Preston keeps pushing my paper."

I reacted in a lesser version of rage, but quickly. "Preston, get out! I will not tolerate this behavior."

Preston, a naughty prepster in the making, with his collar flipped up and his feet slipped into sockless loafers, blushed but stood defiantly, knocking back his chair. Then he casually picked up his books, smirking from the side of his mouth, and headed for the door. A final hush fell over my class and the students worked productively for the last fifteen minutes of the period.

After class, I brought Nathan and Preston into the room and turned on my stern charm. Nathan showed some remorse and Preston grinned, employing his own charm to return to my good graces. They agreed to reel it in under penalty of being taken to the next level of authority and then their parents. I agreed to let them try again.

By the end of the day, I learned that Milo had a bloody nose. Preston and Nathan were the culprits. Apparently, Milo generated the energetic naughty behavior in my classroom, according to these perpetrators, in addition to tattling on Preston. My sources told me that they plotted their revenge while out in the hallway, banished from my room. I had created the perfect conditions for their diabolic planning—what a disaster! What a miserable classroom management failure!

All year, I taught from a place of disoriented anxiety. I could not trust myself to get control of these children and never knew when the hormonal beast would rear its head. We enjoyed moments of pure delight as they sat for an hour listening to stories I wove of the Masada and Chinese folk lore. Individual children thrived as they learned to test their critical thinking and communications with debate over the Palestinian-Israeli conflict. I saw these children grow! But I taught in tension, fear and hope confounded; I never felt like I was a good teacher to them.

• • •

A year later, I applied my creative energy to my sixth grade class. Having a year of World Cultures under my belt, I felt more confident straying from the old syllabus and employing the tools I had acquired through the "History Alive!" professional development course I took over the summer. The course provided practical strategies for applying Gardner's Multiple Intelligences in the Social Studies curriculum. The theory was all the rage in graduate school and it had been trickling into pedagogy for the past few years. It made sense to me and my philosophy to do whatever I could to meet the needs of every student and challenge them so that they could grow in my class. In fact, the theory and its

Social Studies pedagogy seemed an all-inclusive tool and so I set about using it with vigor, designing every unit with every intelligence in mind. I coupled it with my historical method/thinking pedagogy and felt my classes were pretty strong as a result, rigorous and engaging for every student.

Christopher's mother disagreed. She perceived my project-based instruction as fluff. She advocated for her son with the Upper School Head. Mary defended me and even sat in on the parent-teacher conference. We educated this mother on the theory of multiple intelligences and its applications in my student-centered pedagogy. We explained to her how this pedagogy was better for Christopher and his classmates. She complained that he wasn't challenged and insisted that Christopher receive the kind of educational experiences constructed by my colleague, Joe. Joe was a sixty-something retired lawyer who saw teaching as the do-gooder phase of his life. He loved history and pontificated from the front of the classroom, often regaling students with his stories gleaned from his travels and reading. He expected his students to take detailed notes and he tested them regularly on their retention of his lectures. Joe was old school and so proud of it that we couldn't have pedagogical conversations in our department meetings. Any other method of teaching was a waste of time and he certainly had nothing more to learn. His knowledge deposited into his students was education. Period. Full stop.

I was irked by this mother's assumption that I did not know what I was doing and infuriated that she found Joe's teaching superior to mine, and yet, her advocacy of her son called attention to a slight disturbance that had registered in my considerations of Christopher. Something about my instruction did not quite fit Christopher. His projects consistently shattered even my highest expectations both in the quality of thought and in the execution. Christopher meticulously completed assignments; engineers with drafting boards could not match the precision of his visual projects. His written work expressed analysis beyond the contours of the given assignment in cogent, persuasive form—with handwriting that may as well have been typed it was so neatly shaped. When engaging in group assignments, Christopher's quiet, agreeable disposition was not an asset. Both he and his group inevitably became frustrated when Christopher's ideas and work consumed their time or pushed the group to do more than time or individual capacities allowed.

Sweet, curly-haired, blue-eyed and polite, Christopher became the bane of my existence that year. I could not make him fit into the theoretically ideal educational experiences I created. And his mother's opinion of me and my rival colleague only made the situation more untenable for me. Christopher and his mother made me question my professional expertise, only I could not do that because I did not know what else to do. I was enacting the current best practices in my field for the grade level I taught. I even attempted to differentiate by giving Christopher assignments with a bit more rigor, such as adding a higher level of question from Bloom's taxonomy or allowing him to work alone instead of in a group. When I did this, though, I felt like a hack. I felt like I wasn't equipped and so couldn't do a good job. I couldn't sit with that level of insecurity, so I blamed Christopher's mother. My colleagues, my friends, supported me with the usual attack on parents at this school: entitled elites used to getting their own way even if they had no idea what was what ... you couldn't tell them anything. It was an easy narrative to buy into. Later that year, when the parent committee bestowed their "Caring Teacher" award on me, we all gloated that Christopher's mother was in the audience and I showed her! This distinction, recognized for my efforts "above and beyond the call of duty" spoke volumes about my teaching. In our minds, the majority opinion silenced hers. It was not valid.

And yet, Christopher lingered in the discomfort in my heart. Did I not fulfill my responsibility to him? Or was the problem with him and his mother?

•••

The long-standing and storied promise of autonomy bestowed on teachers in a private school still drew and held many of my colleagues to their jobs at this school. We had freedom to select our content and our methods of instruction, as well as our assessment tools. This is what many of us believed and valued. But this firmly held tradition in the hearts and minds of the teachers could have negative consequences for students. Furthermore, great tension arose between faculty and administration that seemed to belie respect for teachers' autonomy, both on the side of the faculty and on the side of the administration.

But I will begin with the students. Because the individual teachers had control over the curriculum of the course they taught, they were not accountable for the experience of the students year to year. The first through fourth grade math teachers loved a new program called Everyday Mathematics for the conceptual understanding and practical application it promoted. The fifth grade teachers found the incoming fifth graders ill-prepared for the fifth grade curriculum, which required a strong algorithmic foundation. These teachers fought quite bitterly about which program was better. You could feel their disdain for one another around the faculty lunch tables, muffled by stiff, polite smiles. In private, or when a rival wasn't present, these teachers bemoaned the lack of quality education received by the children in the other math classes, but few seemed to prioritize the experience of the children over their preferred pedagogy.

This problem existed in other departments, though to a lesser extent. We rolled our eyes quietly at Joe's pompous proclamations of how best to teach history, but the Social Studies department could still do a tequila shot together at the annual holiday party. Despite our shared joviality, the children in our care bounced between varying philosophies of education and every year they were subject to their teachers' pet preferences and projects in history. This was a similar trend throughout the school. Some classes learned about frogs three years in a row because their first grade teacher loved frogs, their second grade teacher kept a frog in the classroom, and their third grade teacher relied heavily upon a textbook in which frogs featured prominently in the unit on amphibians.

Revisiting subject matter was not what troubled me. Instead, it was the lack of attention to the children's total experience as they progressed through the school. In fact, even within a grade level, teachers held vastly different expectations for the children's organization, including whether or not they wrote their homework assignments in a notebook or had to bring pencils or pens to class. Teachers rarely spoke with one another about their standards for skills shared among the disciplines, such as note-taking or writing. I was greatly discomfited that we prioritized our teaching autonomy above a thoughtful, coordinated educational experience for the children in our care.

This problem of autonomy was further frustrated by significant tension between the faculty and the administration. The current headmaster, Karen, replaced a man who had served the school for almost thirty years the year prior to my arrival. Karen's entrance coincided with revelations about the previous headmaster's tenure. He had paid teachers according to his discrimination, starting from the premise that if the teacher was not supporting a family then they didn't need as much money. You might imagine the kind of old boys' club he fostered during his tenure. The men he left behind pined for him and interpreted Karen, our new head, and her strong, brash leadership style as bitchy and undermining. Many of the women on staff joined their grumbling and gossiping, distrustful of any administration supported by the same board of trustees who allowed the injustices under the past headmaster. The tension and negativity stunned me, though I will admit that being welcomed into conversations with these adults and fed juicy tidbits of gossip felt pretty great. I participated at first, reveling in the salacious details. Over time, however, it became frustrating. My colleagues and I complained a lot. We were victims of parents, victims of an administration who didn't protect us or look out for our needs, and victims of a board who cared more about façade—literally putting millions into new, arguably necessary construction—than about salaries and compensation. Some of my colleagues, the ones I began to admire because they maintained a positive attitude, shared their philosophy with me: "I shut my door and I give my students my best. I don't get into the rest." The prospect of confining my perspective to my small classroom, combined with the nagging suspicion that the children and their education were being compromised, kept me from embracing this philosophy.

Thus, when the headmaster announced that the school would undergo a period of self-reflection and strategic planning, I leapt at the chance to serve as a faculty representative to the steering committee. She embraced my participation after hearing how passionate I was about addressing the big picture. In a large meeting with board members and alumni, my fellow faculty representatives and I offered our take on the lack of a unifying curricular mission. This created some angst initially because the headmaster and members of the board thought we had one already. To their credit, they listened to the teachers who regularly had to function without an organizing, coordinating framework.

A curriculum committee was formed and from their work, the headmaster brought in an expert on curriculum mapping. This tool, both a framework and software program, allowed teachers to journal their curriculum as they taught it over the course of the year. It was a living document as opposed to a binder of intentions left on a shelf to be consulted when a new teacher took up a position at the school. But the hope was that this living document might be a communication tool among the faculty where we might recognize replication or gaps, for example. The framework also prompted teachers to consider the essential questions and rationale underlying their curriculum, and so it was an opportunity for teachers to reflect and think critically about their work, as well.

As a member of the committee, I became a mentor for my colleagues as they attempted to frame their practice with this curriculum mapping tool. A few teachers already intuitively approached their practice this way but many more were frustrated. They were used to thinking about their practice in terms of units of content, the knowledge or specific skills they wanted their students to learn. Framing content by discovery was unfamiliar. Even pinpointing specific learning objectives mystified some who had for some time driven their content with pet projects and fun activities.

Through the mapping process, some teachers went from defensive despair to a bright, engaged thoughtfulness. The transformation was something to witness with one particular fourth grade teacher. As a result of her engagement, she was no longer a victim of the project. She was driving her curriculum, but from within a context that expected her to stretch beyond her former way of seeing. While she endeavored to grapple with unfamiliar ways of thinking and see her work differently, she knew that this work would be shared with her colleagues so her energy, thought and creative growth would be shared as well.

I myself moved from a sympathetic, yet self-righteous mentor to a team mate and believed that she and I were laying the groundwork for real teamwork among her grade level colleagues.

I'm not sure all of the teachers had such positive experiences with mapping, but I did feel the whole school effort to move everyone to the same page contributed to an overall enlivening of the faculty. For about a week after these professional development sessions, the atmosphere of the school was different. There was a bit of hopefulness in the air.

The hope dwindled, inevitably. A new Upper School Head, Steve, replaced Mary and he contributed to the administration/faculty contention by having the audacity to take Karen's side. Despite my attempts to rise above the fray after my first few years, I could not stay positive. I found myself grumbling a lot, a victim to Karen and her policies. Midway through what would be my final year at the school, I received word that Karen would not fund my travel to a national history competition in DC for which my students qualified after two earlier levels of competition and a lot of hard work. I relayed this information to my colleagues. They pounced on my grievance and we quickly formulated that this was yet another example of Karen abandoning the teachers. I did not have the funds for this trip and I was indignant that Karen would not support me when my work reflected so well on the school. I took my case to Steve, who listened stone-faced to my complaint, which I squeezed out through the self-pitying sob in the back of my throat.

"Christy, didn't you just submit a receipt for payment for a professional development course?" Steve spoke dryly.

"Yes, but that was for last summer!" The sob released in a tidal wave of self-righteousness. Dogs barked across the neighborhood at the pitch of my cry.

"But you waited to submit it and now it is taken out of the budget for this year. You've used up your allotted funds." And he turned his back and walked away.

Confusion whirled in my head. But, but, but ... Shouldn't she still support me? My god, is my lack of responsibility screwing with my ability to support my students?! Shouldn't she have budgeted for me this year the same amount? Wouldn't there be a surplus? Oh, oh ... Karen did lecture us about submitting our receipts in a timely way. She gave us strict but clear boundaries for funding this year. Oh, god, am I in the wrong?

"No way!" My colleagues exclaimed. "She should support you!" "She's arbitrarily exercising her power!"

When the newsletter mentioned my students' achievements without the usual thanks to the teacher, my colleagues and I confirmed that this was Karen's hand. Karen was exacting her revenge because I was leaving the school that year to teach at the school led by Paul, our former Lower School Head. To Karen, it may have felt like a slap in the face. I wasn't leaving to try public schools, as I thought I might, or to teach high school, another reason I submitted when I resigned. My future institution differed ever so slightly. In fact, she confronted me.

"I thought you wanted a change? I didn't know you wanted to teach fourth grade. You should have said something. I could have found something for you here!"

Many of my colleagues shared her confusion. I had been talking about getting involved with the National Teachers Academy, established that year by the Chicago Public Schools. It was a neighborhood middle and high school in which master teachers would not only teach children but also mentor new teachers. It seemed to fit me. My nagging ethical dilemma about caring for the needs of less privileged children in public schools never went away and the joy and fulfillment I felt working with my colleagues during the curriculum mapping experiences left me aching for more. But as I jumped through the bureaucratic hoops of CPS and state licensure, waiting endlessly for someone with the NTA to return my calls and emails, another offer came to me. Paul, the family friend who brought me to my current school, reached out to me. He left the school a year before to assume the headship at a private elementary school for gifted children, also outside of Chicago. When he heard through the grapevine that I wanted to leave, he approached me. I was languishing on a bureaucratic limb waiting for everything to come together for the public school option and soon realized it may not come through before the next school year. Paul's offer was a gift—a job—at a school led by an honorable, exciting educator. I took it even though it so closely resembled my current employment.

And so, I stammered a bit when asked, "Christy, really, tell us the real reason you are leaving." I felt accusation and judgment from Karen and sensed a conspiratorial tone from other teachers. I told them I needed a job closer to home. I wanted to try teaching gifted children, after my experience with Christopher, which was the mission of the new school.

But the real reason I left was the tension between faculty and administration. By the end of my final year, I read every move of the administration as an assault. And the self-victimization of the faculty was palpable. In my mid-twenties, I was still working on establishing who I wanted to be as an adult. This environment created constant tension in my soul. I didn't want to turn into a person who couldn't work with my colleagues, including the school's leadership. I didn't want to ignore school-wide, student experiences for the sake of self-preservation. And I didn't want to swim and breathe in stormy, negatively tainted waters. If I stayed there another year, I would either burst at my seams with untapped passion and underdeveloped practice or shrink to a version of myself I could not respect.

Upon exiting that school, I carried with me shame for my complicity in a negative work environment. I was embarrassed by my self-pity, confounded by how little we teachers exercised our voice in productive ways, and enraged at the deaf ear turned toward teachers' concerns by those in authority.

1.5   *Becoming a (Professional) Teacher*

When I asked Paul why he thought I, a passionate and skilled secondary Social Studies teacher, could teach the fourth grade, he told me that I had a quality—a gift, a perspective—that would enable me to teach anyone. Paul, the headmaster of an elementary school for gifted children, flattered me, no doubt, but I did feel drawn to thinking about teaching and learning in many contexts. Why, just last year, didn't I lead the curriculum mapping initiative with teachers at the Day School? I had been thrilled by the opportunity to walk alongside my colleagues in their frustration and excitement as they reflected upon and framed their practice. So, maybe Paul was right. Maybe I could teach fourth grade despite having training and experience only in 6th–12th grade Social Studies. Several experiences made me wonder.

•••

Leonard was a quiet but mischievous fourth grade boy with a mop of bowl-cut brown hair framing his bespectacled brown eyes, cheeks with remnant of baby chub and a big goofy mouth he was still growing into. Leonard was gifted. His IQ tests qualified him for a place at this private school for gifted elementary and middle school students. Leonard excelled in math. No, Leonard thrived in a relationship with mathematics. He devoured problem solving cards designed for use with grade levels far above his own. Night after night, Leonard dug into the boxes of cards or rustled through the folders of extra practice to "play" with math at home.

But Leonard's teacher possessed experience and training in 6th–12th grade Social Studies, and I had stopped taking mathematics seriously when my tenth grade math teacher, aka Hotpants McCants, took up some bizarre form of competition with me, humiliating me in front of my peers and vindictively rounding grades down on my progress reports. It didn't help that I'd bitten off more than I could chew the year before taking on honors geometry as a freshman. With some embarrassment, I dropped down to regular geometry after six weeks of high school. Never mind that all the way through elementary and middles school, I worked at least two grade levels above most of my peers in math. By the time I was an adult, I felt out of my depth in mathematics, frequently joking of my mathematical ineptitude. Needless to say, I did not feel prepared to engage or challenge children with exceptional abilities or interest in math.

As Leonard's teacher, I shared teaching responsibilities with a co-teacher. Together we taught 32 children in two adjacent rooms and split teaching responsibilities along disciplines. As the teacher with lesser seniority, I taught the subjects rejected by my partner: Social Studies (yay!) and math (yikes!). We shared language arts in order to share the burden of grading writing assignments. My preference would have been to spend five days a week, two hours a day on Social Studies and humanities projects and lessons. The school's curriculum, national standards, and parental pressure made my desire a moot point. Math and reading held the place of honor in the class schedule: an hour of each before lunch, recess and maybe art in-between.

Daunted by the professional challenge before me, I assumed I could at least rely on the trusty textbook and teacher's manual to guide me, as I had done during a long-term subbing assignment in science years before. I soon learned that I was required to use the University of Chicago Math system and curriculum. Everyday Math was the latest trend in math education. It eschewed "skill and drill" algorithmic pedagogy for "conceptual understanding." Children learned complex and multiple algorithms for computation, for example, in order to tease out numeric concepts. This program stood in direct contrast to the way I was taught math. In addition, the students' workbooks were arranged thematically, covering a variety of topics. The workbook assumed every child in the course grasped concepts in a synchronized and uniform manner, and it did not offer extra practice. The idea was that students would continue to revisit these concepts and understand them over time.

Initially, I panicked. Not only would I have to teach math to gifted children, but I would have to do so using very unfamiliar pedagogy. And I questioned the pedagogy. No skill work? No problem solving? No alternate pacing possibilities? I chafed at the obligation to strictly adhere to the workbook and program. I called my dad and my good friend, both math teachers at two different levels of experience in their practice, seasoned and early career. Both teachers were familiar with the program; my friend Mel struggled within her math department trying to determine its value and place in the middle elementary school years. Both teachers concurred with my assessment of the program, shaking their heads in frustration at the ever-present bandwagon effect in education: everyone jumping onboard and throwing the baby out with the bath water.

I tucked away my intuitive nudges and the confirmation of trusted colleagues for the first six weeks of school. I plunged into Everyday Math. Actually, I found that some of the new algorithms helped me to understand computation at a conceptual level. I discovered that a lot of my mathematical knowledge consisted of knowledge of rule application. It felt wonderful to know something deeply, owning it, rather than apply the rules with crossed fingers trusting the magic to work because I followed instructions. Score one—Everyday Math.

My personal discovery occurred at the blackboard in front of the children as I fumbled through a long division problem. I got the answer wrong twice while applying the rules. Finally, I turned to the students with a big confident smile and said, "I'm just trying to see if you can do this! Who wants to show me what I'm doing wrong?" Hands waved excitedly, children tickled that they could help their teacher. It was a successful move pedagogically to engage the children, and I'm so thankful I possessed knowledge of that kind of pedagogy in my tool box. But as I "aha-ed" with new conceptual understanding through observing my students apply that same knowledge—inwardly, I felt like a fraud. I was having light bulb moments and learning content right alongside of my students ... not even the night before in preparation!

As I observed and came to know my students a bit better, my intuitive inklings about Everyday Math as the sole determinant for the curriculum were confirmed: the children all needed greater challenge. Every single child in that room was academically talented. To say any struggled, without providing the context that they were all at or above grade level, would not convey an accurate picture of my dilemma. I sought to challenge and engage my students with a curriculum and pedagogy that was unable to do so in its current implementation. To leave things as they were would have been to teach to the middle of the group and designate the rest as "low" or "high." I wanted to provide a learning environment in which they all had to strive and engage to grow. No easy A; no debilitating failure. Through this lens, I could see some required more practice; the thematic presentation of content was too diverse and they had difficulty transitioning between skills. Other students raced through the workbook pages, without requiring much instruction. They sought, even demanded deeper thinking and an accelerated pace. Leonard was one of the latter. The fifth through eighth grade math teachers, my colleagues and yet the final authority on my curriculum, would not allow deviation from the school's commitment to Everyday Math. I decided then to supplement the program.

To differentiate my instruction, I needed to address the pace, depth, and complexity of the children's experience with mathematical concepts and understanding. I knew I needed materials and I knew I would have to adapt my instruction. I designed my response by drawing from knowledge I felt in my bones, old knowledge gleaned from and deposited by my parents' conversations, sometimes including me, as they wrestled with the application of gifted education research in daily practice at the private, independent school they started when I was in third grade. The summer before I started teaching at Paul's school, comprised exclusively of children who measured "gifted" on the Stanford-Binet, I borrowed books from their personal-professional library to connect research and literature to the professional knowledge forged at my family's kitchen table. That fall, the entire school attended a regional independent school conference, and I participated in a workshop on differentiation. I returned confirmed and inspired to do the work that would enable me to meet the needs of my students.

So on this base of knowledge, warranted by my parents and research, I created a plan that was focused on the students in my room.

Based upon my understanding of the students, I placed them into four groups (I saw fifteen at a time, while the other half of the class participated in their reading class): one group generally paced more slowly and needed more skill practice, one group devoured math work quickly and sought more, and two groups of students varied by concept and interest. I added the students who it seemed had greater capacity than interest to the group that was paced more rapidly. In doing so, I hoped the challenge and excitement demonstrated by that group might encourage deeper engagement by the uninterested students.

In my mind these groups were not fixed. Every unit included a pre-test. All of the students completed this assessment and I organized the groups based upon their current understanding, keeping in mind the factors above. At times, I found that once I began instruction a student might struggle or excel in a way I hadn't anticipated, so I simply moved the child after we talked about my observations and he or she appeared to understand my rationale. Thus, the groupings were somewhat fluid by concept and level of engagement.

I tackled resources next. I explored the back rooms of the school, and I went to the dollar store and the bookstore in search of practice problems, extension ideas, and problem solving materials. Before every unit, I would spend several evenings standing over the copy machine. Having estimated how much practice each group might need and what kind of depth or extension activity might be appropriate, I Xeroxed and organized worksheets into folders. Each group had their own folders arranged in order and set up in a designated area of the classroom. The folders contained work that required repetitive practice, application of the concepts, and additional related concepts. There were more or less of each category depending on the group. The children could then work independently and ask each other for help around their group's round table, as I provided direct instruction through manipulatives or board work, initiated activities, or assessed the children one-by-one.

To the independent content work and my differentiated instruction, I added the self-driven problem solving work. The school had several product lines of problem-solving cards in varying levels and we participated in a number of math competitions that provided practice resources. Students were free to do as much or as little extra problem solving work as they desired (beyond the scope of the problem-solving embedded in the curriculum I constructed related to the content). I provided charts and stickers so the students could keep track of their work. I also incentivized the more complex competition problems that usually required more time: five completed problems for a miniature candy bar. This approached seemed to induce students who were reluctant to take the risk of engaging in unfamiliar or outside-of-the-box mathematical thinking.

What remained was to introduce this idea to the students. My teacher partner Linda and I wanted to counter the narrative that differentiated instruction affected children's self-esteem. We had a sense that self-awareness and a sense of accomplishment would do more for children's self-esteem than teaching the group as a whole and pretending they all worked and understood to the same degree, at the same depth of understanding, and at the same pace. To that end, we imagined a classroom in which the children honored themselves and one another for who they were—struggles, accomplishments, and personalities altogether. We decided to have a naming ceremony. We considered the children's characteristics and named them in silly but dignified ways according to their gifts and possibilities. A smiling but easily frustrated girl became Princess Positive, for example. We designed place cards with their new names and drew up programs for our ceremony. When they returned from gym early in the second quarter, I held them outside my door while Linda finished arranging the room. The class buzzed with excitement and rushed to their seats to see what was the big deal. One by one, we asked them to stand and we "dubbed" them with their new name, encouraging applause and hoorays. Each child giggled as they rose to receive their new name: some stood proudly, others were embarrassed but grinning. We munched on some treats together in celebration, and then I stood and explained that we are group of wonderful and very different people. I tried to inspire them to honor this as we worked together.

As we shifted into math and reading classes, I explained to each class how this would apply in math. I pointed them each to a designated group and table. Each group named itself, which I allowed in an attempt to cast a shadow on which group was the "highest" or "lowest." They figured it out quickly, but thankfully I had the language from our naming ceremony to construct another way to think about our groups. We settled in. The combination of these accommodations to content, pedagogy, and environment seemed to work for my class. We hummed along together for a few weeks. Until Leonard became a problem.

Leonard flew through the content work, although it seemed that once he figured out how long this kind of work might take, he slowed and chatted with friends. But his work was always completed on time. His approach to our hands-on activities and projects were thoughtful, more than cursory attempts to follow the directions and finish the assignment. As I mentioned earlier, Leonard exuberantly tackled the problem-solving work. At every free moment, he asked to do problem solving cards. He requested five competition problems every night. He and his dad worked on them together, as a bonding experience his mother related to me. All of this did not seem to be enough. Leonard showed signs of boredom with the regular content. I felt, while he was learning new concepts, everything I provided for him did not cause him to engage his person. In other words, he didn't have to work very hard. It was all coming too easily—with the exception of some of the competition problems. I ensured that there were always plenty of problems and added more with greater complexity.

The trouble was that if Leonard could not find the answer to a problem and did not understand how to find the answer, often, I could not do the math or I could not explain how to do the math. Thankfully, the competition problems came with explanations in the answer key. When Leonard brought me such a problem, I would buy time. If I couldn't get away with taking it home and working it out with my engineer-husband, I would distract Leonard with a task or busy work and then discreetly pull out the answer key. Hunched over my desk with my arms hiding the book, I would frantically try to piece together enough understanding to explain Leonard's missteps in solving the problem. Linda was a co-conspirator; she did her best to keep the students occupied when I would find myself in this predicament. One awful time, I couldn't figure it out either. Leonard's dad asked for the answer key and determined there was a typo! Again, deception served me well and ate at my soul.

I met with Paul, the head of school, my partner teacher, and the fifth through eighth grade math teachers. I described my observations and suggested that Leonard's needs could be met in part by an accelerated math curriculum. He simply did not need the time most children needed to understand new mathematical concepts. It was as if he almost understood them intuitively after glancing at the first presentation of the new skill or concept. Could he not join the fifth grade for math? He could at least be taught by a math specialist who might better differentiate due to her content knowledge. I was met with an unequivocal "NO!" by the math teachers. Their reasons were two-fold: first it would be too complicated to adjust the curriculum year after year for him, and that it would be inappropriate for him to be with older peers. "We do not skip children here." The headmaster, only two years into his tenure, acquiesced to tradition.

I returned to my classroom baffled. My best efforts pacified Leonard and offered only glimmers of possibilities for his giftedness (or simply capacity, talent, and interest) in mathematics. He was in a school whose mission it was to serve children exactly like him, but the school's way, its best intentions, did not serve Leonard or honor its own mission. And I was complicit. I felt like I had to do SOMETHING to help Leonard engage in math in a way that helped his person grow. I zeroed in on Leonard's Achilles heel: his very sloppy, elephant-letter handwriting. I justified taking points off his homework assignments because his manuscript demonstrated a lack of care for his work. I kept him from getting an "easy" A. All year, I felt as if I did him a great disservice by my lack of content knowledge. And even though I maintained my tough position on handwriting with Leonard, I didn't fool myself. That pedagogical and philosophical choice did not allay my regret for Leonard's experience as my student.

Contrary to Leonard's experience, I believe my differentiated, tweaked Everyday Math curriculum supported Benjamin in a wonderful way. A small, bony boy with enormous blue eyes, Benjamin's mousy light brown hair reflected his aura. His personality didn't grab you; he didn't lead his peers. But oh, was he delightful. Benjamin's disposition was sweet and respectful. He loved to be in on the joke and laugh and laugh. Benjamin loved math, but he worked slowly and often did not grasp concepts even after the third and fourth time. He needed lots of practice problems to support his understanding, and I found them for him. He did not seem to mind his group placement. In fact, Benjamin seemed content. He worked at his own pace, but because I designed the whole curriculum to address their various needs, he often finished his work in time with his peers. Benjamin enjoyed the problem-solving cards, taking some home every night. Actually, Benjamin's only problem, I think, became ME when I reacted to his parents.

•••

Benjamin's dad was a mathematician. His mother may have been as well; what I remember for sure is how highly the family valued mathematics. This information came to light just prior to spring parent-teacher conferences and the final written progress reports. You see, we made decisions about middle school placement at this time of year, and Benjamin's dad was determined to have Benjamin placed in the upper level math class in fifth grade. Two years previously, Benjamin's sister had not been placed in the upper level. Benjamin's parents and the fifth through eighth grade math teachers went twelve rounds before, during, and after the placement. The teachers finally acquiesced and placed her in the upper level, but felt Benjamin's sister suffered in the subsequent two years, and they were resentful because they had to support her far more than they needed to support other students at that level. They did not believe she was appropriately placed.

When Benjamin's dad insisted that Benjamin follow his sister's footsteps, I was unaware of their history with math placement at the school. I was a bit surprised by this request, at first. Did Benjamin's parents really believe he could handle advanced math? I realized they did not have the context of Benjamin's progress relative to the rest of the class and my differentiated instruction and content. I went to the head of school and he organized a meeting with the upper level math teachers. As they spoke about this family, the faces of these middle aged women—who dedicated themselves through a career of diligent service to this school and to gifted children—flushed and their nostrils flared. They were indignant that this family was challenging them yet again. They argued vehemently against the parents' wishes, laying out every piece of evidence they could conjure from their vast experience, including their tenure with Benjamin's older sister. They recalled her stumbles; the many readjustments to the curriculum. They worried about her self-esteem due to her struggles; and they lamented the additional work required for her when the regular math curriculum at her grade level would have suited her so well. Ever amiable, Paul bobbed his bulbous red nose in agreement with these women. The message to me was clear. It was my responsibility to draw the line with these parents. In no uncertain terms, I needed to ensure that Benjamin's parents would not become a problem for these teachers again. Benjamin's parents needed to be put in their place, and their opinion was not to be affirmed in any way. After all, what did they know about math education?

I discussed this charge with my co-teacher, and as I did I also voiced my concern that we were so dismissive of the parents' concerns and desires for their children. Linda shared my discomfort and we agreed that when we met with Benjamin's parents we would listen to them first. I mean, they were his parents. They had a right to see their child challenged and engaged in a way they thought was suitable, didn't they? Or didn't they at least have a right to advocate for their son without there being a foregone conclusion?

On the afternoon of our meeting, my stomach fluttered anxiously. How would I break it to these parents that their son isn't as bright as they think he is? Is there a way to do it gently? I reminded myself that I would listen first, and I think I trusted that the truth would emerge as we all just wanted what was best for Benjamin. They would see that he was bright but could be accommodated in the regular upper level math courses.

Benjamin's parents warmly received our greeting and we sat together around a student table. Mr. J was a slight man with large glasses. He wore an open-necked white and pale blue striped shirt under a navy blue blazer. Mrs. J stood by his side—a foot smaller than her husband, if that was possible.

"Mr. and Mrs. J, what would you like to talk about today?" I smiled and tilted my head to indicate I would listen closely.

In a tone that belied his size, Mr. J carried on at length about the outrageous treatment of his daughter by the math teachers. He swore that he would not let the same thing happen with Benjamin.

"What level are you going to recommend for Benjamin in fifth grade?" Mr. J demanded. He shook visibly, and Mrs. J put her hand on his arm. He stopped talking and Mrs. J resumed.

"We would like to be heard," she explained. "We know our son. We know what is best for him."

I could not argue with her. But I also had information they did not. They knew their son to be gifted. And he was! His IQ was a prerequisite for his enrollment here. But giftedness is relative in a school for gifted children, so I attempted to paint a picture of Benjamin's progress in math. First, I concurred with their understanding that Benjamin loved math, even thrived when learning math. I provided examples of his enthusiasm and delight when he acquired a new skill or understanding. Then, I explained how I differentiated content and instruction, assessing and organizing the children. I related the fact that Benjamin never fell within the accelerated group because he required a steady, methodical pace in which to work out and practice new content. I did not show them his work or the work of students who worked at a level beyond Benjamin's. I was trying to be diplomatic.

Diplomacy failed me.

Mr. and Mrs. J continued to insist that I recommend him for advanced math next year. I didn't have the guts to say no. I just kept smiling and listening and speaking in soothing tones. I did not tell them I would do it, but neither did I tell them "no" flat out.

When they left, Linda and I just stared at each other in a kind of stupor. It was as if they didn't hear a word we said. What was I supposed to do now?

I really didn't have a choice. I had known what I had to do ever since I left the meeting with the other math teachers. My older, more experienced colleagues, and my boss, our headmaster, would not "allow" it. To recommend Benjamin, to support his parents' wishes, would have meant my disobedience.

And yet, how dare Benjamin's parents ignore my professional opinion, established through careful observation and work with their son?! How dare they ignore the professional experience of my colleagues? Why do they even have him at this school if they don't trust us?

It was in this fit of indignation that I wrote his end-of-year report. Summoning my mathematical "prowess," I figured out that Benjamin was in the bottom 5 percent of his class based upon assessments and observations. I wrote that number and sentence in his permanent record, determined to get his parents' attention and make them hear me. I gave them mathematical proof that he was not a candidate for the recommendation they demanded. That would show them. I saved the document and sent it to the main office for delivery.

Linda shook her head. "Christy, why are you putting this in his permanent record? How will it hurt to just send him on?"

I left that school and elementary school teaching that year. In later communication with Linda, I heard that my report created quite a stink: furious parents and an administrator's nightmare.

Benjamin's delighted face lives in my heart. Caught between my sense of professional authority and fear of disobedience, Benjamin, his expression, causes me to wince. I fear, ultimately, that I hurt him. Did he read that report? Did I stop on his enthusiasm in my attempt to exact respect for myself as a professional? What other choice did I have if I was to stay in line with my "team"? How could I have hurt Benjamin when I started by just trying to help him?

My experiences with both Benjamin and Leonard left me pondering my qualifications to teach "anything" just because I might have a "gift." Was it ethical for me to take the job outside the boundaries of the knowledge I had accrued? Was it ethical for the school to provide ME as the teacher to these children?

2   Disturbances

> I cannot understand my own behavior. I fail to carry out the very things I want to do, and find myself doing the very thing I hate ... for although the will to do what is good is in me, I cannot carry it out.[1]

Dear Ruth and Joy,

I share these stories, and their subsequent retellings, with you, my newbie teacher-friends, because it has been in my thinking, writing, and conversation with others about these memories that I have found a kind of understanding of my experience, which opened up new opportunities for me in my teaching and my Being in the world. I know, it seems like wild exaggeration to make so much of my "worst," inexperienced days of teaching. And I hesitate to share these lest you interpret my sharing as generosity from an older and wiser educator. This is not my intention at all. I do not assume that I have figured out teaching and learning simply by the years I have logged in the profession. In point of fact, I have not. Quite the contrary, teaching and learning and schooling and curriculum and pedagogy have become less clear and more complicated.[2] Actually, in all my experience, more precisely in the reflection upon and meaning I have made from that experience, I have found a kind of liberation in not knowing, in being uncertain, and more to the point, in being unfinished as a growing teacher and human. And this freedom energizes me to be the kind of teacher and person that I am proud of because of how I attend to the people in my life, including myself. If there is anything I wish for you, it is for you to engage in a similar struggle for this kind of freedom.

But I did not always cherish the complications. I assumed tidy explanations and executions of teaching. I expected learning by students in return for my efforts. I'm reminded of Jack Donaghy, played by Alec Baldwin as the straight-laced, right-wing, high-level executive in the TV sitcom *30 Rock*, who explained he didn't need to talk to anyone about his feelings because he put any potential problems in his "mind vice" and CRUSHED THEM until they simply did not exist.[3] ☺

To be honest, the fact that I experienced teaching as something other than that clean, simple exchange was bewildering to me.[4] As I experienced these teaching moments, you can tell, I did not quite know what to make of them. The residue of these moments and the snap judgements that followed were funny feelings and a longing to put the discomfort out of sight and mind. By the time I came into doctoral study, these anomalies, which I've portrayed, in an otherwise satisfying and sometimes laudable teaching career, became a significant frame through which I perceived myself as a teacher. I had confidence in myself as a teacher and yet these experiences seemed to say something about me, about my teaching, which was very unsettling. I could not abide the sense of confusion that what I knew did not yield the results I anticipated. Because I did not know what to do, because I was many times left with feelings of guilt for reasons I could not explain, I thought I was doing it all wrong or I blamed the kids and their parents. Mostly, I was ashamed of myself for not getting it right. But in order to survive (who can bear facing shame?!), in order to "grow" along professionally responsible lines, I long ignored my feeling of shame and powered on, determined to be the best I could be according to what I understood the standards to be. That was my job for the sake of the kids in my classroom. As I embarked on doctoral study, I focused on helping other teachers by getting to know everything I needed to know to support them in what I perceived to be their weaknesses.

But these memories that I attempted to exclude from my story kept rearing their heads, insisting they belonged. They butt into conversations with my study group of professors and my teaching fellow colleagues also in the doctoral program with me, and they clamored for attention through my revulsion when seeing myself in my adult students. My study group engaged in dialogue mostly around critical incidents we experienced as teachers of an undergraduate pre-service teaching course, Social Foundations of Education. Later this continued when I was co-teaching a graduate course, Curriculum Studies, for future administrators. We brought to the discussions insight and discourses from our current reading as well as contemporary cultural concerns relevant to education that came up in the media. The critical incidents usually represented interactions with students that caused us frustration or surprise.[5] Why couldn't they see or receive alternate ways of viewing education other than what they had experienced as students? This dialogue, incorporating as it did so many perspectives (students, professors, peers, scholars represented in their discourses, current public narratives) was incredibly rich. As a result of this on-going dialogue over several years, supplemented by compelling dialogue with discourses thought my own coursework, I was able to make sense of these anomalies. Further, I could see that by incorporating, rather than ignoring, their difference, I could tell my story in ways that permitted me to seek and try alternative ways of Being, as a teacher and a person.

When I returned to graduate school, I also encountered the work of educational philosopher Maxine Greene, who encouraged teachers to pay attention not only to the children in their care but also to themselves. Who we are as human beings mattered as much if not more than what kind of curriculum and pedagogy we used.[6] After all, education is not about getting a good job or about saving the national economy or reputation, right? We've talked about this a lot, so I think it's safe to say we share this belief. Education is about the development of the individual into and toward the person (woman, mother, citizen, teacher, friend, neighbor, etc.) she might become. It's about the idea that that "Becoming" never ends, right?[7] And so, education, as John Dewey liked to say, is the intentional constructing and reconstructing of experiences to make meaning for our Being and Becoming in our world.[8] Of course, then, who we are in our role of teacher, in our place in the formal structuring of experiences for others, *matters* in terms of what we understand this process of growing and Becoming to be.[9] That means my struggle for freedom was not merely individual, either. As a teacher, my Becoming has social and ethical dimensions as well.[10]

I was captivated by this view of the teacher. The idea compelled me to think that my responsibility was more holistic than knowing the right pedagogy to get kids to learn and knowing enough of my content to get them to understand. It certainly seemed to match my experience. My central difficulty was in not knowing enough and so not having success getting kids to do what I needed them to do for their own good, such as learning content and how to be a good citizen, to name a few of my expectations. I believed that I'd live up to my ethical responsibility if I just had the right body of knowledge.

What I found in Maxine Greene's work was her idea of Naming embedded in her existential and phenomenological view of teachers as human beings. She proposed that if we pay attention to the disturbances, the tensions, the sense that something is missing, we might find our way into greater freedom in Being who we imagine we can be. The idea of Naming is to look at our circumstances as we have not before and to find language for the feelings we have that something isn't right. Something is in the way of our human need to Become who we might Become. In other words, instead of striving to do something better, or ignoring what is troubling me, I need to pause and face it with a critical, questioning, curious perspective. She suggests paying attention to the unsettled feelings that emerge from experience. Why? Those feelings tell me that there is an obstacle to my Becoming. I am somehow impeded in my deep-down impulses to care for myself and others in our growing together.[11] Paying attention to those feelings means paying attention to what kind of human being I am.

Highlighting discomfort or embarrassing feelings seemed counter-intuitive, especially since as a teacher I was supposed to know what I was doing. If I was uncomfortable or unsure or confused, then I couldn't be doing my job right. Focusing on myself felt, well, selfish, and my small problems did not seem to warrant service when there are so many, even my own students, who suffer real issues. But I tried Naming professionally. Not only had this worked for me personally, to some extent, but I also could not abide the tension and shame anymore. Something wasn't right. In fact, something about my way of Being felt downright wrong, and I didn't want to intrude or impose myself on students without figuring this out.

I think we three, and most teachers we know, would leap to answer in the affirmative to the idea of doing whatever we have to do for the sake of the kids. But when it comes right down to it, it is pretty painful to focus on what feels like we haven't gotten right. Many of us, I think, don't relish the thought, let alone dive in, to do this kind of internal work. To do this is to let go of safety, of what is supposed to be, and trust ourselves to find the right way forward. It's scary to think about freedom in an unknown context and end. Sometimes, though, not being the person and teacher we yearn to be is painful enough, or troubles us long enough, that we are compelled to figure out what's going on so that a new way of Being might be possible.

Well, this letter represents my engagement in that struggle to make sense of what it has meant and what it does mean for me to be a teacher. I hope it will demonstrate the power of a Naming praxis and the freedom made possible through such a praxis.[12]

•••

To begin, I have to address the troubling inklings that something was off in the experiences I shared with you. I have to confront the feelings that stayed with me for over a decade after I left those classrooms. You may recall, I felt: discomfort, desperation, confusion, pain, shame, guilt, and uncertainty. I felt, at times, as if something was missing. What also arose in the stories were my feelings of certainty, clarity about the way things were supposed to be. You can see that, due to this uncertainty, I carried with me a lot of judgement, too, toward myself, my colleagues, the students, and their families.

Maxine Greene always advocated coming together with others in shared projects of freedom.[13] Dialogue offers multiple perspectives regarding the dialectic, how we experience the world, mediating internally and externally.[14] We make meaning of our experiences through interpretation; we reconstruct what happened to make sense of it all according to what we believe or value about the world and ourselves. Within dialogue, we engage with our interpretation of experience through language. By taking our interpretation out of our head and putting it into language, we "try on" meanings. The richer the dialogue, the richer the possibilities for meaning as a foundation for our Becoming.[15]

This is where the dialogue comes in, such as the kind I had with my study group which I described in an earlier letter. Through it, I started to focus on three things. First, I removed the pillow from atop the uncomfortable feelings I had been smothering and let them live more openly in my mind and heart. Next, I searched for similarly troubling perspectives which seemed to resonate with my experiences and/or my interpretations of those experiences. Finally, I borrowed language that seemed to describe what happened or what I thought happened to me. These three actions of attention helped me to reinterpret, to reconstruct, to Name the obstacles to my Becoming.[16] This thinking work in language within the context of my discomfort helped me to be free of an interpretation that stilted how I *was*; it allowed me to think and so BE differently.

In Naming, then, I focused on dialogic engagement.[17] I allowed the voices in my head—the versions of my Self I thought I was supposed to be or wanted to be—to converse with the discourses represented by my peers and the scholars I encountered in doctoral study.[18] In these conversations, I addressed my emotional response and initial intellectual interpretations of those concrete, lived experiences in my early teaching days. Through honest engagement with multiple perspectives, I began to see several themes emerge that troubled my professional sense of well-being: the way my own experience of education positioned me for teaching, my expectations regarding classroom authority, my understanding of professional responsibility, compliance, aims of education, and ethical responsibilities. In what follows, I will describe to you my Naming process from the narratives of my teaching experiences. You will find, as I did, that they do not fit neatly into separate categories or descriptions, but I will do my best to keep things clear!

• • •

When I entered the teaching profession, you may recall, I highly valued my experiences as a student. I believed that I'd had a wonderful education in many ways. My assumption was that those experiences meant that "I knew what good education looked like." Further, I then knew what it meant to be the teacher creating that good education. You can trace in my narratives my attempts, especially at Teachers College and in my student teaching experience, to replicate my own educational encounters for my students. Those stories tended to end in my confusion that the students did not experience those encounters as I had. I blamed the kids: Ruby only had the capacity for "candy books," Nate was defiant—perhaps due to his background, Maria just didn't want to do the work. And I was frustrated with myself. What was I missing? I executed what I knew to be the best of my experiences in reading, analyzing a primary source, or writing, and yet, I didn't get the simple exchange of students learning that content or skill for my teaching effort. When I taught my peers at TC, I was baffled that my own experience in these kinds of discussions was not enough to lead them.

The second theme I noticed in my narratives was fear, frustration, and confusion regarding my authority. I was certain that I needed to make the children obey me and conform to my expectations. I was offended by disrespect. Students' disobedience was on par with mutiny; I used battle metaphors to illustrate my defeat. You can see in the narratives how firmly I believed that managing the classroom was my responsibility. My execution of successful classroom management, my control over the students, was what was best for them. Moreover, I understood order and obedience among the students to mark my skill and success as a teacher. My strong sense of righteousness on this point, I think, is clear in the narratives as well.

If I am honest, the most difficult scenarios of classroom mismanagement arose when I taught minority children in low-income public schools. At the time, if you had asked me, I might have been able to tell you that I was struggling with classroom management. I saw the problem as another simple exchange: I should exert enough of the right kind of authority to get obedience; the students should respect me as their teacher, positionally endowed with authority. It did not occur to me to acknowledge anyone other than the individuals directly or tangentially involved in the scenario. At the most, I might extend blame for bad parenting. However, in retrospect, I can hear a deeply buried voice inside me that simultaneously blamed and excused the behavior of these children on the basis of their race or ethnicity and its culture, which I surmised may not have taught them any better. I would not or could not have spoken this aloud at the time. My liberal prioritization of the asocial-cultural individual meant that "good teaching" worked for any child, regardless of their culture. This meant that what had worked for me would work for them. Whether or not they were a minority, or even more whether or not I shared the same culture as my students, did not seem relevant to their education or my job at all.

Instead, I focused on my professional responsibility according to perceived standards. I attempted to create an environment conducive to learning, which included maintaining and exercising my authority over my students to control their behavior. Further, I assumed that as the teacher, I should have expertise in my content knowledge and pedagogical knowledge. All teachers should. This definitive assertion explains some of my disdain for my colleagues as well as my impetus for involvement with the curriculum mapping project. Given my position as a teacher, then, I should be respected for that professional expertise. This was evident in my indignation when parents did not trust what I was doing in my classroom with their children. But I could question and should question whether my expertise was up to par. I felt like a hack or a fraud if I did not know enough content or couldn't figure out the best practice to get children to learn something. I believed that I alone was at fault for not knowing enough. I bore shame. Convinced something was wrong with me, I determined to fix myself according to the standards for professional expertise I assumed. I must not know enough, I surmised. Over time, I had also begun to recognize that I and the other educators in the building bore responsibility for the experiences of students in our school beyond those in our own classrooms. This also became a standard by which I judged my colleagues and myself. This "should" drove my imperative to grow as a teacher, as well, and colored my relationships with other educators.

One particular assumed standard became quite apparent in these early teaching experiences: my compliance. I felt obligated to powers greater than myself. With regard to professional expertise, I was bound to the expectations of my field, curriculum standards and content goals. Getting through the material was my responsibility. Employing subject matter expertise and implementing "best practices" such as those stemming from Howard Gardner's multiple intelligence theory demonstrated both my submission to the wisdom in the field of education and my identification as a "good teacher" for following that wisdom. Further, I felt subject and duty-bound to the powers-that-be within my schools. I had to be a "team" player and "stay in line" with the team's wisdom and decisions. Sometimes, it felt like a matter of self-preservation to do what was expected of me. Often, the team was simply represented by the administration, the "we" of the institution invoked in expectations. My narratives, especially in the private schools, express a feeling of having no choice. Quickly, I found myself identifying as a victim, expressing self-pity in grumbling. I did not like who I was Becoming. I became complicit in the negative work environment. My work and life bore a strong tension of emotion, which became untenable. I think it was best expressed after wiping my eyes from the cup of ice thrown at me by children on a bus: righteous anger at the violation of clear, significant expectations and penitent acceptance of punishment for my failure to be what a teacher should be.

Abiding in this triangulation of expectations, assumptions, and perceived standards was essential to me because my teaching bore an ethical and moral imperative related to the aims of education in my view. In my narratives, you can see I held two primary purposes for education. First, education should develop the human being so that she could live a meaningful, rich life, including service to others. Second, American education should prepare citizens to engage thoughtfully in our democracy. These were high aspirations, and if I were to be a vehicle of their realizations for children, then I had better be the best teacher I could be. Scanning the horizon of my field, my profession, and my school to identify the components of the highest level of teaching was my moral duty if I was to give my students the best. In other words, being the "best" teacher was an ethical commitment; it involved knowing the right "best" things. Controlling their behavior, making children work hard and aim high, selecting the "best" materials and pedagogy are examples of the kind of work I needed to do to give these children optimal opportunity to have a well-lived life, contributing positively to American democratic society.

But these aims also provoked ethical questions for me. Who should receive the benefits of my teaching? I know there's a lot of ego there, but really, to whom was I ethically obligated in a democratic society? Public school children? To whom am I accountable for use of my skill and knowledge? What's my part in this democracy? In our society?

More soon!

Christine

3   "We" Know: Beginnings of Discursive Naming

> Man goes beyond his own decision,
> Gets caught up in the mechanism
> Of swindlers who act like kings
> And brokers who break everything[19]

Dear Ruth and Joy,

From the most unlikely sources, in my mind, I discovered that I am not at all alone in my experiences; in fact, conundrums and troubles like mine have been studied and discussed by teachers and scholars. I say "unlikely" because the ability to re-interpret my experiences—in ways that opened up possibilities for my teaching rather than clamming me up in shame and paralysis, did not come wrapped in neat packages of "solutions." I didn't discover one right action or body of new knowledge that would fix the simple but disrupted equation of teaching and learning among a handful of individuals in a classroom. Instead some historical, critical, ethical, and ontological discourses claimed by the fields of Social Foundations of Education and Curriculum Studies provided alternate ways of looking at my earlier circumstances and my interpretations of them.[20] Taken as a whole, these discourses provided language and possible re-interpretation for my experiences. Through my dialogic engagement with them, I Named what I could only once feel. I could make sense; I could make meaning upon which to direct and re-direct my Becoming as a teacher and person. In what follows, I will lay out some of these discourses in order to critically interpret the themes I identified above. These multiple interpretations revealed what bound me and created alternative ways of thinking and Being than I hadn't considered before. You may find they converse with each other and I hope you will feel the freedom to engage with them yourself. Do they resonate with you? What would you add? What thoughts of yours resist the discourses?

• • •

"If I was a good student, then I know how to be a good teacher."

Apparently, I am not alone in this early teaching experience and interpretation. Deborah Britzman, whose research with new teachers comprises a seminal text in teacher education, describes a central difficulty with new teachers. "Teaching is one of the few professions where newcomers feel the force of their own history of learning as if it telegraphs relevancy to their work."[21] We stumble through our own remembered experience as students while we attempt to shape our identity as teachers, as if our interpretation of experience-as-student might typify that of every other student. As if our interpretation is broad enough to denote the kinds of pedagogical moves which help every other student learn. It's curious that we who are usually driven into this profession by our desire to care for others would not notice that our focus is on ourselves rather than "how others learn, what learning means for them, and what one's efforts as a teacher have to do with that."[22]

While humbling to realize and acknowledge this about myself, I have to say that this insight, and the research and discourses that warrant it as a substantive difficulty for teachers, comforted me, while also providing direction for my further study of teaching—my teaching, in particular. Britzman and others suggest that the move from student to teacher is fraught with unexpected pressures, with uncertainty. We have already constructed a reality of formal education for ourselves through our interpretation of our own schooling experiences.

Somehow the collective "we" seems to understand the role, the identity, the work of the teacher in a similar vein. Some, like Britzman, attribute this to the fact that "we" all occupied schools, as law required our attendance, and thus carry a shared understanding of teaching. Furthermore, those schooling experiences were reinforced by the stories we tell each other within our culture. It's a part of our student experience. Didn't our parents' reactions to our teachers for good or ill shape some of the "should-ness" of our interpretation? And as we became adults, could we not just feel it in the air? But beyond our days as students, political and cultural narratives pervade our consciousness beyond our own relationship to teachers. Our cultural milieu bears symbolic meaning through popular texts. From the "hero" teachers who single-handedly save a child or group of children to the vitriol found in the "Comments" section in our digital world, the pervasive quality of media creates images which are either truly aspirational or eviscerating. In both cases, they demonstrate the cultural understanding that teachers are integral to our ideals for our society and its members. And we could feel this personally. We aspired to be teachers because of the great power teachers wield in shaping HUMAN BEINGS! What an honor to be part of such a noble process. Friends and family nodded, noting how our character and temperament are suited to such work. And yet sometimes, when questions about our chosen profession are asked and answered, people shake their heads. "You could do so much more." "Only a teacher?" they wonder.

I think it might be easier to bring these elusive, seemingly invisible, "shoulds" or normative assumptions to light in yet another story. This one is not about me but about the construction of the American Teacher in our cultural mind.[23]

To tell this story, I will have to tell it several times within several discourses. As I layer the interpretations, I use this language to Name my experiences. The first interpretation is one I pieced together as I studied the history of American Education in history texts written through the late 19th century into the 21st century. Consider it a "textbook" version of how we may have come to constitute the idea of the American Teacher.

...

Four score and many more years ago, round about the 17th century, Europeans brought forth on this land newly imagined, ideal ways of living together, which they hoped to maintain and perpetuate in America. Survive, and then thrive. [24] Of high importance was the preservation of religion and authority.[25] Both New England and Southern colonists intended to create a new society, with religious and economy-driven aims. Education came to represent the vehicle for their ideological aims. In the North, colonial society took the view that education could perfect a good person and create a good society. Education could help a person follow God and the government, control the inherent evil in children, and confirm or confer social distinction and material prosperity of the society.[26] In the South, colonial society ensured its self-perceived cultural and moral superiority by using education to train the "Indian" out of the indigenous peoples they encountered and included in their New World economy.[27] The role of American colonial teacher was played initially, in the North, by women who taught their own families from the Scripture, and in the South, by both tutors and then ministers in parson schools.[28] As colonial society grew, young educated men were hired by towns to instruct the young. These teachers hailed from upper class backgrounds and entered a short tenure in teaching in order to benevolently serve the community. This American Teacher was responsible for imparting subject matter and consciously shaping the character of his students, whose population was comprised of boys.[29] His position was honored for his task as a noble and necessary one. The young teacher boarded with a family; he was required to be of high moral standing; and the eyes of the community followed him to ensure this standard for their children. Having served their time, most of these men left teaching to begin their "real" careers in law or medicine.

Upon the birth of our new nation, education retained its ideological purposes and subjected them to the principles of the republic. Our nation required education that might mold a virtuous citizenry and provide tools for the exercise of political freedom. The role of the mother as educator was elevated in patriotic duty as literacy and civic morality became an imperative for every member of the new nation.[30] Young men, recently graduated from Harvard and the like, continued to serve as instructors of boys in schools. The American Teacher continued to convey Enlightened ideas but now also bore the responsibility of shaping citizens who would determine the future of American republican democracy.[31] Teaching became patriotic duty, as well.

In the 19th century, schooling and teaching took on increasing social responsibility. With industrialization came capitalism and immigrants—two realities that swiftly disrupted the notion of a virtuous republic based upon shared values. With capitalism came vice, and with immigrants came very different ideas of American family values.[32] Formal education became an instrument of government policy, the central institution for control and maintenance of the social order.[33] This kind of schooling was embodied in the "common school," an education made free to all children of the state. This model demonstrated society's growing belief that schooling had the power to ameliorate social ills. The schools were not only intended to amend the problems created by an industrialized society, but the implication was that now, with increasing immigrant poor populations, only the school could be trusted to assimilate diverse populations, inculcating the values American society required.[34] The common school could provide national unity through the common ideology, based upon Anglo-American Protestant culture, promoted through the common school curriculum.[35] The goal of the curriculum was socialization: 1) make children fit as adults to bear the honor and responsibility of democratic citizenship, 2) prepare children for work through obedience and compliance, 3) provide moral instruction. Horace Mann, the primary proponent of the common schools, asserted that the common school teacher's central responsibilities included training children not to transgress and in this the teacher could replace the police. The American Teacher, through the common textbooks and other instruction guides that depicted particular Biblical virtues, was expected to deliver a common moral education in addition to the political education expected during the nation's infancy.[36]

A growing population in need of socialization demanded more teachers. Who better to contribute to a virtuous and moral cause than women, who had been inculcating Biblical, civic and now—through the transformation of the "home into a haven in a heartless industrial world" —moral virtue in their homes for three phases of American life?[37] The gentler sex, surely, were well-suited to attending to the character of the nation. As teaching positions were initially designed as work for single, middle class women, these ladies moved easily into this respectable, nurturing employment for which, in many ways, they had been trained their whole lives to do. Catherine Beecher created the first seminaries for training women in … wait for it … the domestic arts! (I told you that women's informal, in-house curriculum would enter the tale at some point). Once trained, these women, the American Teacher, mostly headed West to fill vacancies in new communities. Women in the teaching force also brought down the price of teaching because, do I even need to say it, they could be paid far less. Within a few short decades, by the latter half of the 19th century, teachers were recruited from within the immigrant and lower classes as well in order to meet the demand. The combination of poor, ethnically diverse, and female characteristics further substantiated the lower cost and need to oversee the American Teacher. Like their male peers who came before, many of these women boarded with community members who could keep tabs on the teachers' behavior.[38]

As the American Teacher was feminized, the men who had remained in formal education first became "principal" teachers—leading by practice and experience, then administrators—overseeing and ordering the work of teachers, and then—spurred to action by Horace Mann and the common school call for local control over local schools—political and cultural superintendents of formal schooling. Education had become a profession. Teaching could become a stepping stone for greater ambitions. Many professions in the late 19th century were organizing and establishing themselves as fields of study in the universities as well. But the study of education had a patchwork past. It began as the preparation of teachers. The American Teacher first had intellectual training in academic disciplines through the course of study of the young colonist and early citizen. With the common school and the instruction of female teacher seminaries came the Normal School. Devoted to the moral formation of teachers first, the normal school also offered raw experience and methodological training to prospective teachers, eventually formalizing training to "guarantee superior work." Those who structured these experiences hailed from schooling practice themselves; they were not scholars from within the academy. In order to establish a place for education as a field of study, the education programs subordinated the academic disciplines to studies in pedagogy. Pedagogical research and science-based methods became the foci of university study in education in order to demarcate scholarship that could not be claimed by the liberal arts. Thus, more and more, the American Teacher found herself on the bottom rung of a profession struggling for professional and academic legitimacy.[39]

The voices of American education echoed in hallowed university halls by the late 19th and early 20th century. Raucous debates ensued regarding the best pedagogy for training citizens for democracy and for work. These debates only intensified as floods of immigrants seemed to necessitate compulsory school laws to keep wayward children off of the streets and out of the sweat shops. Progressives brought to light a notion of the "whole child," human beings as more than mind; children's experience as a vital component of learning; and learning as a process of problem-solving and "doing," rather than merely thinking abstractly.[40] Liberal arts' proponents decried the loss of depth in the disciplines and intellectual rigor that these progressive ideas seemed to eschew.[41] The population of teachers swelled and yet among the voices invited into the debates, the American Teacher was not one. In fact, even school leaders were subdued as the arguments raged among academics.

Without a voice, with little power in the face of scientific management, the American Teacher addressed her needs through the formation of unions.[42] Professional organizations such as the American Medical Association set professional standards and provided learning opportunities for professional practice, but teachers' unions focused on issues of power, such as wages and working conditions. The lack of autonomy and voice experienced by the American Teacher caused her to position herself with uneducated, blue collar laborers in order to address her basic needs.[43]

With the rise of nationalism in the mid-20th century, politicians entered the schooling debate. Patriotism and international superiority in the face of communism dominated the country's narrative about why education was so important and what its contents should be. Sputnik sent fear shivering up our national spine and drove funding into science and math.[44] The American Teacher became responsible not only for the character and academic growth of the democratic citizen but also for the nation's standing in the world. And strength was to come from within, as well. The growth of federal intervention in the field of education intensified the common school objectives for the school to address social ills. The first Elementary and Secondary Education Act of Congress passed as part of a War on Poverty.[45] The American Teacher had to work toward national well-being on top of international prominence.[46]

When our economy got rocky in the 1970s, so too did confidence in our nation's schools. Standards for learning and standardized tests to asses that learning became the norm with the federal report "A Nation at Risk," which framed the solution to the country's education woes (and thus economic woes) into a narrative of economic/business reform that persists to this day.[47] Education policy increasingly became the purview of the federal government, changing multiple assumptions within education including the concept of accountability.[48] Once our nation was attacked at the turn of the new millennium, confidence dipped to new lows. Fear driven and desperate for action, politicians intensified their quest for accountability in schools.[49] The American Teacher, it was discovered through "research" was the single most important factor in a child's learning in schools.[50] Standardized tests increased and schools that did not see gains in student learning according to these measurements were defunded or closed.

And the American Teacher was evaluated for her effectiveness and blamed accordingly. Business saw opportunity and began to profit off of the new technology and scripted curriculum schools and districts "needed" in order to pass these tests and retain their very existence.[51] Billionaires influenced policy.[52] The great debates were now fought among elite industrialists and their political counterparts, and their arguments began to sound like fundamental agreement on corporate reform measures.[53] The voices of academics were diluted.[54] School leaders might not even be educators and, likely, if they did have a say in the national conversation, were instead business men and women.[55] And the American Teacher made noise through unions but was quickly dismissed for being argumentative for petty, selfish reasons.[56] The American Teacher's responsibilities were the future and stability of these United States. Moral character, academic excellence, civic duty—she was to instill these into children in order to ensure for the nation: social equality, a thriving economy, and distinction as and protection for the most powerful country in the world.

And the American Teacher failed. Failed children. Failed the republic. Failed society. Failed the nation. Over and over. Decade after decade. By 2015, she was honored rhetorically by a handful of politicians, but by most and in the cultural narrative she was shamed. Her ranks fell. It was widely believed, through the proliferation of Teach for America ideology, that "anyone" could teach and with little experience beyond a successful tenure as a student.[57] The passage of the federal Every Student Succeeds Act (ESSA) at the end of 2015 even included language that undermined the validity of teacher education in universities at all, while still suggesting that teachers were the lynchpin of quality education.[58]

• • •

Have I demoralized you fresh-faced educators yet?! Sadly, while I've relayed a story you may not have heard before, I know that you both struggled with the perception of teachers embedded in our culture today. It is still seen as noble work, but it isn't seen as particularly intellectual or challenging work. There is no sense of power, autonomy or creativity in the aura of being a teacher. In fact, usually the word "just" precedes identification as a teacher. This image gave you brilliant, capable women pause as you entered the profession; it continues to do so, I know, as you grapple with whether there's "enough" in teaching to keep you excited and growing.

For me, because teaching ran in my family and was seen as intellectual work, I didn't really see this image early in my career. Of course, twenty years ago, the profession was not as diminished in honor and respectability. There was some trust, as the story indicated, that if well-educated and trained, teachers would change the world. I entered the profession with a sense of calling and also with a huge sense of individual responsibility. The failure, which I and other teachers experienced, was of our own making. It was our responsibility to figure out what's gone wrong and to fix it ... for the sake of the kids!

This first historical story of the role of American Teacher began to take shape for me within the first few months of doctoral study. Just understanding that there were the historical forces at work, framing expectations, gave me language to reinterpret my story of individual failure. I started to see that perhaps being in the role of American Teacher meant that I would be inhabiting a web of power relations in existence before I even got there. Social expectations. Social value. Professional expectations. Professional value. I discovered that my own intentions, values and aims were rooted in cultural understanding of the obligations of formal education in America. As I talked with fellow-teacher friends at this time, I realized that while I could blame my upbringing and personality for my oftentimes intense approach to my profession, I could no longer assume that my experience was unique and completely of my own making. Even with our vastly different experiences in America's public, private, urban, rural, and suburban schools, so many of us embodied these dynamics as we exercised ourselves in our role as American Teacher. I want to highlight a few of the dynamics that arose in the historical narrative by representing some of the discourses I "conversed" with through my studies. That dialogic engagement, which follows, changed me.

More to follow!

Christine

4 Naming a Feminized Profession

> In the days of Shamgar son of Anath,
> in the days of Jael, the highways were abandoned;
> travelers took to winding paths.
> Village life in Israel ceased,
> ceased until I, Deborah, arose,
> until I arose, a mother in Israel.[59]
> To tell the truth is to tear aside the conventional masks, the masks adopted due to convention or compliance, the masks that hide women's being in the world. It is to articulate a life story in a way that enables a woman to know perhaps for the first time how she has encountered the world and what she desires to do and be.[60]

Dear Ruth and Joy,

You know, as a history major, I could trace the roles, responsibilities, and perceptions of the American White Woman through time. I knew that politically and legally she was inferior to men. She did not have a privileged position or power. In many ways, her freedom was limited, unable to choose her own life, as so much of it was defined for her. Confined by law and social mores, she created her life within and against expectations.[61] What I had never considered was that the role of American Teacher might be embedded in these same gendered social, political, cultural, and legal dynamics. Several scholars in the field of Curriculum Studies brought these to light so that I could see being a teacher not as an isolated phenomenon but as a product and instrument of culture.

The field of Curriculum Studies points to the early 19th century as a beginning for the study of public curriculum issues, but it must be said that these beginnings of course were founded on conceptions of gender, which claim earlier roots.[62] Primarily, female participation in education as students or teachers rested upon the idea a woman could contribute to society based upon her feminine character (biological and/or virtuous) and sphere of influence (roles and responsibilities).[63] Thus, while girls entering educational spaces traditionally intended for boys were seen as a victory for the equal competency of women's minds, the goal of this allowance was to produce wives and mothers who functioned intelligently and wisely within the home.[64] The virtue and behavior of girls would also have a civilizing effect on their male peers: the boys "would presumably cease acting in an unruly fashion."[65] Female teachers, then, would have a wonderful effect on the future. One of the most vocal proponents of coeducation and female teachers, Catherine Beecher, emphasized women's submissiveness and their inclination to self-sacrifice, purity, and domesticity, as evidence of the moral superiority they would dispense into schools.[66] As cottage industries faded into industrialized systems, single white women moved out into the world out of necessity and opportunity.[67] Schools welcomed and encouraged their contributions based upon their femininity. Surely they would create "happy home-like schools."[68] And their participation in schools, practicing virtue, would only serve to strengthen that capacity once they returned to the home as wife and mother.[69] Curriculum theorist, Madeleine Grumet, writes that in the role of schoolteacher the "good daughter had found a way to advance women into the public sphere without disturbing the dominance of patriarchal authority."[70]

The problem, according to Grumet and other feminist curriculum theorists,[71] is that while school men and the society they purported to represent desired the feminine gender ideal, schooling itself had acquired a very different gendered character. In her seminal work on women and teaching, Grumet contextualizes teaching within conceptions of mothering.[72] She points to the attributes of mothering experience and expectations, and she notes the lack of these attributes within teaching. Grumet draws on history, not unlike the historical narrative in my last letter, and demonstrates how, for example, the aims and formation of common schools, compulsory school laws and citizenship education directly undermine not only the feminine ideal but also contradict our own experiences of such nurturance.[73] "The feminization of teaching became a form of denial as the female teachers in the common schools demanded order in the name of sweetness, compelled moral rectitude in the name of recitation, citizenship in the name of silence, and asexuality in the name of manners."[74] Grumet argues that the heart of nurturance is the visceral, concrete, lived experience of the relationship between mother and child. She then presents historical evidence of female teachers idolizing and emulating male teachers' maintenance of order among students, of schools boasting of their pupils' total submission of their bodies and minds to the direction of their teacher. In such examples, Grumet demonstrates that nurturance rooted in relationship collapses "into strategies for control" in the role of American Teacher.[75]

The discourse of control extended to self-control, Grumet asserts through the compelling example of Father Cyrus Peirce. A normal school instructor (a teacher of teachers), Father Peirce becomes renowned for his teaching philosophies and methods. His students' notebooks reveal his instruction that they find within themselves a "deep well of patience, obedience, self-abnegation, and loving-kindness."[76] He establishes a method of moral suasion to inculcate in students (his teacher students and subsequently their child-students) the desire to do good. Thus, Father Peirce creates an idealized teacher image through his own presence as moral superior, teaching and training through his own execution of virtue. His instructional rhetoric promotes this image by setting clear personal virtue objectives, desirable teacher qualities being, among others, "patience, mildness, firmness and perfect self-control."[77] What his image and rhetoric belie are his tremendous frustration, anger and resentment as he deals with his students. His own journals are filled with annoyance at ill-prepared students who are lazy. He is distressed by their lack of attention and enthusiasm. He bemoans the future comprised of such disengaged educators-to-be. In this way, for his own teacher-students, he mystifies the actual experience of teaching. The picture painted for the new teacher is one of success built on personal endeavor, an emphasis on doing it right rather than paying attention to the state of one's Being. While this historical picture details a male teacher's experience, Catherine Beecher exacerbates the poignancy of the problem for female teachers when she theorized that meekness and orderliness were essential properties of femininity. For a new female teacher, then, the errant student or disorderly classroom makes a case for her incompetence not only as a teacher but as a woman. Grumet conjectures that many a young woman left teaching, "chastened and humiliated, interpreting their failure as proof of their own frailty, weakness of will, and essential incapacity to function in the man's world."[78]

Can you see, thus far, where the roots of feminizing teaching left patterns on the contemporary American Teacher ... on my own experiences as a teacher? The incongruence of expectation with experience is threaded throughout the history of the American Teacher as a feminine phenomenon. Further, the mirage of the ideal pointed over and over again to the individual teacher's very character and correct action, judging and condemning the person for not possessing the qualities she *should* have.

But oh, ladies, it just gets more complicated, and yet so clarifying in terms of Naming my experiences. I learned that as education professionalized itself from the late 19th through the mid-20th centuries, teachers were marginalized because they were primarily women. Because women's work outside the home was considered temporary, women were mostly excluded from leadership positions. Men first assumed leadership in practice, as principals and superintendents. Women's (teachers') livelihoods were dependent upon their relationship with these men and thus compliance became integral to the identity and responsibility of the teacher. Because of this gendered division of power, some scholars argue it became easier and easier to undermine the creative agency of the American Teacher.[79] Gradually men in intellectual and professional leadership also came to dominate the identity, culture, and direction of the profession. Historian Joel Spring describes this process as the "rise of the expert," beginning in the early 20th century.[80] The field and profession of education was built around the concept of scientific management. The "first" and early education professors and curricularists advocated dispassionate analysis, emphasized procedural precision, and minimal waste of instructional time.[81] With an eye toward models of business and industry, these schoolmen developed curriculum as a means-ends proposition, using objectives as a primary tool for efficient delivery of knowledge and skills required for adult life.[82] Psychology became an important component of education as these experts analyzed human activity for curriculum development and administered tests to children to benefit their efficient instruction.[83] As expertise in management, curriculum development, and psychology grew, so too did hierarchy and bureaucracy in the schools, increasing the space between teachers' work and the agency with which to make decisions about that work.

Scientific management pervaded teacher training as well, historian Herbert Kliebard argued.[84] Experts defined traits of good teachers and conducted job analysis to both judge teacher quality as well as to discern those methods which best worked in the production of good students. The field of curriculum development thus specified end products, and teaching became an application process, a "standardized means by which predictable results might be achieved."[85] Teacher education then could be yet another process "by which teachers were transformed into efficient manufacturers," thereby making teaching a technology.[86] In this way, becoming a teacher came to mean becoming a part of a system, playing a role with defined responsibilities.

Critical theorist Michael Apple asserts that these responsibilities shifted from designing one's own curricula and teaching to mastering a wider range of technical skills, such as assessing and assigning grades quickly, deciding which skill group to put a student in, and efficient management of groups. Apple and others call this process deskilling, in which skills of workers (teachers) are broken down and re-appropriated by management to enhance efficiency and control.[87] As this happens, teachers lose control over "timing, over defining appropriate ways to do a task, over criteria that establish acceptable performance."[88] As standardization of educational processes has increased in the last decades, so too has intensification, Apple writes. Intensification is the erosion of teacher privileges like having time for bathroom breaks at the very least and time for creative thinking at the other end of the spectrum.[89] In fact, the intensification of procedures (for the sake of efficient and standardized practices and management) may even result in "cutting corners" by the teacher but definitively creates the feeling for the teacher that she doesn't have time for the intellectual work of her job and must rely more heavily upon experts.[90] Her "professionalism" then stems from her ability to consume the intellectual work of experts and make quick management decisions in her classroom based upon what others have deemed generally appropriate.[91] In this way, compliance becomes the American Teacher's professional responsibility.[92]

As you read this, you may believe I am anti-expert, anti-objectives, anti-analysis, anti-accountability, etc. This is not my aim nor my point. What strikes me is the framing of the field and profession in such a way as to elbow teachers out of the conversation and yet expect teachers to shoulder the enormous task of ensuring the student exit schooling as the "outcome" the experts, representing the public, desire and expect.[93] It's funny, even progressives who fought to overturn the scientific paradigm, to turn educators to the child's experience and concrete rather than abstract educational encounters, relied on the individual teacher to effect this change. The underlying framework of the field and profession reveals that we have removed autonomy from the American Teacher and her work and yet directed incredibly intense, collective focus, as a profession, and in the last several decades as a nation, on the accountability of the American Teacher in her work.[94] William Pinar, another curriculum theorist, Named the consequences of this framework, which I felt as I taught.

> Instrumental rationality is to blame ... attention to pedagogy, teaching, instruction sets intellectual and political traps for the teacher. Power and responsibility accompany the command of attention. It becomes the teacher upon whom the student depends in order to learn –that is the intellectual trap. It is the teacher who becomes responsible for student learning: that is the political trap. The locus of responsibility, the very site of education, is the teacher then, not the student.[95]

The accompanying pressure on the American Teacher to maintain a professional stance such as this is tremendous to say the least. The American Teacher cannot afford to be wrong. It is her professional duty to know more and do more for the child than even the child's own parents.[96] Can you see, then, how I could get to dismissing Benjamin and Christopher's parents?

This all becomes possible, scholars argue, because those most connected to the educational encounter, the teacher and the student, are severed from their human need and ability to create and control that encounter. No one hears them (or listens to them) say, "Hey! This isn't working! This doesn't feel right!" And this dilemma arose due to the view of teaching as women's work.[97] Whether a man or a woman in the role of teacher, such persons embody a feminized role, which has pervasive normalized expectations and responsibilities that have marginalized him or her, as well as his or her knowledge and experience, from the public and professional discourse.

But being a woman within a feminized role may create added tension. Out from extensive collaborative work with teachers, Janet Miller observed that "attempts to professionalize teaching seem to have simply reinforced the internalized conflicts of many women who are encouraged to move beyond the confines of women's work and yet who still are being molded by external definitions of their profession."[98] Further, research on women's ways of knowing in the last four decades reveals that the abstract, rational, subject-object epistemologies so prevalent in education may be contrary to ways women have historically made sense of the world.[99] In their groundbreaking study of women's ways of knowing, Mary Belenky and her colleagues assert that reasoning or what is labeled "thinking" involves considering the abstract and impersonal, "while those [processes] that deal with the personal and interpersonal fall under the rubric of 'emotions' and are largely relegated to women."[100] The "one best system" created by schoolmen in the last century forced denial of emotional, intuitive knowing as well as knowing grounded in relationships.[101]

Teachers' legs are taken from under them as the very language and nature of conversation most detrimental to themselves and their work is written off as decidedly emotional and female; irrational and unquantifiable. Grumet sums up the tension well, "Dominated by kits and dittos, increasingly mechanized and impersonal, most of our classrooms cannot sustain human relationships of sufficient intimacy to support the risks, the trust, and the expression that learning requires."[102] Furthermore, the professionalization produced through a professional culture always looking up to authority mitigates a collaborative, collective spirit among teachers. This isolation disrupts the historical tradition of women gathering with one another.[103]

My compliance, my strong sense of responsibility to professional standards, my need for others to respect my professional authority made so much more sense in the context of these discourses and history! I was relieved in some ways. This kind of thorough explanation allowed me to try again to make sense of my experiences. To rise up. I even felt like somewhere in this new understanding there was a little bit of space to maybe even rework how I could see myself in a different way both as a woman and a teacher. To create another way of being a teacher, one that paid closer attention to how I understand what's going on in my classroom and in my own heart and mind ... one that maybe used her voice a bit louder ... one that maybe could effect change if she spoke loudly enough?

I didn't realize that in some ways I was still bound. My freedom was still limited. The troubling feelings felt a lot more faint. But they lingered. Thankfully, I could begin to count on my dialogic encounters with my study group and with scholarship to Name the elusive discomfort of my teaching experience! Re-interpretation awaited although I had no idea how the discourses I encountered would both give volume to the unsettled whispers and shatter my sense of righteousness.

Still with me? ☺ More soon!

Christine

5 Naming Hidden Work and (Mis)Understanding

> When those who have the power to name and socially construct reality choose not to see you or hear you, whether you are dark-skinned, old, disabled, female, or speak with a different accent or dialect than theirs, when someone with authority, of a teacher, say, describes the world and you are not in it, there is a moment of psychic disequilibrium, as if you looked into the mirror and saw nothing.[104]

> We who are in education cannot know, cannot truly know how it was, how it is. But we can attend to some of the voices, some of the stories.[105]

Dear Ruth and Joy,

What also became clear through my historical and critical study was the idea that the American Teacher was expected to do much more than teach reading, writing, and arithmetic. I thought I was using the academic disciplines to teach critical thinking so my students would be equipped to keep learning and growing and be effective citizens in a democracy. But I was doing, and expected myself to do, so much more. Philip Jackson's discourse on the "hidden curriculum" in schooling initiated a Naming in this vein.[106] The very structure of school as an institution—its routines, rules, and physical daily "sameness"—immerse students over time in a way of Being and Being together. As a student, I was socialized in this same way. I then taught my own students what it means to be socialized. I reinforced an understanding of the teacher-student relationship which prioritized order: students should respect and obey; teachers were responsible for providing an education in which students learned how to do that.

Critical theorists fleshed out this Naming in political and economic terms. They drew on historical aims of education, that industrial America required good workers and their critiques of schooling, for example, pointed to the myriad ways that students were socialized for factory work: bells delegating the use of time; their own work confined to others' design and approved by outside standards; movement constricted by designated areas such as box-like classrooms and desks within straight columns and rows. These and other features comprised what has come to be known as the "factory model" of education. Jean Anyon and other theorists went further and her research suggested that schools that drew from different socio-economic populations socialized the students through hidden curriculum of class to participate within their own social class.[107] Whether this relationship created 100-percent causality is not the point; for me, the pattern was enough to point to forces outside of myself compelling me to "be" a certain way as a teacher, forces I had not yet examined or evaluated because I simply had not considered this possibility.

Although it was interesting for me to understand the hidden curriculum in economic terms, the cultural implications of the hidden curriculum helped me again to reconstruct some of my early teaching experiences. In the historical story that I wrote, did you catch the formation of curriculum based upon Anglo-American Protestant culture? Did you notice that both colonial and industrial Americans sought to inculcate non-Anglo-American Protestants with particular values, and in doing so possibly communicated a lack of respect and acceptance of their own family/ethnic culture? Teacher training programs and colleges taught first those domestic arts that represented the value system of the Anglo-American Protestants who established them.[108] Thus, whether Anglo, American, Protestant or none of the above, the American Teacher would come to understand her role within the context of that culture. I have to say I was floored by the idea that what I believed to be "true," and fundamental "givens" could be a construction of culture rather than a universal truth.[109] Shouldn't all children respect their teacher; be quiet unless spoken to; know to obey when asked a rhetorical question such as "Why don't we take out our books ..."? I was baffled and I discovered through further dialogue with discourses that my inability to see my own culture, to see it in its dominant power in schools, is something I share with many other teachers.[110] You'll see in the following discourses how our shared blindness and complicity may exist despite our deep desire to do good. And in that dissonance may lie the roots of our frustration and confusion.

I have to explain myself a bit before I dive into this next story of Naming. You may find that not everything in this story has a one-to-one relation with my teaching experiences. There's a lot here, but I include it all because it was the depth of the cultural difference and the consequences of the lack of acknowledgement of those differences that struck me most profoundly. In fact, I do not have clear hindsight regarding a possible rationale for my confusion and frustration. Instead, this story changed my attitude toward myself. I realized that it is quite possible I had no idea what I was walking into; that I could only BE and BEHAVE according to the culture and perspective in which I'd marinated. I began to have some compassion for myself—for that young teacher and for her students. It's the same compassion that I had for you, Joy, when you blogged about how you exuberantly shared the victory of Martin Luther King, Jr. and the Civil Rights movement with your fourth grade class. "Now African-American children and white children can go to school together!" you exclaimed. The response of one little boy in your charter school class, comprised entirely of minority children in inner city Cleveland, was to echo in surprise, "We are allowed to go to school with white kids?!" When you told this story, you related so well your own bewilderment evolving into chagrin that somehow you had taken the lesson you learned in school as reality and missed the one experienced by the children seated before you. I had so much empathy for you in that moment, Joy. We don't see, until, well, we do. Ah. I'm so thankful for that kind of seeing, painful though it is, because it opens up the possibility to live more closely aligned with what felt like an ethical calling to teaching. So I wanted to share with you part of my own process of grappling with these cultural realties.

In them, I became aware not only of my own culture, but that of my students as well. And I recognized in myself the race-less identity of the American Teacher. This is my Naming and Seeing.[111]

In the field of Social Foundations of Education, some scholars such as Lisa Delpit, Gloria Ladson-Billings, Ann Arnett Ferguson, Gary Howard, and Herbert Kohl, reframe the problem of student "mis"-behavior as a problem of culture. To be clear, these scholars do not locate the problem within the culture of the student, as has become popular: pointing to a "culture of poverty" or a deficient racial or ethnic culture. Rather, the discourses that represent their work, including those framed by critical race theory and anti-racist education, highlight the culture of school as it is expressed in institutional norms and traditions as well as the teachers' practice and their own culture. Both the school and teachers' cultures tend to be the dominant social culture.[112] One scholar states, matter-of-factly,

> Public education, like any other aspect of public policy that has a cost attached to it, is directed by elected public officials according to the values they hold and the extent to which they see all students as worthy of high levels of education. The decision to provide a high-quality education is affected by officials' views of race and ethnicity as well as the role they saw for students of different racial/ethnic backgrounds in American society.[113]

In these discourses, scholars recognize race as a system for organizing culture, and further as a device for reproducing inequality in the contemporary United States.[114] Delpit points out that "most institutions in our society are created to reflect the realities of a particular cultural group, mainly the white, academically oriented middle class."[115] Thus, white culture holds the privileged position in our society. Ladson-Billings argues "the creation of a racial hierarchy with White and Black as polar opposites has positioned all people in American society and reified whiteness in ways that suggest the closer one is able to align oneself to whiteness, the more socially and culturally acceptable one is perceived to be," and African-American culture is seen as a corruption of white culture, rather than a distinctive culture of its own.[116]

What is troubling is that this remains unacknowledged by most of white America. In fact, with a Black president, some argue we are in a post-racial America. Critical race theorists suggest this ignorance or naiveté exists because racism is normalized in American society, "so enmeshed in the fabric of our social order it appears normal and natural to people in this culture.[117] In other words, we are typically unaware of the Foucauldian references we make, comparing everyone and their culture to a standard of whiteness.[118] As Delpit puts it, "when the privileged see others who operate from a different worldview, they can often comprehend them only as deviants, pathologically inferior, certainly in need of fixing ..."[119]

American public schooling makes clear the Foucauldian reference, perpetuating the larger society's racism within the schools.[120] Delpit explains, "In the educational institutions of this country, the possibilities for poor people and for people of color to define themselves, to determine the self each should be, involve a power that lies outside of the self. It is others who determine how they should act, how they are to be judged."[121] This emerged historically and will sound familiar to you given the history I constructed in my last two letters. "The emphasis on a 'one best system' emerges from the 19th century Americanization model that was designed to merge all students, regardless of ethnic and cultural origins into one ideal American," argues critical historian Joel Spring.[122] And just as they were intended to unify the Anglo-American culture, the actions of the American Teacher within and through schools were meant to "deculturize" Native Americans, Asians, Puerto Ricans, African-Americans, and immigrants.[123] This continues today. For example, African-American children, especially those from urban areas with high levels of poverty, are labeled as "at-risk" and culturally disadvantaged before they come into the classroom. In this way, labeling children as "culturally deprived" positions white middle-class cultural expressions as the normative or correct way of being in school and society.[124] Ladson-Billings clarifies this point.

> Being at risk became synonymous with being a person of color ... This works to construct a position of inferiority ... Diversity, like cultural deprivation and the state of being at risk, is that "thing" that is other than White and middle class.[125]

Much educational literature denigrates African-American culture. It is seen as an oppositional counter-productive culture in reference to white culture. It is not seen as a useful tool for meeting the needs of African-American learners and is thus delegitimized in the classroom. "Schools and teachers treat the language, prior knowledge, and values of African-Americans as aberrant and often presume that the teacher's job is to rid African-American students of any vestiges of their own culture."[126] This attitude can be traced to the 1950s and 1960s when cultural deficit theories emerged describing children of color as "victims of pathological lifestyles that hindered their ability to benefit from schooling."[127] The two most popular explanations for low achievement (of children who are seen as different) locate the problem in the children themselves or in the families.[128] The popular refrain reflecting these attitudes include phrases like: "parents just don't care" and "they aren't ready for school." Programs were and are then created, such as Head Start or Title 1, which rest on a foundation of cultural and social inferiority. Ladson-Billings reasons, "If we begin with the notion that some children lack "essential" qualities deemed necessary for school success, how is it that schools can correct or compensate for those missing qualities?" The goal of school, then, is to remove the children of such families and/or "to compensate for those perceived inadequacies."[129]

The result of these attitudes and goals is a poor education for African-American children in poverty. "Teachers and administrators assume that poor children are so inherently different that they cannot be treated with human dignity and humanity. They are trained to not place high academic expectations of these children because the primary purpose of school is to bring order to their lives."[130] Ladson-Billings continues and expounds that the perspective that

> "these children don't have enough exposure/experiences" … causes classrooms to be filled day after day with experiences but little, if any, teaching. (And) when teachers espouse "You poor dear" syndrome not only do they focus their energy on sympathizing, but this sympathy also turns into a set of excuses for why they cannot expect much academically from underserved students. Most grievous is that this attitude on part of the teacher gives children permission to fail, which can be contrasted with what teachers seem to do with White, middle-class students, namely "demand success."[131]

One of the first obstacles children of color run into is the American Teacher, who is most often white. A majority of teachers in urban classrooms are white, while their students are increasingly diverse.[132] There are several issues related to this particular obstacle, including the way educators perceive black children and their culture, the teacher's own culture, and the teacher's practice and pedagogy which represent her culture and the way she was trained. Many of these teachers come from "predominantly White neighborhoods and predominantly White colleges of teacher education."[133] This means that the American Teacher brings with her the vision and dynamics of White dominance. Often, the American Teacher attributes academic and behavior problems to the children themselves, not recognizing the impact of the clash of cultures the students' experience on a daily basis.

The question of authority is a good place to begin this discussion on cultural misunderstanding. In White culture, authority is established primarily by acquisition of an authoritative role. The (White) American Teacher understands that she does not need to exert personal power because of the position she holds. Through rhetorical questions, she may ask veiled commands, such as "would you like to sit down now" and the children in her class who do understand authority as she does understand that this question is a command to be obeyed no matter how "indirect, soft-spoken, or unassuming she may be."[134] But African American children may understand authority in terms of their Black culture in which authority is earned and exhibited by personal efforts and characteristics. "The authoritative person gets to be a teacher because she is authoritative," Delpit explains.[135] Thus, a veiled command uttered without power is not necessarily seen as a directive. In fact, the (White) American Teacher portrays herself to these children as weak and "incapable of taking on the role of being the teacher (so) there is no need to follow her directive."[136] At this point, typically, African-American children can then be seen as the problem, disobedient and uncooperative, in need of behavior management. My expectations of respect in Evanston and Harlem were based upon my positional authority as the Teacher. My manipulations and pleas dripped of powerlessness, however. My assumption—rather than exertion of power—confused us all. Scholars note this exhibition of personal power is also a way that many African-American children understand that their teacher must care about them. Delpit's work in particular reflects that

> Research has shown that motivation in African-American children from low socioeconomic groups is more influenced by the need for affiliation than for achievement. [Further] research suggests that children of color value the social aspects of an environment to a greater extent than do "mainstream" children, and tend to put an emphasis on feelings, acceptance, and emotional closeness.[137]

These studies contend that African-American interpretations of the environment determine the amount and kind of effort students will expend on classroom tasks. The American Teachers, however, are expected to be "dispassionate arbiters of knowledge and tasks."[138] Emotion is not supposed to exist beside rational scholarship and objectivity. Displays of emotion are equated with "losing control" and upset behavior management systems intended to deliver logical consequences. This is classic White, academic culture, as we discussed in earlier letters, and it contrasts widely with a Black culture that ties emotion with affiliation. When an African-American child sees a teacher as non-responsive, this is often interpreted as non-caring. Again, the cultural difference produces a misunderstanding detrimental to the child's well-being and learning. In my teaching, I struggled so much to hide my feelings, put on a stern face and expect obedience and respect. But, from their perspective, why cooperate with an adult who does not even care about them? I could see this with Nate. The level of focus and effort he exerted could be interpreted as proportionate to the time I spent at his side.

Behavior problems emerge both from misunderstandings within academic work and because language, language patterns, and narrative of different cultures figure prominently in school work. These differences lead teachers to assume African-American students have inferior academic potential. I will later discuss the resulting behavior issues, but for now hopefully the following will provide a rich picture of how deep the cultural misunderstandings run in the work of teaching. For example, in studies, "black students were unaccustomed to responding to the 'known answer' test questions of the classroom. Students would lapse into silence when direct factual questions regarding information just covered were asked [whereas they] responded actively to questions probing students' own analyses and evaluations."[139] Teachers, unaware of such cultural interpretation assumed the children did not know the answer in the former scenario.

Delpit cites another study reflecting the difference in cultural storytelling and the subsequent underestimation of the competence of African-American children. White and Black first graders were asked to tell stories in this study. The stories of White children focused on a single event, while the Black children told episodic stories usually including shifting scenes related to a series of events. After listening to these stories, White adults commented that the Black stories seemed incoherent. These adults further assessed the children having only heard the stories. Their assessments included the assumption that the children have reading or language problems, if not serious family or emotional problems that "might hamper academic progress."[140] Conversely, the Black adults found these stories to reveal children with great gifts. To them the stories were "well-formed, easy to understand and interesting with lots of detail."[141]

Another language difference, dialect, led not only to similar problems but studies indicate that the way teachers handled these perceived problems led to real learning troubles for the children. Studies found that "constant correction of dialect ... blocks reading development."[142] Delpit explains this arises when children are constantly corrected for dialect differences such as "here go" instead of "here is":

(1) Overcorrection means this child will be less likely to become a fluent reader than other children who are not interrupted so consistently.
(2) Complete focus on code and pronunciation blocks children's under-

standing that reading is essentially a meaning-making process (the child who understands the text is led to believe she is doing something wrong, and instead encouraged to think of reading as not something you do to get a message but something you pronounce).[143]

Further, the linguistic form many African-American children bring to school is intimately tied to loved ones, community, and personal identity. The constant correction communicates to the children that their identity and culture is wrong. Delpit asserts that "heritage is central to identity. To be disconnected from that identity means losing not only the ability to explain one's essence to others but also any potential for self-knowledge as well."[144]

These academic problems can result in behavior problems when children resist the practices that alienate or denigrate them and their culture. Herbert Kohl believes this resistance emerges out of an understanding that learning what others want you to learn can sometimes destroy you. Not-learning, he writes, is a personal choice and exercise of free will in an environment that limits or oppresses identity and agency.

Not-learning tends to take place when someone has to deal with unavoidable challenges to her or his personal and family loyalties, integrity and identity. In such situations there are forced choices and no apparent middle ground ... To agree to learn from a stranger who does not respect your integrity causes a major loss of self. The only alternative is to not-learn and reject the stranger's world.[145]

Through Kohl's research, he found a number of academic scenarios that seemed to produce a response of not-learning from students. These situations parallel those found by Delpit: reading, language, and authority. While some students were failing because there were real learning problems, others, he found were making a conscious positive choice in their life not to learn. Was this the case with Nate? With his friend John? Kohl's work provoked this kind of wondering:

> For some, not-learning was a strategy that made it possible for them to function on the margins of society instead of falling into madness or total despair. It helped them build a small safe world in which their feeling of being rejected by family and society could be softened. Not-learning played a positive role and enabled them to take control of their lives and get through difficult times.[146]

But not-learning is interpreted negatively by the American Teacher and the education system she represents. This kind of resistance is a threat to the entire system, and measures are taken to discover and solve the *problem*. Inevitably, it is found, the problem is located within the child as he or she is found to be disturbed or dumb. And the system itself is protected from change.[147]

It is not hard to see how authority exercised through behavior/classroom management emerges as an important discourse in teacher education given this perspective of African-American children, their culture and their experiences in school.[148] When the problem is located within the child or his family, then clearly "management" becomes a priority in order to mitigate distraction. It becomes the professional responsibility of the American Teacher. But anti-racist scholars emphasize "the need to address systemic barriers that cultivate and sustain racism, particularly within educational settings."[149]

Following this line of thought, Ann Arnett Ferguson, in her extensive case study research, found behavior management or "punishment [to be] a fruitful site for a close-up look at routine institutional practices, individual acts, and cultural sanctions that give life and power to racism in a school setting that not only produces massive despair and failure among black students, but that increasingly demonizes them."[150] As a result of her study of punishment in schools, she concludes that institutional operations themselves, rather than the cultural difference, determines the pattern of punishment.[151] What we see in punishment is the clash of educational structures with student resistance. "Institutional practices continue to marginalize or exclude African Americans in the economy and society through the exercise of rules and purportedly objective standards by individuals who may consider themselves racially unbiased," Ferguson clarifies.[152] The resistance appears when students reject the cultural modes that make them "different."[153] African-American students, Ferguson demonstrates, recognize the school's alienation of their culture and themselves, and "kids recoup a sense of self as competent and worthy under extremely discouraging work conditions ... by getting into trouble."[154] And in doing so, they enter the punishing system. Ferguson elucidates this concept quite definitively.

> The punishing system is supported by nothing less than the moral order of society—the prevailing ideology—which simultaneously produces and imposes a consensus about a broad spectrum of societal values, manners, presentation of self, including style of dress, ways of standing, sitting, tone of voice, mode of eye contact, [and a] range of facial expressions ... It is also assumed that the rules, codes, social relations, and behaviors adjudicated by a school's discipline system are about the transmission and enactment of a moral authority from adults, who are empowered to transmit and enact, to children, who are seen as lacking the essential values, social skills, and morality required of citizens.[155]

Ferguson's study revealed the school labeling practices and the exercise of rules operated as part of a hidden curriculum to marginalize and isolate black male youth in disciplinary spaces and brand them as criminally inclined. Although, few educators involved in this school would frame the problem with race. In fact,

> In relation to this study, the position was that children were sent to the Punishing Room not because of who they were, but because of what they did. The institutional discourse was that getting in trouble was not about race but a matter of individual choice and personal responsibility: each child made a choice to be "good" or "bad." The homily "the choice is yours" was printed at the top of the list of school rules to emphasize this connection.[156]

But African-American educators in the building suggested that race was a factor, intimating that White teachers were afraid of or did not know how to discipline Black boys. (If I'm being honest, hadn't I been afraid?)

Ferguson found children were sorted by the narratives teachers told themselves. Educators believed "at-riskness" was a consequence of apathetic or dysfunctional families. (You may recall I addressed these narratives as I confronted troubling new circumstances in Harlem). Mothers and mothering were blamed for children's behavior. The narratives continue: The "worst" behaved children are black and male. They score far below grade level. Their attitude toward school is terrible; they refuse to work. Their actions reflect this attitude: they eat candy, fight, chase, instigate, and cut school. "They are defiant, disrespectful, and profane."[157] Those who misbehave come from the (low-income, Black) neighborhood, which is not a good neighborhood because you can see the drug dealers on the street. Black children need special attention because they do not get it at home. They are rarely in the gifted program but instead are sent to compensatory education specialists for their "impulse control and attention disorders."[158] Both the parents and the children are in need of special training programs. Conversely, as the narrative goes, well behaved children are also the best and the brightest, who come to school ready to work and know how to resolve their disagreements with others in socially acceptable ways. This is due to the fact that their parents are good role models who oversee their education. They are almost all White.

These narratives seemed to express the natural order of things, but Ferguson's study uncovered a hidden order that instigates and perpetuates inequality. Through the lens of radical schooling theory, she argues that "the function of school is to reproduce the current inequities of our social, political, and economic system."[159] Using Foucault's theory of disciplinary power, Ferguson demonstrates how the educational institution reframes the consequences of racism in the institution as problems with individual students.[160] School rules become the centerpiece of discipline. Conformity to school rules is the prerequisite to learning.[161]

Rules operate with other forms of classification such as tests and grades, psychological screening measures, and the distribution of rewards and punishment. These things tell the "truth" about the individual.

> For some boys, the route from the Punishment Room leads to another series of rooms where psychological counseling is offered in order to teach them "impulse control" and how to get along better with their peers. So trouble making acts become transformed into "troubled" children, with pathological personalities and character flaws that must be documented and treated. This psychologization of "troublesome" behavior is linked with a discourse about the nature of the problem as an individual disorder rather than one that is social and systemic.[162]

In additional to "neutral" rules, teachers seemed convinced that their own practice is impartial, but cultural displays of emotion or use of Black English, for example, became significant factors in teachers' decisions about academic possibilities for students. These determinations were made against their own and institutional standards for what is ideal or normal, in other words against the standard of White culture. Ferguson attempts to demystify this concept of a race-less interpretation.

> This apparent absence of race in whites, this presence as raceless, permits their cultural forms to be known as, even experienced, as individuality. The reproduction of racial order in the United States today is made possible by the invisibility of operations that seem to be about natural dispositions and character rather than about racial frictions.[163]

But Ferguson's study also recognized that African-American youth understood that their backgrounds, experience, and modes of expression "were detrimental to their achievement and ... must be eradicated." She continues,

> As discerning observers and participants, the boys know they must be actively engaged in discarding or making up for these unbecoming elements of their biography. They must make themselves over to succeed in school and to accumulate the cultural capital that is the prerequisite

for achievement. They must ... shed the distinguishing features of "Blackness" by approximating whiteness by acting white.[164]

Her study then highlighted the conscious choice many African-American children, especially boys, made with regard to how they would behave in school. The boys chose to become Troublemakers or Schoolboys. Schoolboys operate with the notion that their Blackness is a problem for their achievement. Internalizing the idea that academic prowess is an individual choice, these boys consciously work to align themselves positively with authority. In contrast, Troublemakers defy the argument that they as individuals are the problem. They see their behavior as a critique of a racist institution. They refuse to accept the "upward mobility strategies that require black youth to distance themselves from family and neighborhoods and to reject the language and the style of social interaction, the connections in which identities are grounded."[165] Troublemakers enter the punishing system, which has long-term effects that substantially increase one's chances of ending up in jail.[166]

There is significant tragedy here. Ferguson urgently asserts that

> There is overwhelming evidence that African-American kids enter school not with an oppositional orientation at all, but full of promise and eager to learn. There is also evidence that somewhere early in the fourth grade this motivation and intense excitement about school learning dwindles markedly so for African American boys in what has come to be known as "the fourth grade syndrome." This is the point at which African-American boys appear to begin to disidentify with school and to look for other sources for self-evaluation. It is my contention that this diminished motivation to identify as a "scholar" is a consequence of the inhospitable culture of school that African American children encounter rather than a consequence of peer pressure.[167]

When behavior is framed by these discourses, emphasis on the American Teacher's control and "management" strategies are a Band-Aid at best and unethical treatment of children at worst. To remake schools into hospitable spaces for children of color, many of these scholars call first and foremost for educators and institutions of educational training to recognize the existence of White dominance in our society and the pervasiveness of White culture in the American Teacher. Ferguson contends,

> If we want to work seriously on the issues of inequality for Blacks and other oppressed people ... we must begin not with the "problems" of mar-

ginalized groups but with the fundamental social flaws that have been created by White dominance.[168]

Emphasis on authority and control issue from an educational framework that ignores racism and the educational mechanisms that perpetuate it. In doing so, it too becomes part of a disciplinary system that individualizes children and locates problems within the individual, thereby ignoring race, culture, and systemic inequities. Equally troubling are the low academic expectations and inferior educational programming, also resultant from this classification. Children recognize this ranking and many resist by choosing to defy the rules meant to order them. Rather than managing the children at this stage, the discourses I have referred to in this letters suggest addressing White dominance in educational institutions and within the American Teacher herself, as well as honoring the humanity of African-American children by incorporating their culture and providing high quality educational programs for them.

When I synthesized these discourses in this way, with some anguish, I cringed. And once or twice, while reading Ferguson's book, especially, I wept. My God, how violent is ignorance—not seeing. I repeated to my teacher-self in cautionary tones, "Be careful. Be so very careful. You know not what you do." In other words, I didn't find any neat and tidy solutions to the problems of my early teaching days in Evanston and East Harlem. I was suddenly very aware that culture was most likely a major factor in my confusion and frustration. The tragedy of what could happen when teachers "miss" culture was so palpable. And in the context of our earlier discussion on "professional responsibility" I was further cautioned. The proliferation of "ideas" about how to manage students, especially students of color, has become yet another *must-digest-and-execute* responsibility bestowed by "experts." To be honest, after such a Naming of my experiences, I have to say that I became less and less convinced that educational "experts" held expertise in matters that really concerned me as a teacher. I felt a new professional responsibility toward my students. I needed to understand their culture and how they might interpret mine. I needed to pay attention to the ways in which I included or excluded their experiences. In what ways did being an American Teacher, as I understood it, undermine their Becoming? How did it undermine my own Becoming? Certainly my current interpretation and thinking bound us both, but, in Naming the limitations, suddenly there was the possibility of alternatives, whether I could define them yet or not.

Always searching for hope,

Christine

6   Being Ethical

> How *can* one act on one's commitment and at once set others free to be? This seems to us to be one of the crucial questions confronting the self-conscious teacher?[169]

Dear Ruth and Joy,

At this juncture, you may have noted how the good student/good teacher assumptions, the historical story, the feminized professional discourse, and anti-racist explications provided critical language for me to Name some of the discomfort I acknowledged in my teaching narratives. That language, to this point, also helped me to make sense of how I came to my understanding of my role and responsibilities as a teacher. I relied heavily on external standards such as theory, management, administrative approval, cultural expectations, normative understandings for "being a teacher" (just the way things are)—such as getting respect and having enough of the right kinds of knowledge. This led to distrust of parents, disdain for colleagues, and self-victimizing in the face of authority. While I had colleagues who were friends, in many ways, teaching was an individual endeavor, a challenge for me to tackle, so that I could be my best and help kids be their best. This also meant I alone was to blame for not getting it right.

Even after identifying the web of forces that construct the sense of the American Teacher, it was clear that these discourses helped me understand my thinking and behavior, but it didn't necessarily explain the specific tensions I felt. In our study group sessions, my mentor Noreen Garman would often assert that because we, as a society, force children by law to be in schools, we have a moral obligation to those children. This statement stung me. It bugged me. And I could not shake it over the course of the next ten years. At some point, I acquiesced to its insistent voice, engaged dialogically with it and discourses representing this idea, and let them guide further Naming for me. I shifted my gaze for a moment from myself and my internalized standards to the children I taught.

I look back at my teaching narratives, and I found many emerge from situations in which I was at a loss with a particular student. In other words, my inner turmoil and thus the fertile space of re-interpretation occurred within a relationship with another person. Quite often, I was puzzled because I acted to make the appropriate thing happen and I did not get the outcome I predicted. It seemed like there was a SHOULD on one end and the specific, living child in front of me at the other. And I couldn't always reconcile them. That inability to make them fit together was a deep source of frustration. Should Ruby *not* read *Jane Eyre*? Should Nate and his classmates be permitted to disrespect me and carry on in the class according to their own whims? Should middle school children be allowed to dance and listen to music loudly when they have been asked by someone in authority to turn it down? Should Dustin not be disciplined for plagiarism? Shouldn't seventh graders learn how to get along and work together? Shouldn't Leonard learn to write legibly? Should a trained Social Studies teacher instruct a burgeoning gifted mathematician in math? Shouldn't Christopher and Benjamin's parents respect the professionals? Could I not claim some degree of expertise and therefore expect respect for my decisions for students based upon my hard won knowledge and experience? In each scenario, this living child in front of me seemed to be the opposite of what SHOULD have been.

This was the most profound and most common tension in my teaching: this child before me and the right thing to do in my head. How could they be polar opposites? It became an indictment on my professional ability and/or on the child's willingness and ability to learn. Either way, one of us was to blame. I resorted to manipulation and weird passive aggressive acts to claim my authority or justify my expertise.[170]

Honestly, this was the deepest source of my shame. How could I be doing the "best," aiming for acquisition and execution of the best knowledge, and hurting my students? I could not understand why I could not understand this and fix it. I found myself, ironically, entrenched in a quintessential battle in the field of education … but in my own head. Make the child my focus or the curriculum (and its aims)?[171] It's pretty black and white, dualistic thinking. And the silo effect of the academy offered answers but not to my questions. Scholars of discipline pedagogy reinforced the notion that if I, as an individual teacher, would just know and use the right pedagogy, I could get the right results. Critical theorists fleshed out a richer picture of the constraints of culture, politics, class, and systems embedded in my experience of teaching; they even offered the possibility of resistance and voice. But many steered clear of how I might reconcile all of this within my daily practice confronted by particular children and my particular school environment. The aggressive attack on the practical tools available for teachers left me with little but a sense of the enormity of the problem.

When I stumbled upon Parker Palmer's interpretation of the concept of paradox, however, this "other way" of thinking about "opposites" refined my understanding of Naming while also Naming the challenge for me in each of the incidences portrayed by my narratives.[172] Paradox, Palmer suggests, offers us a fruitful way to grapple with life as contradiction, a study of dissonance rather than harmony. "The heart of the human experience is contradiction, not consistency or chaos; the world is not monolithic, things are not locked in place."[173] This resonated with me as I wrote these visceral memories that could not be reconciled into a cohesive narrative about who I was as a teacher. And I could, of course, identify with the picture he paints of avoidance of the uncomfortable dissonance of human life: "Much in our human nature resists living the contradictions [and] wants to avoid the tension that comes from being torn between poles."[174] But Palmer insists that the contradictions point to larger truths. Logic, of our mind, wants to separate and divide, but "the seeker looks for life's hidden wholeness."[175]

I do not think that he is talking about seeking a monolithic narrative that smooths out the dissonance. Rather, his aim, like Maxine Greene's, is a freedom that enables us to move into new and richer possibilities for Being in the world. He describes a process of accepting the contradictions, owning them as my life. In this comes a sense of powerlessness, and a fatal sense of death … "of self that insists on being in charge, the self that continually tried to impose its own idea of order and righteousness on the world. We have finally accepted a difficult reality."[176] Out of acknowledgement, we can face it for what it IS: an imposition to our growing, an obstacle to our Becoming. We can transform those contradictions, or "larger truths," into paradox, moving deeper into them to allow us to see differently. "In the tension of my fear, I am open" to other possibilities for being.[177]

As I pressed into the paradox of my narratives (children and professional responsibilities at either end), what did become useful were discourses in feminist and alterity (otherness) ethics. Based on my narratives, I would say that my ethical commitments were to know and do the best of what my profession demanded so that I could set up my students to become thoughtful, engaged, fulfilled, growing adults who contributed responsibly to our democracy. Achievement of my ethical commitment was based upon my "right" enactment of external ideals in my daily life and interactions. After this incredibly lengthy letter, I am quite certain that you may have come to the conclusion that I was having a bit of difficulty realizing an ethical existence as a teacher with these commitments. As I've mentioned, my only recourse was to believe that either I wasn't doing it right or that the kids weren't.

Feminist ethics in education, specifically those represented by Nel Noddings, sparked my imagination in the sense that they offered a way of being I hadn't considered while also identifying, or Naming, why I might find myself in such an untenable ethical position. Noddings grounds ethics in the nature of human beings in the world, rather than spectators outside of it. The premise is that every human being at least has an "inkling of having been cared for … and this is the root of our responsibility to one another."[178] In this sense, principles of ethics are useful insofar as they restore a more intuitive or "natural" caring among people. Interactions can rely then on the mutual and spontaneous regard that characterizes healthy caring relationships. This is contrasted with principle-based ethics in which moral questions can be divorced from lived interactions and determined in solitude. "Thus," Noddings suggests,

> instead of turning to a principle for guidance, a carer turns to the cared-for. What does he or she need? Will filling this need harm others in the network of care? Am I competent to fill this need? Will I sacrifice too much of myself? Is the expressed need really in the best interest of the cared-for? If the cared-for is a stranger, I might ask how I would respond to her or him if she or he were a member of my inner circle.[179]

These were a lot of my own questions, but I felt wrong asking them. The confines of the American Teacher, which I embodied, strongly tied me to referencing standards and responsibilities beyond the relationship and certainly beyond the child. These standards told me what was best for the child, and I was supposed to impose what was best for the child. An ethic of care, however, "insists that caring does not reside entirely in the attitude and intentions of the carer. We must ask about the effects on the cared-for."[180] This gave me pause just as Noreen's reminder about our moral responsibility to children in schools. And it made me wonder about the implications of where I directed my attention.

Sharon Todd had similar concerns, but she also challenged the idea that understanding and empathizing with the "other" in a relationship was ethical.[181] Like Noddings, Todd found problematic the idea of teachers acting based upon their knowledge of the good or best outcomes or their knowledge of others and their concerns.[182] If I try to operate out of my knowledge of the other person, I now make that person an object for my purposes. I am "exercising my knowledge over the Other ... and the Other becomes an object of my comprehension, my world, my narrative, reducing the Other to me."[183] She sees the potential for a kind of violence, in not allowing the other to be different. Instead, since we cannot reconcile the Being that is "me" and the Being that is "you," we could direct our attention to the relation between us. The relation is the encounter; it has "qualities, texture, time, history, and above all, tension and limitations."[184] This begs for our attention to what is there in the interaction. For teachers, this is a pedagogic encounter and we would pay attention to the Becoming that happens in that interaction, what we (teacher and student or student and student) are Becoming as a result of the encounter. Our posture then is one of "mindfulness, attentiveness, listening."[185] I am therefore learning from the Other, from the students and what they are Being or Becoming within our interactions. This informs my own Being and Becoming as a teacher of this student. Ethics then is based in our attention to difference, not commonality or previously learned knowledge about others and their needs. The relation fraught with paradox becomes the site for Naming.

I know this is heady stuff. I still need more study, but I wanted to bring it up because just dipping my toe in these discourses, and, being open in dialogue, transformed my thinking about my presence and "right" actions in the classroom. And it's so close to this idea of Naming as a part of my teaching practice because attention to the relation is potentially attention to the site of paradox. Someone might read this letter and assume that I have thrown out ethical principles or am disgusted by discussion of "best practices," that I have no use for theorists, administrators, or politicians, and that I am completely disregarding democratic or Aristotelian aims of education. But the fact is that all of this Naming led me not to reject these things but rather to both reprioritize and re-imagine. I wondered—and wonder today in trial and error—what would my teaching look like if I repurposed pedagogical and critical knowledge, for example, as resources rather than ideals? What if I set social and academic aims as a backdrop, but led with observation and intuitive disturbances regarding my students and their present Being and possible Becoming as I emerge from my encounters with them? I wonder if my attentiveness to the dissonance would connect me not so much to an ideal and normalized American Teacher but to myself, to my project of Becoming in my interconnected, lived world. What would it mean to honor myself and my students in that way?

•••

I'll give you one practical example of the nature of my teaching since engaging in this kind of Naming. Joseph is a kindergarten student this year. He can read through a sixth grade level, although his comprehension falls several grades below that. He can conceptualize (not just process) numerical concepts through the first grade level. For a small part of every day, kindergarten instruction (small group, play, and manipulative-based) is differentiated, so Joseph is working every day at a place that is right where he is at cognitively, not too easy and not excessively challenging. But he is a total "space cadet." He wanders not only away from the group but out of the room, down the hall and who knows where else?! He enjoys his peers, but he doesn't spend time with any of them during the day. He sits and reads or wanders.

Prior to engaging in Naming as a way of Being a teacher, I would have assessed him as a problem and a frustrating anomaly. I would have adjusted my pedagogy, rifling through my resources representing best practices, but been confused when Joseph still left the table repeatedly to wander or read. I would have reached deeper into my professional knowledge and noted developmental issues and proceeded to subtly blame the parents for putting him in kindergarten too early. He's barely five years old. He's too young, see! He can't do what the other kids can do in terms of his focus. He should be in preschool. Or maybe they should get him tested? He really has trouble with his focus. Nothing would really have changed as a result of this stance, except this would give me some relief from my ownership over a problem I couldn't, though I "should," solve.

Somewhere in the middle of graduate school, in the early days of Naming, I would have recognized a red flag, sought discourse/dialogue, and dug deeper for critical knowledge, social and cultural knowledge. His family is from Uganda. He's never been in an institution, let alone a culturally American one. He's never seen snow. Oh, ah ha. This complicates, or makes richer, the knowledge I have about Joseph. I would have had more patience, allowed him time to grow by suggesting he repeat kindergarten. Not only could he mature, he might also need the time to adjust to being in an institutional culture with particular expectations and norms. Critical knowledge would have granted me some depth of understanding and a richer ethical posture, potentially.

Instead, in taking my present posture of seeing Naming as making visible a paradox of a "should" and a child, I pay attention to the Becoming of both Joseph and I in our encounters. I might notice how when he reads, whether or not he understands it, his sense of competence emanates from his smile. He wants to show me, to read to me, to read to his parents and friends. And that smile lingers through long periods, even twenty to thirty minutes of reading. I know this about his smile because after several encounters with Joseph I learned his sense of self was affirmed and growing through reading, and I made a pedagogical choice to give him the time and space to read for as long as he could sustain his focus. I learned from him that, right now, much of the vitality of his Becoming is through reading. Given what I know about the development of self-worth, his sense of competency is a huge priority.[186] Reading often and for long periods of time supports this growth, this Becoming. I don't discount the other parts of the curriculum (the other side of the paradox), as being useless to his Becoming. However, I do not let the external standard define his experience and growth or mine.

Given what I am learning from him and given what I know theoretically about development and cultural competency, I am constructing educational encounters for and with him that attend to this specific unfolding of Joseph. We create time for him weekly to talk about his home country, and the children engage in conversations about family and home, similarities and differences;

it's a jumping off point for climate and environment, among other things. I attend to what I learn from him by noting what he pays attention to as well. I've learned from him that math engages him for a certain period of time and with methods of instruction before his eyes glaze and his feet move. I plan for those encounters very specifically, drawing on my knowledge of the four-year-old brain, math pedagogy, and my wealth of resources (including dialogue with my fellow teachers and discourses/research in teaching to which Joseph's situation may point) to create a possible engagement for Joseph that matches his cognitive urge to play with math *and* his demonstrated developmental ability to attend to a task and exercise self-control. Over time, I will tune myself to Joseph's expression of thriving and competency to sense whether these encounters can be stretched over a few more minutes, whether they are sufficiently challenging, and also whether he is able to exercise greater bodily stamina. On the face of it, I still employ a great deal of abstract, theoretical knowledge, standards, and benchmarks acquired through study of discourses and people, but my practice, my study, and Becoming, center on the interaction I have with each student. This is where I can be not only sensitive to discomfort, but also to the space in which I can embody new ways of Becoming as a result of the Naming process, which I may choose when the discomfort arises. I think this is the fruitful soil where, subtlety, wisdom grows.

I know this resonates with you both differently. Ruth, as a teacher in a small town public school, you have greater autonomy over your curriculum and pedagogy. Based on our conversations, Joy, I can hear your frustration as a teacher in a large metropolitan school district. "I don't have that kind of flexibility!" Yes, you are micromanaged through testing that "evaluates" you, bureaucracy that robs you of your humanity (and bathroom time), and a lack of respect and therefore power to educate according to your conscience. Joy, what we know to be true is that the most humane educative experiences happen in relationship. Thus, the unique wisdom of teachers emerges out of the meaning we make within our relationships with the children in front of us within our given context. Unfortunately, we have this experience of the horror of how children are being treated, let alone educated, and then we take to the streets or the negotiating room or facebook. "It's unrighteous!" Yes, it is unrighteous, unethical, and even immoral. For several generations now, the shout and fight to address these issues still leave teachers perceived and feeling as if we are victims. This Naming practice, attending to the children right in front of us and how our experience together in our particular circumstance informs our ways of being, enables us to articulate and frame the issues wisely. The attention to our own Becoming within the relationship and encounter with children brings us to an awareness of our own limited sight; we recognize we are not victims but participants. We begin to practice our agency and see our power generate healthier, more ethical ways of being together with children. It is this kind of teacher wisdom, experience combined with whole-being critical reflection, especially when pooled collectively among educators, that generates structural change.[187]

Theologian and activist Barbara Holmes suggests that as we continue to jump from cultural trauma to action without first noting, understanding and healing the trauma, we find ourselves forever stuck in cycles of systemic injustice.[188] A Naming praxis which begins with you and the children before you engenders this deep understanding and critical work necessary for more ethical possibilities in schools. In this way, we are truly dependent on one another, wherever we teach, to do this wisdom work, and therefore, we are …

In this together,

Christine

7   Becoming Possibilities

> Now that I'm free to be myself, who am I?
> Can't fly, can't run, and see how slowly I walk.
> Well, I think, I can read books.
> "What's that you're doing?"
> the green-headed fly shouts as it buzzes past.
> I close the book.
> Well, I can write down words, like these, softly.[189]

Dear Ruth and Joy,

I am so appreciative of your willingness to read my letters, full of many stories. I hoped to show you the good Naming, as a praxis, has done for me. To have a praxis of Naming is to keep myself "wide-awake" to my unfolding, to pay attention when I am disturbed because my Becoming may be obstructed.[190] To do so in teaching is to be present and attuned to the encounter with the student. Upon recognition of disturbance, a Naming praxis points me toward dialogue. With whom can I converse to more deeply understand the dilemmas of my particular situations? What interpretations will provide language to birth thought—freedom to see and Be alternately?

For me, Naming also enabled understanding and compassion for myself. The role of American Teacher is so tightly wound in normative assumptions and behaviors, I was left to blame myself for my apparent failures. I could not see myself, my virtue, or my ethical missteps. Naming also proved useful in resisting those normalizing tendencies, as it ushered in deeper understandings of my circumstances. I no longer see myself as a victim, with no choice but to comply. I am free insofar as I can Name and Imagine alternate possibilities.

Naming revealed my connectedness, foregrounding the dialogic nature of my Being in the world. My best hope of freedom in Being was in dialogic engagement, not in the isolation in which the profession and my interpretation of it had imprisoned me. I need my colleagues. They need me. We need to engage with one another, to tell our stories. And we need access and willingness to thoughtfully converse with scholarship, discourses, and language that open new ways of seeing. I've started to pay attention to what others express and recognize it as valuable to my own Becoming. I've also learned that telling my own story might be useful to them. Naming emboldens me to seek community. I *am* my community.

Most profoundly, Naming unlocked the notion of Becoming for me and gave me access to my emotions, my heart, my intuition, where before I confined my Being as a Teacher to my "rational" mind.[191] And in this, in my connection to my Being, I reclaimed my ethical commitments. I am empowered in my agency. I have found that Naming grants me access to an embodied ethics that I enact in very practical ways with floppy-haired, goofy-smiling, bright-eyed, integrity-filled Becoming children.

I want to pause here, in the midst of the joy of imagining possibilities, to remember for you the anguish of Naming, for just a moment. I do not want to leave you with the impression that Naming is a simple detachment from past interpretations so that I can better do my job or live a freer existence. Naming has always presented itself to me as an option in my distress; that much I believe is clear. But I also experienced anguish as I Named. See, in Naming, I face two apparent impossibilities. Those interpretations WERE my Being. A version of my Being built upon a kind of certainty and clarity. I also had to defy the often beloved or respected voices and communities representing those discourses that informed my interpretations. And in order to enter into Becoming, I needed to enter into a kind of death. To let go of that certainty, that "real" version of myself, especially to let go for an unknown Becoming, often felt like dying. There is a space of unknowing and blind Becoming that Naming engenders ... and it is not for the faint of heart. My fear of uncertainty is an existential fear because I don't know who I am yet. So, my friends, what I've come to believe is that in the midst of these layers of fear and discomfort, I need faith in my very humanness. I've come to believe that my deepest ache is for freedom to Become, and to Become in ways that allow me to give and receive love within boundaries of mutual respect. It's messy and scary, but I keep this deepest ache as my banner. It is for this that I willingly engage in the suffering it tends to create. For the joy set before me, I embrace the gifts of Naming.

I hope in relating this process, I have not been condescending. I hope I have provided enough space for you to engage dialogically with me, with these discourses, and with your own experiences and interpretations. Our conversation isn't finished, is it? What is your response to my chatter? Are your experiences different? Call me so we can sit around my fire with tea and wine and chocolate and popcorn to tell each other our stories.

With love and respect,

Christine

Notes

1. Romans 7:15, 17, adapted from the *New International Version*.
2. William Pinar, *The Character of Curriculum Studies*," 1. "Curriculum studies is a complicated *conversation*. Structured by guidelines, focused on objectives, and overdetermined by outcomes, the US school curriculum struggles to remain conversation. It is conversation—efforts at understanding through conversation—among students and teachers, actually existing individuals in certain places on certain days, simultaneously personal and public. The fact that students and teachers are individuals complicates conversation considerably, and often in welcomed ways, as each person brings to whatever is being studied his or her own prior knowledge, present circumstances, interest, and yes, disinterest ... Add to these the locale or region where the curriculum is enacted, the nation (its history and present circumstance), the state of the planet, [the individual school] ... and one begins to appreciate just how complicated the conversation about the school curriculum is, can be, and must remain"
3. Tina Fey and Kay Cannon, "Chain Reaction of Mental Anguish," *30 Rock*.
4. Janet Miller, "Teacher Spaces," 12. What captured "our attention ... were the examples of variation, the uncharted, the exception in our classrooms. These constant anomalies often contradicted a tidy description of a successful teaching approach reported in a journal article ... or a surefire combination of methods and materials that we remembered from our teacher preparation programs."
5. Within Social Foundations courses, "critical incident" may be seen as a moment in the work of teaching for teachers to reexamine their personal biography within and against the institution and larger social and cultural dynamics. Julie Carter, "Critical Incidents in Social Foundations: Reflecting on Theory, Connecting to Practice," in *Becoming a Teacher*, ed. Blake and Blake.
6. This notion is discussed by a number of scholars, including Greene in *Existential Ecnounters*, 155. The teacher ... must acknowledge somehow that his effectiveness, like his authenticity, depends to some degree upon the nature of his personal commitment. He must acknowledge that he cannot live in two domains—private and professional." It is expressed well by Palma Suzanne George Millies, "The Relationship Between a Teacher's Life and Teaching, in *Teacher Lore*, ed. Schubert and Ayers, 24: "A teacher's school experience is inseparable from the rest of her life. Teacher's life outside of teaching contributes to the kind and quality of teacher she will become, and her personality, assumptions, and values impact her teaching directly and indirectly."

7 Greene, *Existential Encounters*, 4. "They are to be educated, in other words, to make their own way as persons, if not as producers; they are to be educated so that they may create themselves."
8 Dewey, *Democracy and Education* and *Experience and Education*. Millies in "The Relationship Between a Teacher's Life and Teaching," describes it as "a form of thorough inquiry that asks questions of the experience in order to better understand it" (25).
9 I like Virginia Jagla's articulation. In a qualitative study of teachers responding to question of the use of their imagination and intuition in teaching, Jagla finds, "It is our becoming as human beings that spawns our becoming as teachers … Being in tune with one's insights, building a capacity for trustworthy intuition and being willing to act upon it—are all part of a philosophy of life that can lead to better teaching." Jagla, "Teachers' Everyday Imagination and Intuition," in *Teacher Lore*, ed. Schubert and Ayers.
10 Greene, *Releasing the Imagination: Essays on Education, the Arts and Social Change*, 197–198. "The central questions will continue to haunt us. How can we reconcile the multiple realities of human lives with shared commitment to communities infused once again with principles? … It is out of this kind of thinking, I still believe, that the ground of a critical community can be opened in our teaching and in our schools. It is out of such thinking that public spaces may be regained … The principles and contexts have to be *chosen* by living human beings against their own life worlds and in the light of their lives with others, by persons able to call, to say, to sing, and—using their imaginations, tapping their courage—to transform."
11 Parker Palmer in "The New Professional" suggests that staying close to emotions can generate "energy for institutional change, which might help *everyone* survive."
12 "Praxis is a particular type of cognitive action which crucially involves the transcending or surpassing of what is. Those who treat knowing in this fashion refuse to take the social cultural matrix for granted as a given. This means that they pose their relevant questions and pursue answers with a sense of a reality to be produced and with the intention to bring about the projected state of affairs." Greene, *Teacher as Stranger*, 163. See also Miller, "Teaching Spaces" and Grumet, *Bitter Milk*, who imagine that praxis also highlights teachers' knowledges that evolve in human relationships. Such knowledges … "emerge from the reciprocal movement of theory in practice and take shape in the variety of relationships that teachers forge in their daily work," 16.
13 Greene writes in *Dialectic of Freedom* that freedom is "personally achieved when we each make decisions we believe to be fully our own. They are decisions more often than not based on shared principles or shared perceptions of what is good and right; but they remain personally achieved," 101.
14 Greene's use of the dialectic is hermeneutic, related to understanding and interpretation. In the *Dialectic of Freedom,* she described this dialectic as the back and forth consideration of one's inward consciousness and existing external structures of the material world. "The dialectic [involves] the subject/object relationship. [We are back to] the realization that freedom can be achieved only in an ongoing transaction, one that is visible and legible to those involved," 83.
15 Greene, *Dialectic of Freedom*, 21. "Human consciousness is always situated; and the situated person, inevitably engaged with others, reaches out and grasps the phenomena surrounding him/her from a particular vantage point and against a particular background consciousness … The perspectives available are always partial. The individual sees profiles, aspects of the building entered in the morning, the school or the agency … There is always something more to be discovered each time he/she focuses attention. As important, each time he/she is with others-in dialogue, in teaching-learning situations, in mutual pursuit of a project-additional new perspectives open; language opens possibilities of seeing, hearing, understanding. Mul-

tiple interpretations constitute multiple realties; the "common" itself becomes multiplex and endlessly challenging, as each person reaches out from her own ground toward might be, should be, is not yet."
16 Greene, *Dialectic of Freedom.*
17 Sidorkin, *Beyond Discourse.*
18 Miller, "Teachers' Spaces," in *Teacher Lore,* "I struggled to make explicit the ways in which I had internalized others' expectations for myself as woman and teacher ... Those passive and unconsciously complicit assumptions not only had shaped my professional and personal life but also had reflected psychological, social, political, economic, and historical constructs which, heretofore, I had assumed as immutable and beyond questions," 19–20.
19 T-Bone Burnett and Elvis Costello, "The Scarlet Tide."
20 See footnote 19 in *Letters to Maxine.* See also Pinar, *The Character of Curriculum Studies* and *Standards for Academic and Professional Instruction in Foundations of Education.*
21 Deborah Britzman, *Practice Makes Practice,* 1.
22 Britzman, 2.
23 What I attempt to do here is craft the beginnings of a Foucauldian genealogy of the concept of teacher, although I do not claim it to be so definitively. A brief look at the historical conceptions of the work and role of teachers in America since the colonial era, coupled with critical and feminist interpretive discourses, helps me to piece together a widely-accepted normative discourse about what it means to be Teacher in this country. This story focuses on the ways in which power relations operated to norm teaching in the cultural mind and more specifically in the beliefs and practices of teachers themselves. The discourse both includes and excludes particular language, and in doing so clearly articulates what Teacher *is* or *should* and what Teacher *is* or *should not.* Using a Foucauldian framework to "Name" the limitations of my Being created opportunity for critique I could not access prior. I tell the story here within the idea of Foucauldian framework to demonstrate the hint of another way of looking at my experience as a teacher. I do not mean to suggest that this is a complete genealogy. That is a project for the near future! I explore it here as a theorist to determine its possibility as a future project to complicate the individualized ahistorical image of the American Teacher both in education discourses and in cultural narrative.
24 First, my "once upon a time" is an exclusive beginning. I'm talking about a concept of Teacher in America, but it is one that did not start with the First Americans. It began with the European, primarily Anglo-Saxon, colonists who shaped a social and political culture, and then nation, which soon required "Teacher" to exercise a role to help realize these cultural intents. What I mean is that colonists did not arrive on this land, turn to the Native Americans, wonder aloud how they might establish a social order like the tribes, and investigate the system of tribal education. Rather, with violence and rhetoric which claimed the superiority of European, Christian beliefs, the colonists established colonial culture in America as the dominant authority of this land. In order to maintain this culture, with its values and beliefs, colonialists asserted. See also Joel Spring, *American School.*
25 Historian Merle Curti, in *Social Ideas of American Educator,* would suggest that what was new about the colonists' attempt was to align religion with civic authority in the North and to create a gentry class from those on the fringes of the dominant class in Europe at best. Thus, the role of education was to preserve a new and therefore potentially tenuous order of authority. See also a discussion of representative discourses in Urban and Wagoner, *American Education: A History,* 22.
26 In his historical work *Pillars of the Republic, Carl Kaestle* demonstrates that Protestant-Calvinist culture embedded in the colonial schools served to define school culture into and throughout the 19th century. It marked the boundaries of what and who was acceptable. In

this way, even white Catholics found themselves aliens of school culture, required to leave their family culture outside of the classroom and embrace as "academic and American" a culture rooted in another religion. Colonial communities assumed their teachers would embody these values and principles as members of the community. That assumption remained for the American Teacher except now those values and principle simply represented "American" school culture.

27 Spring, *American School*
28 Urban and Wagoner, 24.
29 Here, as with indigenous education, we find the education received by girls missing from our narrative, and that while girls and women did receive an education in reading the Word of God, house and family care, and arts or crafts, this particular education was not privileged and formalized into schools. Thus, at this juncture in our story, its inclusion does not help us to understand our notion of the American Teacher today. But, patience, my feminist friends, it would not be excluded for long. (Education of slave, black and other minorities are addressed below and in the next section).
30 Republican Motherhood represented a social ideal. Young citizens of the new republic must be instilled with republican virtue and literacy. These became the unique responsibility of women in the home, thereby extending their sphere of influence beyond the home economy to the political sphere, albeit removed from direct participation. Linda Kerber, "The Republican Mother," 187–205.
31 Lawrence Cremin, *American Education*.
32 Spring, *American School*.
33 Urban and Wagoner address the exclusion of African-Americans and Native Americans from the common school through segregation and Indian Schools. Indian schools, and thus exclusion from the common education, are affirmed and approved by Thomas Jefferson himself, as the schools clearly created the "industrious and virtuous citizens Cherokees," 89.
34 An 1853 statement of the Boston School Committee claims, "The parent is not the absolute owner of the child. The child is a member of a community, has certain rights, and is bound to perform certain duties, and so far as these relate to the public, Government has the same right to control over the child, that it has over the parent ... Those children should be brought within the jurisdiction of the Public Schools, from whom, through their vagrant habits our property is most in danger, and so, of all others, most need the protecting power of the State." In Grumet, *Bitter Milk*, 40.
35 David Tyack and Elizabeth Hansot, *Learning Together*.
36 Grumet suggests this was not only white Anglo culture but also a growing middle class that favored homogenizations of culture, 34.
37 Nancy Cott, *The Bonds of Womanhood*. The Cult of True Womanhood or Domesticity was a social ideal in which women were commended to attend to the domestic sphere with moral authority. That moral authority was her responsibility to cultivate and inculcate in every member of her family. Her husband required it as well since he was now a victim of the influence of the immoral industrial world. The social values embedded in this ideal were primarily embraced by white, middle class women. Immigrant women, likely, worked outside the home for the family's survival and thus could not embody the family values that had come to be reified for the American family at this time. Black women, mostly being slaves, and Native American women, were aberrations of this ideal as well.
38 Grumet, *Bitter Milk*, 38.
39 Discourses on the history of the professionalization of the field of education include with rich explication especially: Christopher Lucas, *Teacher Education in America*; Geraldine Clifford and James Gutherie, *Ed School*; Paul Mattingly, *The Classless Profession*.

40 Examples of the shift and call of progressive education described here can be found in Dewey, *The Child and the Curriculum* and George Counts, *Dare the Schools Build a New Social Order?*
41 Maurice Berube, *American School Reform*.
42 Spring, 319.
43 Wayne Urban explains in his history of teacher unions, *Why Teachers Organize,* that teachers sought to improve wages and working conditions, as well as secure seniority.
44 Berube discusses this move historically. America could no longer afford for education to be left to "professional educators" announced educator Admiral Hyman Rickover in his 1959 *Education and Freedom* essays. This indicated the move of authority from educators to government over the next few decades culminating in establishment of a federal department of education. Teachers took their cues now from government policy.
45 Signed by President Johnson on April 11, 1965. It was the most expansive federal legislation of education to date and fell under the umbrella of Johnson's War on Poverty. The law intended to lend government financial support to the poor for education, including job training programs and Head Start initiatives, among others. Expansively, over time, it came to include federal education initiatives for special education, female access to higher education and sports, etc. See Christopher Cross, *Political Education*.
46 Joel Spring, *The Sorting Machine*, 402.
47 *A Nation at Risk* was the report commissioned by the National Commission on Excellence in the mid-1980s; "it asserted that the United States was at risk of losing preeminence in the world as a consequence of slippage in its competitive edge in the global society because of an educational system fraught with inadequate standards that had failed to produce the quality of workers, as well as the science and technology necessary to remain number one. This line of criticism argued that the root of the problem lay with public schools—their loss of clear direction ..." writes Sandra Jackson in "A Matter of Conflicting Interests?, 55–56.

"The curriculum reform era has been replaced by a standards-based reform era focusing primarily on outcomes, a basic utilitarian approach that focuses more on ends (e.g., test scores) than means, but that affects both. Much of the impetus and continued support for standards-based educational reform comes not from educators, educational researchers, or the public, but rather from corporate business. In fact, a main current in the history of education in the United States is the effort of corporate leaders ... to shape public education to the ends of business. The four National Education Summits held since 1989 have been key events in the rise of the accountability movement in schools and intensified efforts to transform schools to meet the corporate expectations." Sandra Mathison and E. Wayne Ross, "The Hegemony of Accountability," 93–94.
48 We saw major cross-party agreement with the second reauthorization of ESEA or "No Child Left Behind," which had been gathering since the Clinton era education policy such as GOALS 2000—legislation that explicitly tied education to the acquisition of skills for use in the market. A significant feature of this agreement was around the idea that the adults in the system "must be held accountable for performance based on academic content standards. Content standards, reflected in the curriculum, must be carefully aligned with tests, whose results would hold children accountable for learning and teachers accountable for students' learning." Cross, *Political Education*, 113.
49 With the terrorist attacks of September 11, 2001, Kenneth Saltman argues that a new neoliberalism intensified "articulation of economic growth and consumerism as issues of patriotism and national security" and defined public education as a site for protecting national security. For example, in Chicago, curriculum frameworks and models with daily lessons were designed by the Military Command and General Staff Council. Increasingly, educa-

50 RAND Corporation, Teachers Matter: Understanding Teachers' Impact on Student Achievement. I use air quotes around *research* to highlight the web of power relations operating to produce neoliberal interpretations of schooling. This report was conducted by economists and has been referred to repeatedly by those arguing for stronger accountability and disciplinary measures for teachers. It has been widely critiqued, though that critique lacks the mouthpiece of corporate media, by critical and curricular theorists in education as well as education practitioners who assert that poverty and other aspects of social inequality are stronger indicators of student achievement.

51 A heightened critique of reform in the last thirty years stems from a critique of neoliberalism, which asserts the increasing role of corporate and privatizing influences in the schools (market solutions to all individual and social problems, privatization of goods and services, etc.). "Remediation by test companies and educational publishers means that this 'accountability'-based reform was in large part set up as a way for these testing and publishing companies to profit by getting federally mandated and state-mandated business." Kenneth Saltman, 166. Their business improved enormously when the Obama administration made the availability of federal dollars for states dependent upon a competition won through high stakes test results. The demand for teacher-proof, scripted material soared. Pinar, *Curriculum Studies in the United States*, 10.

52 The move of billionaire tech company owners to influence education policy has become so prolific that it is almost "comical." From Bill Gates to Mark Zuckerberg, billionaires, whose companies arguably profit from the privatization and corporate reform agenda, have spent millions of dollars in order to dictate within schools, districts, states, and even federal reform policy. An illustration: Charles Pierce, "What Does the Netflix Guy Have to Say About Public Education?"

53 Certainly, education reform has made strange bedfellows in the era of corporate, high-stakes accountability reform. Members of both political parties (and their operatives), liberal and conservative think tanks, as well as corporate leaders have joined forces in initiatives such as the #teachersmatter movement.

54 One area in which the role of education professors has been eroded is in the creation of curriculum and coaching and assessment of teachers' preparedness, as this has been outsourced to companies like Pearson who evaluate teachers through videotapes and lesson plan documents. Pinar, *Curriculum Studies in the United States*, 10.

55 For example: Valerie Strauss, "Business leaders inject themselves into School Reform."

56 An example of the cultural narrative in which unions attempt to advocate for students on issues such as testing but are denigrated with implications that teachers are self-serving: Kate Taylor and Motoko Rich, "Teachers' Unions Fight Standardized Testing, and Find Diverse Allies," *The New York Times* (April 20, 2015).

57 A fascinating history of the rise of alternative teacher training programs and credentialing can be found in Christopher Lucas, *Teacher Education in America*.

58 This bill allows states to use federal funds (and federal aid programs) to create, operate or use alternative training models, by-passing schools of education within the university. The alternative academies would be permitted to ignore certain state rules and standards of higher education, as well. These are just a few of the policies that potentially undermine education academics and professionals.

59 Judges 5: 6–7, adapted from the *New International Version*.

60 Greene, *Dialectic of Freedom*, 57.

LETTERS TO NEW TEACHERS 185

61 Pinar et al., in *Understanding Curriculum* concur and account for feminist discursive territory—including, but not limited to Beauvoir (1974), Friedan (1981/1963), Millet (1971), Greer (1970), and Firestone (1972)—which took women's oppression as the starting point for analysis and transformation of prevailing social conditions ... and marked "Patriarchy, the entire system oppressing women, as the subject of feminist analysis and critique," 364. I take this as the starting point but do not wish to suggest that patriarchy defines the female experience. It helps to mark boundaries of acceptable behavior and assumption of roles and responsibilities in terms of constructing a historical genealogy of the American Teacher.
62 Pinar et al., *Understanding Curriculum*, 70.
63 Pinar et al., *Understanding Curriculum*, 360; Grumet, *Bitter Milk*, 37.
64 Tyack and Hansot, *Coeducation*, 40.
65 Pinar et al., 360.
66 Grumet, 40.
67 Some suggest that the opportunity was to escape, for a time, the stricter confines of the feminine role defined within the boundary of the home as daughter, wife, and mother. Spring, *The American School*.
68 Louisa May Alcott as quoted in Pinar et al., *Understanding Curriculum*, 362.
69 Catherine Beecher claimed that "the great purpose in a woman's life –that happy superintendence of a family-is accomplished all the better and easier by preliminary teaching in school. All the power she may develop here will come in use there" in Grumet, *Bitter Milk*, 37.
70 Grumet, 40.
71 Grumet, *Bitter Milk*, and among a number of scholars see: Jo Anne Pagano, *Exiles and Community* and also Kathleen Weiler, "Feminist Analyses of Gender and Schooling."
72 Comparing teaching to mothering can be found in the early theories of education upon which the common schools were founded. See Urban and Wagoner, *American Education*, for a discussion of these, including Pestalozzi on maternal teaching.
73 Grumet, *Bitter Milk*, 45.
74 Grumet.
75 Grumet, 43.
76 Grumet, 51.
77 Grumet, 51.
78 Grumet, 52.
79 Michael Apple, *Teachers and Texts*. See also Grumet in *Bitter Milk*, Pinar et al., in *Understanding Curriculum*, and Spring, *American School*.
80 Spring, *American School*, 286.
81 Herbert Kliebard, "The Rise of Scientific Curriculum-Making and Its Aftermath," and specifically, Franklin Bobbit, "Scientific Methods of Curriculum-Making," 42.
82 Iconic and representative of this movement are Ralph Tyler, "Basic Principles of Curriculum and Instruction" and W. James Popham, "Objectives."
83 Spring, *American School*, 299.
84 Kliebard.
85 Kliebard, 35.
86 Kliebard, 36.
87 Critical theory emerges out of the Marxist critique of class, thus the use of the term "worker." Hereafter in this paragraph, the term teacher is in lieu of "worker" but still articulated within this Marxist context.
88 Apple, "Controlling the Work of Teaching," in *The Curriculum Studies Reader*, 195.
89 On teacher work environment and conditions in the face of high stakes accountability, see, for example, Margaret Crocco and Arthur Costigan, "High Stakes Teachers."

90 Apple, "Controlling the Work of Teachers," 188. In the intensification of high stakes accountability policy, this "cutting corners" has taken the form of cheating scandals on high stakes tests whose results determine whether teachers keep their jobs. See for example, the investigation by the Atlanta Journal Constitution of the Atlanta Public Schools' cheating scandal. This news organization initiated a 50-state investigation of cheating in 2008 due to the pressures of high stakes accountability testing on teachers.

91 Apple, "Controlling the Work of Teachers," 191.

92 Urban in *Why Teachers Organize* tries to explain the confusing notion. "Teachers sought to preserve their existing employment conditions and therefore labeled attacks on the 'unprofessional,' while administrative reformers labeled their innovations attempts to professionalize the teaching force," 41. Spring in *American School* adds, "Thus for some teachers the word professional meant greater teacher control of educational policy and for administrators it meant improving the quality of the teaching force through scientific management. Administrators thought teachers were acting in an unprofessional manner if they resisted administrative control," 320.

93 Spring in *American School* explains that the "expert was representative of the public as the politics was forbidden in schools."

94 For a thorough explication and critique of the high stakes accountability reform movement which emerged from No Child Left Behind, see Kenneth Sirotnik, ed., *Holding Accountability Accountable*.

95 Pinar, *The Synoptic Text Today*, 152.

96 Grumet in *Bitter Milk* discusses the estrangement of children's teachers from their mothers. "Instead of being allies, mothers and teachers distrust each other. Bearing credentials of a profession that claimed the colors of motherhood and then systematically delivered the children over to the language and rules of patriarchy, teachers understandable feel uneasy, mothers suspicious," 56.

97 Apple, "Controlling the Work of Teachers," 184. "In every occupational category, women are more apt to be proletarianized (deskilled *sic*) than men. This could be because of sexist practices of recruitment and promotion, the general tendency to care less about the conditions under which women labor, the way capital has historically colonized patriarchal relations, the historical relation between teaching and domesticity, and so on. Whatever the reason, it is clear that a given position may be more or less proletarianized depending on its relationship to the sexual division of labor." See also Janet Holland "Women's occupational choice: the impact of sexual divisions in society."

98 Janet Miller, "Women as teachers," 117.

99 Belenky et al.

100 Belenky, 7.

101 David Tyack, *The One Best System*. See footnote 100 below.

102 Grumet, 56. This phenomenon is exacerbated in an age of "teacher proof" curriculum packages. See Peter Taubman, *Teaching by Numbers* for a contemporary description of Grumet's point.

103 Patricia Collins, *Black Feminist Thought*, 262. "Feminist scholars contend that men and women are socialized to seek different types of autonomy—the former based on separation, the latter seeking connectedness—and that this variation in types of autonomy parallels the characteristic differences between how men and women understand ideas and experiences."

104 Rich, "Taking Women Students Seriously," 210–220.

105 Greene, *Dialectic of Freedom*, 88–89.

106 Philip Jackson, *Life in Classrooms*. Michael Apple complicates the notion of a monolithic curriculum in his explication of the "official curriculum" in *Ideology and Curriculum*. Peter

LETTERS TO NEW TEACHERS

      Mclaren further explains in *Life in Schools*, 183–184. "The hidden curriculum deals with the tacit ways in which knowledge and behavior get constructed, outside the usual course materials and formally scheduled lessons. It is part of the bureaucratic and managerial 'press' of the school—the combined forces by which students are induced to comply with the dominant ideologies and social practices related to authority, behavior and morality."

107 Jean Anyon, "Social Class and the Hidden Curriculum of Work," and Ellen Brantlinger, *Dividing Classes*.

108 Best represented in the writings of Catherine Beecher and Horace Mann.

109 Lisa Delpit, *Other People's Children*, 5. "Another invisible aspect that should demand our attention is culture. It's often too easy to see that a different culture exists, but it is not easy to see one's own. One's own culture is to humans as water is to a fish—we are completely unaware of our culture until we are taken out of it. Those Americans who are part of the dominant culture are seldom outside their own culture and are therefore seldom aware of their culture at all."

110 Delpit, xxiv. "These adults probably are not bad people. They do not wish to damage children; indeed, they likely see themselves as wanting to help. Yet they are totally unable to perceive those different from themselves except through their own culturally clouded vision."

111 I wrote much of this as an academic paper as I tried to frame the tension I felt with culture and authority and obedience by drawing on scholars I read over time. This is my attempt to pool the drip, drip, drop of the slow reconstruction of experience through dialogic engagement with each of these texts so that I could wash my glasses and see anew. For this reason, I chose to include more quotes within the text as the discursive language itself served to restructure my perspective. The following deliberation represents meaningful, life-changing Naming in my life.

112 Ann Arnett Ferguson, *Bad Boys*, 50. Social foundations' scholars base discourse around schooling on the belief in the power of institutions to create, shape, and regulate social identities. Schools embody the class interests and ideology of the dominant class, which has the power to impose its views, standards, and cultural forms—its "cultural capital" as superior.

113 Carlos Diaz, "Multicultural Education," 518.

114 Ferguson, 17.

115 Delpit, 75.

116 Gloria Ladson-Billings, "Fighting for Our Lives."

117 Gloria Ladson-Billings, "Preparing Teachers for Diverse Student Populations: A Critical Race Theory Perspective," *Review of Research in Education*, 24 (1999), 212.

118 Ferguson, 52. In *Discipline and Punish*, Foucault describes the normalizing effect of power relations so that in this case "normal" is whiteness and thus anything "not white" would be aberrant to the standard.

119 Delpit, 74.

120 Ladson-Billings, "Fighting for Our Lives," 211.

121 Delpit, xxv.

122 Ladson-Billings, 207.

123 Joel Spring, *Deculturalization and the Struggle for Equity*.

124 Ladson-Billings, "Preparing Teachers," 217.

125 Ladson-Billings, 218.

126 Ladson-Billings, "Fighting for Our Lives," 206.

127 Gloria Ladson-1Billings, "Pushing Past the Achievement Gap," 318.

128 Ladson-Billings, "Preparing Teachers," 218.

129 Ladson-Billings, 217.
130 Ladson-Billings, "Pushing Past the Achievement Gap," 320.
131 Ladson-Billings, 318.
132 Gary Howard, *We Can't Teach What We Don't Know*, 50.
133 Sonia Nieto, *Affirming Diversity*.
134 Delpit, *Other People's Children*, 35.
135 Delpit, *Other People's Children*, 35.
136 Delpit, 37.
137 Delpit, 140.
138 Delpit.
139 Delpit, 56.
140 Delpit.
141 Lisa Delpit, "Lessons from Teachers," 227.
142 Delpit, 56.
143 Delpit, 59.
144 Delpit, 77.
145 Herbert Kohl, *I Won't Learn from You*, 6.
146 Kohl, 10.
147 Ferguson, 41. The state laws and the school rules that put them into effect are treated as if they are universal truths, blind and neutral to differences of class, race and gender among groups of children. They are part of our commonsense knowledge of young people: who they are and what they must be taught. Teachers and school administrators speak of discipline as the essential prior condition for any learning to take place.
148 Amanda Ripley, "Bootcamp for Teachers." This is one example of the types of classroom management training for teachers receiving press and financial support in the current educational climate nationally.
149 Paul Carr and Darren Lund, "Antiracist Education," 48.
150 Ferguson, 19.
151 Ferguson, 20.
152 Ferguson, 19.
153 Ferguson, 20.
154 Ferguson, 22.
155 Ferguson, 41.
156 Ferguson, 17.
157 Ferguson, 46.
158 Ferguson, 47.
159 Ferguson, 50.
160 Ferguson, 52. Foucault conceptualizes discipline broadly as the mechanism for a new mode of domination that constitutes us as individuals with a specific perception of our identity and potential that appears natural rather than the product of relations of power.
161 Ferguson. Rules bear weight of moral authority; rules governing children are seen as basis of order, the bedrock of respect on which that order stands; rules are spoken about as inherently neutral, impartially exercised, and impervious to individual feelings and personal responses.
162 Ferguson, 53.
163 Ferguson, 202.
164 Ferguson, 203.
165 Ferguson.

166 Ferguson, 239. "In the daily experiences of being so named, regulated, and surveilled, access to the full resources of the school are increasingly denied as the boys are isolated in nonacademic spaces in school or banished to lounging at home or loitering on the streets."
167 Ferguson, 204.
168 Howard, *We Can't Teach What We Don't Know*, 50.
169 Greene, *Teacher as Stranger*, Preface.
170 Grumet, *Bitter Milk*, 57. She contends that "a defensive passive resistance by uneasy teachers," leads us "into emotional and intellectual stasis and reinforces our isolation from the community and ourselves."
171 This debate is more than a century old, and I think it can best be articulated in Dewey's *Experience and Education*.
172 Parker Palmer, *The Courage to Teach*.
173 Parker Palmer, *The Promise of Paradox*, 39.
174 Palmer, 43.
175 Parker Palmer, *A Hidden Wholeness*.
176 Palmer, *Promise of Paradox*, 46.
177 Palmer, *Promise of Paradox*, 44.
178 Noddings, *Philosophy of Education*, 222.
179 Noddings, *Philosophy of Education*, 223.
180 Noddings, 224.
181 Sharon Todd, *Learning from the Other*.
182 Michael Gunzenhauser, "From Empathy to Creative Intersubjectivity in Qualitative Research," 70.
183 Todd, *Learning from the Other*, 15.
184 Gunzenhauser, "Creative Intersubjectivity," 70 and 72 when Gunzenhauser explains his concept of creative intersubjectivity situated on the meaning made from the encounter.
185 Gunzenhauser, 70.
186 In this case, I might draw from research such as Edward Deci and Richard Ryan's work in self-determination and competency, much of it compiled in their edited *Handbook of Self-Determination Research* (Rochester, NY: University of Rochester Press, 2010). I don't presuppose that I or any other teacher has specific discursive understanding. Rather, I believe Naming discomfort in the encounter causes me to reach beyond what I know, ofttimes, in order to make better sense of the situation. Thus, work in competency research might be useful in a broader philosophical and theoretical framework which prioritizes the pedagogical relation amongst teacher and student which I attempt to demonstrate here.
187 See Alan Block, *Ethics in Teaching* and footnote eleven in chapter one of this book on the empty power of teacher complaint.
188 Barbra Holmes, "True self relating: The community called Beloved."
189 Mary Oliver, excerpt from "Blue Iris," *What Do We Know: Poems and Prose Poems*.
190 Greene, "Toward Wide-Awakeness," 119–125.
191 Collins, *Black Feminist Thought*, 265. Regarding the Naming dialogue that grants such access, she writes, "Neither emotion nor ethics is subordinated to reason. Instead emotion, ethics and reason are used as interconnected essential components in assessing knowledge claims."

INTERLUDE

Today

I
Do not
Want to step so quickly
Over a beautiful line on God's palm
As I move through the earth's
Marketplace
Today.

I do not want to touch any object in this world
Without my eyes testifying to the truth
That everything is
My Beloved.

Something has happened
To my understanding of existence
That now makes my heart always full of wonder
And kindness.

I do not
Want to step so quickly
Over this sacred place on God's body
That is right beneath your
Own foot

As I
Dance with
Precious life
Today.[1]

Notes

1 Hafiz, "Today," in *The Gift*, trans. by Daniel Landinsky, 128.

Concluding Letter to Fellow Teachers

> On the one hand, [my] quest has been deeply personal; that of a woman striving to affirm the feminine as wife, mother and friend, while reaching, always reaching beyond the limits imposed by the obligations of a woman's life. On the other hand, it has been in some sense deeply public as well: that of a person struggling to connect the undertaking of education, with which she has been so long involved, to the making and remaking of a public space, a space of dialogue and possibility.
>
> MAXINE GREENE (*Dialectic of Freedom*, 1988, xi)

∴

> We have to be braver than we think we can be, because God is constantly calling us to be more than we are, to see through plastic sham to living, breathing reality, and to break down our defenses of self-protection in order to be free to receive and give love.
>
> MADELEINE L'ENGLE (*Walking on Water*, 1980, 71)

∴

Dear Respected Colleague, my reader,

My engagement with Maxine Greene in my capacity as a teacher became a sort of spiritual journey for my whole person. By shifting the work of teaching from an epistemological one, in which teachers must know the right things to do the right things—to a work of Becoming, ontologically, Maxine suggested this deep inner dive. While she may not have directed me toward a depth I call spirituality, I believe she would honor the journey of my Becoming, especially on behalf of children.

Perhaps, on my own time, I might have perused spiritual literature or philosophy or self-help, but due to Greene's attention to the impact of our ontology on vulnerable children, I turned to the mirror that was my professional life. We are not merely conveyors of content, skills and character. Our being in relationship with children is about walking alongside other humans in their own Becoming. We relate as humans. In the last decade, science confirmed Greene's observation that who we are and our states of being interact even without our intention. For example, the HeartMath Institute conducted studies on the electromagnetic fields of the heart, finding the heart "involved in energetic communication."

> (I)nformation about a person's emotional state is encoded in the heart's magnetic field and is communicated throughout the body and into the external environment ... Most people tend to think of communication solely in terms of overt signals expressed through facial movements, voice qualities, gestures and body movements. However, evidence now supports the perspective that a subtle yet influential electromagnetic or "energetic" communication system operates just below our conscious level of awareness.[1]

We exude who we are, influentially, on those around us. Thus, the freedom to socially imagine and endeavor toward greater justice requires work in the depths of our hearts. When I see myself as a victim of my students, the principal or district, parents, and political persons or policies, I am not free. When I blame myself, solely responsible for my perceived failures, I am not free. When I operate in isolation and disconnected from the reality of myself as a dialogic being, I am not free. Chances are that the attitude of victim, martyr, hero, and lone wolf show up in other areas of my life, as well. "I am ... not yet" ... in all things.

I saw opportunity in Maxine's work and through the course of my study. When in an uncomfortable position at all, rather than a defensive or critical posture, I might instead respond with curiosity, dialogue and imagination. I need to feed that. Maxine turned to the arts for such inspiration. I turn to music and mysticism in poetry and prose. But I also need to approach life and teaching "wide-awake" to the possibility that my own Becoming will unfold in richness according to my attentiveness to it. If I only feed the wonder, as we idealists may be prone to do, we are left without much but distraction in terms of dealing with our discomfort.

This is where a Naming praxis becomes a support to us as humans and teachers. We bring that discomfort to the center of our attention. We study it.[2] In that obstacle within our relationship, we find the fuel of our Becoming. I'll attempt to succinctly provide a way forward with Naming that might be useful to you.

First
The fish needs to say,

"Something ain't right about this
Camel ride—

And I'm
Feeling so damn
Thirsty."[3]

The wit of Hafiz wakes me up sometimes. This fish is so honest and without blame! Instead, our fish identifies that there is in fact a problem. We don't hear our fish talk about how wonderful the sites are on the camel ride or excuse thirst by convincing itself that it must have a dry throat by nature or even complain about its camel. It makes declaratory statements about its state of Being: (1) it's not sure about its place and (2) it doesn't feel right. There are external and internal tensions with its Being; possibly they are in opposition to one another, but the fish doesn't go so far to establish relationship or causality. It just speaks what's true to it as a fish in the moment.

Articulating the features of your dilemma as you experience it: this is the start of a Naming praxis I discovered through my study. You are asking yourself, what is the nature of my Being in this circumstance? Identify if you are irritated, confused, frustrated, indignant, any other "yucky" emotion, or just generally, maybe naggingly, disconcerted. Remember that the emotion speaks the truth about how you are experiencing the moment. It doesn't have to be right or wrong objectively, but if you do not acknowledge the emotion, you deny the opportunity to honor how you are coming to understand your circumstances.[4]

Before leaping to the cause of the discomfort, consider the boundaries of the dilemma: who is involved, what happened, what did you want/intend to happen, which of your relationships does this effect? (I am going to use a pedestrian example for the sake of universality but also to emphasize how the power of a Naming praxis is found in the daily relationships of our teaching experiences):

> *Joey didn't turn in her homework. She has turned in only one assignment since school began eight weeks ago. I expect homework returned on time. I am exasperated and frustrated. I am not sure what to do beyond what I've done. This effects my relationship with Joey, possibly her parents. This effects my relationship with myself. Potentially, it effects my relationship with her current or previous teachers if we don't share expectations.*

At this point, we have the facts of the bones of the dilemma and our reaction to this obstacle in our teaching/Becoming. Now it's time for rich dialogue. We need language here to help us Name the underlying issue that is in the way of your relationship remaining purposeful in each of your Becoming processes. Remember, the dialogue is as rich as the perspectives you include in your study of the dilemma. I am not suggesting a doctoral dissertation every time "something ain't right," but, as this studied highlighted for me, humans beings deserve the ethical mercy of multiple and deeper ways of looking at things than our singular impressions.

We need to articulate the tension before we can find a way through. My own assessment and that of others who know me and/or Joey can be helpful here. Curiosity, rather than blame, drives me. (I have to feed the curiosity because if I'm feeling beaten down or cynical, I'll leap to blame rather quickly).

I would start first with my own assessment of what I know about this situation. What do I know about Joey: age, history in my class, background—family, past experience in school, culture, etc. What do I know about myself in this situation? What do I believe about homework? What do I believe about Joey? How would I describe our relationship? Is this homework thing an anomaly or more systemic with her way of being in school? How does my relationship with Joey compare with other children in the class? Which other students may have a similar pattern or way of being in my class?

Then, I would move on to people who know Joey and I. I'd ask her current and previous teachers if they have had similar experiences with Joey. I would talk to her parents if possible. It's likely these conversations and my own considerations would create a clear narrative at this time about homework or Joey or Joey's homelife or sixth graders or the fifth grade curriculum that feeds our classes. Likely, something would come up about her race or economic situation. (Let's be honest, these opinions, sometimes stereotypes, enter our conversations as rationales more often than we'd like to believe).[5] This early work of Naming is significant and often what "good" teachers do. This is reflection, a Deweyan attempt at making meaning of our experience with this child so that I can help us both move into more meaningful experiences in the future.

I would also have conversations with other teachers and friends about myself, all the while asking myself to reflect more deeply. Am I prone to frustration when things don't go the way I think they should? How do I tend to react? What kind of positions have I taken on the topics within the emerging narrative above? Am I known for being a homework advocate? Do I take issue with other "kids like Joey"? What is my take on the role of the fifth grade curriculum in preparing students for my sixth grade learning experiences? Some of this dialogue is also a sounding board for me to hear more clearly the distinct voices in my mind engaging with me on this matter.

All of these considerations in dialogue are meant to highlight the exact nature of the paradox that created this dilemma. What dualism sets this tension? It's hard to know without actually having these initial wonderings and personal conversations, but let's say what emerges, what really hits the tender point of my emotional discomfort, is this story in my mind (writing it down helps me look at the language and concepts I'm working with).

> *Homework is important to me as a teacher because I value it as a unique tool in developing children's self-motivation, time management and time on task skills. Joey is Latina, living below the poverty level. We never see her parents. She's already been held back a year. I believe that by helping her do her homework, I am equipping her with these skills for a better life. Her resistance is in the way of her opportunities. Why won't she comply ... for her own sake?*

My central tension lies between the value/meaning I place on homework and Joey's growth.

It is an apparent paradox because I cannot make the two fit together!

Notice I am not judging my beliefs according to political ideals here. It's imperative to leave space for self-honesty without the insistence of "ideals." The process of Naming addresses the beliefs that we embody, not the ones we espouse.

An educational bandwagon response at this time in Western educational history (2020) would proclaim death to homework. A conservative approach would search for the aberration within the individual instead of the valued principle. This is, sadly, the paradox of many education conversations in our culture. If we stop here, this dualistic approach leaves us without deep thought and left to frame children or ourselves as deficient. It's time for more robust dialogue and a more humane engagement in my relationship with Joey.

•••

Now, I engage beyond the walls of the school, with the discourses that inform and challenge my beliefs/actions and possibly, Joey's. This is important because these discourses are more complex, built over time with study, their own language and internal logic, and fruit. This makes them rhetorically weighty, hard to shake or significantly difficult to dismiss.

If I look at my narrative about my dilemma a few key concepts seem ripe for critical reflection: the purpose of homework in human/child growth and future opportunities; how a student's culture, economic situation or family background my impact their ability to do homework or their attitude toward it; developmentally, what intellectual or emotional capacities are significant for a child Joey's age in formal schooling; what constitutes a teacher's responsibility to students' "better" or future life; student resistance and compliance. Of course, we can also question what makes a "better" life or whether the role of teachers is to "equip." My point is that I have taken my narrative beyond my experience to concepts likely contextualized and informed by broader discourses.

With these concepts, I shape my curiosity with questions. First, what are the discourses on these concepts; who has studied this in greater depth and what does that study provide in terms of richer perspectives for dialogic engagement? This first question leads me into scholarship, research and cultural narratives. These perspectives lend credibility with their strong warrants (evidence) and provoke me to challenge my personal experience. These are not the same as blogs which we tend to scan to support our current beliefs. Doing the work of locating and studying these discourses is different intellectual action driven by an ethical imperative: I study to realize my own Becoming in order to support the Becoming of the children in my care. I'm not afraid of being proven wrong any more. My desire now is to honor my relationship with Joey as an open field for our mutual Becoming.

A second question at this stage is, where did I hear these ideas or whose voice do I hear in my head when I emphatically agree or disagree with perspectives on them? The second question points us toward personal formation and may direct us to reckon with these voices of authority with whom we are obliged to agree. With the latter, note that in my study, I found myself dealing with my gender identity and my parents' educational background when I got to this stage. Personal stuff, informing professional decisions.

These questions now drive my inquiry and action—I'm in the midst of the mystery of human becoming. It's kind of exciting! As I study, I may go back and forth in dialogue with my colleagues again. The depth of my study may lead me to gasp at how I've unwittingly harmed a child or it may further strengthen my intuitive and experiential knowing. My knowing is thereby warranted more solidly and I have clearer language to make sense of the dilemma for those involved to work together. Depending on their developmental age, children may not be able to articulate their part in the tension. This is one of the main reasons the thoughts captured by the discursive language is important. Together with your heart knowing within this relationship, you may be able to talk to the child or her parents about what may be going on. Their input in a discussion you've framed with curiosity and by rich study may yield much insight because of how open you have become. Further, perhaps, I need to spend time with a good friend or mentor. Why is it important for me to hold on to these principles or ways of seeing the world?

At this point, are you wondering if you have to engage in discursive dialogue on every key concept in my story?! Who has that kind of time, you may wonder incredulously. Truly, only you will know the answer to that question. My openhearted approach, my disciplined inquiry and my renewed and re-Named ethical commitment have led me to the knowing the relationship required for further Becoming possibilities. On some level, I have to trust myself in this process. I grant myself that trust because the dialogue has been rigorous and rooted in a way of Being that is exercised to be "wide-awake." Thus, when I am in dialogue with these discourses, I trust the "aha" moment when language resonates with experience. Sometimes, the first concept and line of inquiry Names the experience and reveals the way through the tension. Sometimes, you are challenged all year and into the next. One line of inquiry after another doesn't seem to fit. But your commitment to your own Becoming and the Becoming of the children who follow Joey compels your study forward until light comes and, with it, the middle way through the paradox.

1   **Becoming Together**

> Those practiced in the third way, enter into the Holy of Holies, where the two cherubim face one another and create the Mercy Seat.[6]

Bonaventure's exposition upon this Hebrew image of the most sacred of spaces serves as a useful metaphor for our way of Being as teachers. In our times, we might have to recreate this biblical image by drawing horns, tails and frowns on the cherubim; perhaps a trunk on one and donkey ears on the others. The space between them would gape the length of a continent, creating the Judgement Seat.

Culturally, we are bound and oppressed by our dualism. In education, we are eviscerated by the paradox of fear for our common good and fear for the individual. As the American Teacher, we embody the hope and damnation of an entire society. The children in our care are both utilitarian and promise. The human beings in American education have become objects in this framework. Violated in their humanity by the system itself and those who profit by its proliferation. I could feel my complicity in this violation, and I kept grasping for language to articulate something that felt sacred in teaching which was losing ground to an abomination. My language is strong, I know. And yet, when what stands for education—what Dewey called "life itself"—is no longer engaged in human Becoming and worse defies its possibilities by the burden of the fruit of dehumanization, it's time to find new sensibility and language for this dilemma. It's time to Name again, especially in the aftermath of the coronavirus pandemic. Possibilities for social and institutional re-imaging in hope alongside new ways of profiteering on the backs of children abound.

The human project of Becoming is precious in its inherent honoring of both individual and community. It resolves the paradox of individual and community by its unifying purpose and process. We Become at the intersection of our relationships, because we are all Becoming. Our acts of Naming nurture the richest possibilities for intentional Becoming among us all. I found that it is a sacred act to commit to one's own human Being and Becoming. It is a sacred responsibility to support the Becoming of fellow humans. And there is something definitively holy about nurturing a Becoming relationship with children, bound by law to your care. Holy of Holies. Sacred space of mutual Becoming.

This biblical image of the third way, the Mercy seat, viscerally Names the alternative to the deepest troubling of my heart as a teacher. Where there is paradox and its corresponding tension, we might instead see the two as Guides to a newly imagined perspective of Mercy toward ourselves and one another. Naming these guides and entering the paradox is the praxis of Mercy, a discerned acceptance of what is. Seated, in this rest, we might trust ourselves together in our humanity as we Name and then imagine together the richest possibilities for our shared Becoming. The fruit of this work is empowered (re)creation of ethical, just and humanizing educational encounters.

Dear colleague, we are all and together "not yet." May our wide-awakeness to our Becoming be something we share and may our Naming praxis be something we engage side-by-side. I hope I have been a support to yours through this book, and I look forward to more opportunities to do so in the future.

Together with you,

Christine
May 2021

Notes

[1] Rollin McCraty, *Science of the heart*, 60. "The magnetic fields produced by the heart are involved in energetic communication, which we also refer to as *cardioelectromagnetic communication*. The heart is the most powerful source of electromagnetic energy in the human body, producing the largest rhythmic electromagnetic field of any of the body's organs. The heart's electrical field is about 60 times greater in amplitude than the electrical activity generated by the brain. This field, measured in the form of an electrocardiogram (ECG), can be detected anywhere on the surface of the body. Furthermore, the magnetic field produced by the heart is more than 100 times greater in strength than the field generated by the brain ..."

2 Leading scholars in the field of Curriculum Studies advocate for a conception of "study" to counter the very narrow and instrumental definition learning has come to mean. "No mere 'job,' teaching compels us to study, to engage in ongoing, often complicated conversation with our students, our predecessors, and ourselves for the sake of those present and those yet to come. Professional ethics, then becomes a set of subjective and social intellectual practices -cooperative, yes, even 'collaborative' ... undertakings -with potential for the moral transformation of the self (Bielskis, 2011, 303), the self of each concerned, children and teachers alike." Pinar in *Reconceptualizing curriculum studies*, xiii. See also Robert McClintock's "Toward a place for study in a world of Instruction" and Alan Block's *Ethics and Teaching* as well as *Talmud, Curriculum and the Practical*.
3 Hafiz, "Damn thirsty," in *The Gift*, trans. by Daniel Ladinsky, 198.
4 McClarty, 60. Again, science corroborates the heart or emotional knowing as significant to the way human beings make meaning and decisions. Practically, this might mean, when someone enters the room and you wonder aloud if they are angry, even though this person may have said little and only just moved into the room. The person denies being angry and leaves the room. Cognitively, most of us accept the response. This person told me he is not angry; he did not slam any doors or shout. He must not be angry. And yet there is this lingering feeling that something isn't right despite the observations of your sense of sight and sound. There is a deeper knowing. This is the knowing of the heart. As products of the Enlightenment, we are simply accustomed to dividing heart and mind, privileging the latter. We thereby dismiss what we know to be true and are left to maneuver through logic gymnastics to override the deeper knowing.
5 Since my initial discursive study, the American cultural mileu has shifted significantly in its understanding of race and culture. The impetus to understand our own lens—shaped by our ancestors, our bodies, and our beliefs—and Become more humane collectively is clearly required in order to heal, amend and create a society that better embodies its ideals. Authors such as Ibram X. Kendi and activists like the Black Lives Matter group encourage us to eschew tolerance, diversity and inclusion work in order to actively pursue anti-racist ways of seeing and being with one another, including intentional dismantling of institutional systems which perpetuate the inequities. Trauma specialists like Resmaa Menakem point to our bodies and the generations of trauma and resilience of our ancestors which live in our DNA, shaping our triggered responses to our environment and relationships: white bodies and black bodies and brown bodies and Asian bodies and indigenous bodies experienced different trauma and resilience and so we are all "bound" to heal within our embodied communities in order to engage with one another in healed and aware, rather than triggered and ignorant, states. Further, writers such as Ta-Nahesi Coates and educators such as the Urban Intellectuals have begun to publicly recontextualize our cultural understanding of traditional American minorities so that we begin to see them in their full humanity, as historically contributing to human knowing and thriving, and not simply in their struggle and oppression.
6 Bonaventure, *Soul's Journey to God*, 5, 1.

Bibliography

Anderson, Linda. "Autobiography," In *Encyclopedia of Feminist Theories*. Edited by Lorraine Code, London: Routledge, 2000.

Anyon, Jean. "Social Class and the Hidden Curriculum of Work." *Journal of Education* 162, no. 1 (Fall 1980): 67–92.

Aoki, Ted. "What is it to be Educated?" Paper presented at Convocation I. Lethbridge, Alberta, Canada: University of Lethbridge, 1998.

——. "Themes of Teaching Curriculum." In *Teaching and Thinking about Curriculum: Critical Inquiries*. Edited by J.T. Sears and J.D. Marshall. New York: Teachers College Press, 1990: 111–114.

Apple, Michael. *Ideology and Curriculum*. New York: RoutledgeFalmer, 2004.

——. *Official Knowledge: Democratic Education in a Conservative Age*. London: Routledge, 1993.

——. *The State and Politics of Knowledge*. New York: RoutledgeFalmer, 2000.

——. *Teachers and Texts: A Political Economy of Class and Gender Relations in Education*. New York: Routledge and Kegan Paul, 1986.

——. "Afterword: Telling Stories Out of School." In *Becoming a Teacher: Using Narrative as Reflective Practice*, 209–213. Edited by Robert Blake and Brett Elizabeth Blake. New York: Peter Lang, 2012.

Ayers, Bill. *Teaching Toward Freedom: Moral Commitment and Ethical Action in the Classroom*. Boston, MA: Beacon Press, 2004.

Ayers, William. "Keeping Them Variously: Learning from the Bees Themselves." In *Teacher Lore: Learning from Our Own Experience*, 151–154. Edited by William Schubert and William Ayers. New York: Longman, 1992.

Ayers, William and Janet Miller, eds. *A Light in Dark Times: Maxine Greene and the Unfinished Conversation*. New York: Teachers College Press, 1998.

Ayers, William and William Schubert. "Teacher Lore: Learning About Teaching from Teachers." In *Teachers Thinking, Teachers Knowing*, edited by T.S. Shannahan. Urbana, IL: National Conference on Research in English and the National Council of Teachers of English, 1994.

Bakhtin, Mikhail. *The Dialogic Imagination: Four Essays*. Edited by Michael Holquist. Translated by Caryl Emerson and Michael Holquist. Austin and London: University of Texas Press, 1981/1930.

Ball, Deborah and Francesca Forzani. "The Work of Teaching and the Challenge for Teacher Education." *Journal of Teacher Education* 60, no. 5 (2009): 497–511.

Ball, Deborah and David Cohen. "Developing Practice, Developing Practitioners: Toward a Practice-Based Theory of Education." In *Teaching as the Learning Profession: Handbook of Policy and Practice*, 3–32. Edited by Linda Darling-Hammond and Gary Sykes. San Francisco: Jossey-Bass, 1999.

Ball, Deborah, Mark Thames, and Geoffrey Phelps. "Content Knowledge for Teaching: What Makes it Special?" *Journal of Teacher Education* 59, (2008): 389–407.

Ball, Deborah. "What do Math Teachers Need to Know?" Presentation for the Initiative for Applied Research in Education Expert Committee at the Israel Academy of Sciences and Humanities, Jerusalem, Israel, January 30, 2011.

Bartels, Fred. "Our 1% Problem: Independent Schools and the Income Gap," Independent School (Fall 2012). http://www.nais.org/Magazines-Newsletters/ISMagazine/Pages/Our-1-Percent-Problem.aspx

Bauer, Dale M. "Authority." In *Feminist Pedagogy: Looking Back to Move Forward*, 23–25. Edited by Robin Crabtree, David Alan Sapp, and Adela C. Licona. Baltimore: The Johns Hopkins University Press, 2009.

Beck, Julie. "Life's Stories." *The Atlantic* (Aug 10 2015). http://www.theatlantic.com/health/archive/2015/08/life-stories-narrative-psychology-redemption-mental-health/400796/

Belenky, Mary, Blythe McVicker Clinchy, Nancy Rule Goldberger, and Jill Mattuck Tarule. *Women's Ways of Knowing: Development of Self, Voice and Mind.* New York: Basic Books, 1986.

Benstock, Shari. "The Female Self Engendered: Autobiographical Writing and Theories of Selfhood." In *Women and Autobiography,* 5–16. Edited by Martine W. Brownley and Allison B. Kimmich. Wilmington, DE: Scholarly Resources, Inc., 1999.

Berube, Maurice *American School Reform: Progressive, Equity, and Excellence Movement, 1893–1993.* Westport, CT: Praeger, 1994.

Bobbit, Franklin. "Scientific Methods of Curriculum-Making." In *The Curriculum Studies Reader,* 9–16. Edited by David J. Flinders and Stephen J. Thornton. New York: RoutledgeFalmer, 2004.

Blake, Robert and Brett Elizabeth Blake. *Becoming a Teacher: Using Narrative as Reflective Practice.* New York: Peter Lang, 2012.

Block, Alan A. *Ethics and Teaching: A Religious Perspective on Revitalizing Education.* New York: Palgrave Macmillan, 2009.

——. *Talmud, Curriculum and the Practical: Joseph Schwab and the Rabbis.* New York: Peter Lang, 2004.

Bluck, Susan, Nicole Alea, Tilmann Habermas, and David Rubin. "A Tale of Three Functions: The Self-Reported Uses of Autobiographical Memory." *Social Cognition* 23, no. 1 (2005): 91–117.

Brantlinger, Ellen. *Dividing Classes: How the Middle Class Negotiates and Rationalizes School Advantage.* New York: RoutledgeFalmer, 2003.

Britzman, Deborah. *Practice Makes Practice: A Critical Study of Learning to Teach.* Albany, NY: SUNY Press, 2003.

Brown, Pamela. "Teacher Lore Research." In *Encyclopedia of Curriculum Studies.* Edited by C. Kridel. Los Angeles: Sage, 2010.

Bruner, Jerome. *Acts of Meaning*. Cambridge, MA: Harvard University Press, 1990.
———. "Narrative and Paradigmatic Modes of Thought." In *Learning and Teaching the Ways of Knowing*. Edited by Elliot Eisner. Chicago: National Society for the Study of Education, 1985.
———. *On Knowing: Essays for the Left Hand*. Boston: Beacon Press, 1966.
Burnett, T-Bone and Elvis Costello. "The Scarlet Tide." [Recorded by A. Kraus]. On *Cold Mountain* [CD]. Los Angeles: Sony Music Entertainment Inc. and DMZ LLC, 2003.
Butt, Richard. "Arguments for Using Biography in Understanding Teacher Thinking." In *Teacher Thinking: A New Perspective on Persisting Problems in Education*. Edited by R Halkes and Jane Olson. Lisse, Holland: Swets and Zeitlinger, 1984: 95–103.
Carr, Paul and Darren Lund. "Antiracist Education," in *Encyclopedia of the Social and Cultural Foundations of Education*, 48. (Electronic version: Sage Knowledge, 2008).
Carter, Julie. "Critical Incidents in Social Foundations: Reflecting on Theory, Connecting to Practice." In *Becoming a Teacher: Using Narrative as Reflective Practice*, 153–167. Edited by Robert Blake and Brett Elizabeth Blake. New York: Peter Lang, 2012.
Carter, Kathleen. "The Place of Story in the Study of Teaching and Teacher Education." *Educational Researcher* 22, no. 1 (1993): 5–12.
Clandinin, D. Jean. *Classroom Practice: Teacher Images in Action*. Philadelphia, PA: The Falmer Press, Taylor & Francis Inc, 1986.
Clifford, Geraldine and James Gutherie. *Ed School: A Brief for Professional Education*. Chicago, University of Chicago Press, 1988.
Coates, Ta-Nehisi. *The Water Dancer*. New York: One World, 2020.
Collins, Patricia. *Black Feminist Thought: Knowledge, Consciousness, and the Politics of Empowerment*. London: Routledge, 1990.
Connelly Michael and D. Jean Clandinin, "Narrative Inquiry: Storied Experience," In *Forms of Inquiry*. Edited by Edmund Short, 121–154. Albany, NY: State University of New York Press, 1991.
Conway, Martin. "Memory and the Self." *Journal of Memory and Language*. 53 (2005): 594–628.
Cosslett, Tess, Celia Lury, and Penny Summerfield. *Feminism and Autobiography*. London: Routledge, 2000.
Cott, Nancy. *The Bonds of Womanhood: "Women's Sphere" in New England, 1780–1835*. New Haven, CT: Yale University Press, 1977.
Cremin, Lawrence. *American Education: The National Experience 1783–1876*. New York: HarperCollins, 1980.
Crocco, Margaret and Arthur Costigan. "High Stakes Teachers: What's at Stake for Teachers (and Students) in the Age of Accountability." *The New Educator* 2 (2006): 1–13.
Cross, Christopher. *Political Education: National Policy Comes of Age*. New York: Teachers College Press, 2004.
Crotty, Michael, ed. *The Foundations of Social Research: Meaning and Perspective in the Research Process*. Los Angeles: Sage, 1998. Reprint, Sage, 2008.

Curti, Merle. *Social Ideas of American Educators*. Patterson, New Jersey: Pageant Books, 1959.

Council for Social Foundations of Education. "Standards for Academic and Professional Instruction in Foundations of Education, Educational Studies, and Educational Policy Studies. 3rd ed." (2012) http://csfeonline.org/about/csfe-standards/

Counts, George. "Dare the Schools Build a New Social Order?" In *The Curriculum Studies Reader*. Edited by David J. Flinders and Stephen J. Thornton, 29–36. New York: RoutledgeFalmer, 2004.

Daly, Mary. *Beyond God the Father: Toward a Philosophy of Women's Liberation*. Boston: Beacon Press, 1974.

Darling-Hammond, Linda. "Effective Teaching as a Civil Right: How Building Instructional Capacity Can Help Close the Achievement Gap." *Voices in Urban Education* 31 (2005). Retrieved from http://vue.annenberginstitute.org/sites/default/files/issues/VUE31.pdf

Darling-Hammond, Linda and John Bransford, eds. *Preparing Teachers for a Changing World: What Teachers Should Learn and Be Able to Do*. San Francisco, CA: Jossey-Bass, 2005.

Davies, Bronwyn. "The Concept of Agency: A Feminist Post-Structuralist Analysis." *Social Analysis*, 30 (January 1991): 42–53.

Deci, Edward and Richard Ryan, eds., *Handbook of Self-Determination Research*. Rochester, NY: University of Rochester Press, 2010.

Delpit, Lisa. (2006b). "Lessons from Teachers." *Journal of Teacher Education*, 57, no. 3 (2006b): 220–231.

———. *Other People's Children: Cultural Conflict in the Classroom*. New York: The New Press, 2006.

———. "'Will it help the sheep?': Why educate?" *About Campus* 17, no. 3 (July/August 2012). http://onlinelibrary.wiley.com/doi/10.1002/abc.21080/abstract.

Denzin, Norman and Yvonna Lincoln, eds. *The Sage Handbook of Qualitative Research*. Thousand Oaks, CA: Sage Publications, 2000.

Dewey, John. *The Child and the Curriculum*. USA: Feather Trail Press, 1902. Reprinted The Project Gutenburg Ebook, 2009.

———. *Democracy and Education*. New York, Free Press, 1916. Digitized July 2012, https://books.google.com/books?id=WtdEjwEACAAJ&printsec

———. "Ethics of Democracy." In *John Dewey: The Early Works, 1882–1898*, Carbondale, IL: Southern Illinois University, 1969.

———. *Experience and Education*. New York: Touchstone, Simon and Schuster, 1938. Reprinted, New York: Free Press, 1997.

———. *How We Think*. Boston: DC Heath and Co., 1933. Reprinted The Project Gutenburg Ebook, 2011.

———. *Human Nature and Conduct*. New York: Henry Holt and Co., 1922. Reprinted, The Project Guttenberg EBook, 2012.

———. "Outlines of a Critical Theory of Ethics." Ann Arbor, MI: Inland Press, 1891. https://archive.org/stream/outlinesofcritic00dewerich#page/n7/mode/2up.

———. *The School and Society.* USA: Feather Trail Press, 1899. Reprinted The Project Gutenburg Ebook, 2009.

Duran, Jane. *Worlds of Knowing: Global Feminist Epistemologies.* London: Routledge, 2001.

Eisner, Elliot. *The Educational Imagination: On the Design and Evaluation of School Programs.* 3rd ed. Ann Arbor: Merrill Prentice Hall, 2002.

———. "The Promise and Perils of Alternative Forms of Data Representation." *Educational Researcher* 26, no. 6 (1997): 4–10.

Elder, Linda and Richard Paul. "Ethical Reasoning in Education." *Foundations of Critical Thinking* (November 19, 2001). http://www.criticalthinking.org/pages/ethical-reasoning-essential-to-education/1036

Ferguson, Ann Arnett. *Bad Boys: Public Schools in the Making of Black Masculinity.* Ann Arbor, MI: University of Michigan Press, 2001.

Feiman-Nemser, Sharon. "From Preparation to Practice: Designing a Continuum to Strengthen and Sustain Teaching." *Teachers College Record* 103, no. 6 (2001): 1013–1055.

Fernandez, Clea, Joanna Cannon, and Sonal Chokshi. "A US-Japanese Lesson Study Collaboration Reveals Critical Lenses for Examining Practice." *Teaching and Teacher Education* 19 (2003): 171–185.

Fey, Tina and Kay Cannon. "Chain Reaction of Mental Anguish." *30 Rock.* Season 5, Episode 9. Directed by Ken Whittingham. (Aired December 2, 2010). Long Island City, Queens, New York: Silver Cup Studios East.

Fish, Stanley. *Is There a Text in This Class?: The Authority of Interpretive Communities.* Cambridge, MA: Harvard University Press, 1980.

Foucault, Michel. *Discipline and Punish: The Birth of the Prison.* New York: Vintage Books, 1977.

———. *The History of Sexuality.* New York: Vintage Books, 1978.

Freire, Paulo. *Pedagogy of Freedom: Ethics, Democracy, and Civic Courage.* Lanham, MD: Rowman and Littlefield Publishers, Inc., 1998.

———. *Pedagogy of the Oppressed.* Reprinted, New York: Continuum Books, 2010.

———. *Teachers as Cultural Workers: Letters to Those Who Dare Teach.* Boulder, CO: Westview Press, 2005.

Garman, Noreen. "Imagining an Interpretive Dissertation." In *The Authority to Imagine: The Struggle Toward Representation in Dissertation Writing*, 1–15. Edited by Noreen B. Garman and Maria Piantanida. New York: Peter Lang, 2006.

———. "On Becoming a Dialogic Classroom." Unpublished manuscript, 2007.

———. "Teaching a Moral Craft?" Unpublished manuscript.

Garman, Noreen, Michael Gunzenhauser, Maureen McClure, and Stewart Sutin. "Core 1: The Scholar/Practitioner/Citizen Role," Syllabus for Administrative and Policy Studies Department Doctoral Core: An Introduction to Doctoral Study, University of Pittsburgh." Unpublished manuscript, Fall 2013.

Garman, Noreen and Maria Piantanida, eds., *The Authority to Imagine: The Struggle Toward Representation in Dissertation Writing*. New York: Peter Lang, 2006.

Garrison, Jim. "A Deweyan Theory of Democratic Listening." *Educational Theory* 46, no. 4 (Fall 1996): 445–446.

Gabbard, David A. and E.Wayne Ross, eds., *Education Under the Security State*. New York: Teachers College Press, 2004.

Gilligan, Carol. *In a Different Voice: Psychological Theory and Women's Development*. Cambridge, MA: Harvard University Press, 1982.

Giroux, Henry. *Teachers as Intellectuals: Toward a Critical Pedagogy of Learning*. South Hadley, MA: Bergin & Garvey, 1988.

Greene, Peter. "NM: Defending the Test." *Curmudgucation: Trying to Make Sense of What's Happening in Education* (blog), March 16, 2015. http://curmudgucation.blogspot.com/2015/03/nm-defending-test.html

Greene, Maxine. "Beyond Insularity: Releasing the Voices." *College ESL* 3, no. 3 (1993): 1–14.

———. "Blue Guitars and the Search for Curriculum." In *Reflections from the Heart of Educational Inquiry*. Edited by George Willis and William Schubert. Albany, NY: SUNY Press, 1991a: 107–122.

———. "Curriculum and Consciousness." *Teachers College Record* 73, no. 2 (1971): 253–270.

———. *The Dialectic of Freedom*. New York: Teachers College Press, 1988.

———. *Existential Encounters for Teachers*. New York: Random House, 1967.

———. "Foreword." In *Stories Lives Tell: Narrative and Dialogue in Education*, ix–xi. Edited by Carol Witherell and Nel Noddings. New York: Teachers College Press, 1991.

———. *Landscapes of Learning*. New York: Teachers College Press, 1978.

———. "Language, Literature, and the Release of Meaning." *College English* 41, no. 2 (October 1979a): 123–135.

———. "Liberal Education and the Newcomer." *Phi Delta Kappan* 60, no. 9 (1979b): 633–636.

———. "Metaphors and Multiples: Representation, the Arts, and History." *Phi Delta Kappan* 78, no. 5 (1997): 387–394.

———. "Imagining Futures: The Public School and Possibility." *Journal of Curriculum Studies* 32, no. 2 (2000): 267–280.

———. "In Search of a Pedagogy." New York: Maxine Greene, 2007. https://maxinegreene.org/library/maxine-greene-library/works-by-maxine-greene

———. "Prologue to Art, Social Imagination and Action." *Journal of Educational Controversy* 5, no. 1 (Winter 2010): 1.

———. *The Public School and the Private Vision: A Search for America in Education and Literature.* New York: Random House, 1965. Reprinted, New York: The New Press, 2007.

———. *Releasing the Imagination: Essays on Education, the Arts, and Social Change.* San Francisco: Jossey-Bass, 1995.

———. *Teacher as Stranger: Educational Philosophy for the Modern Age.* Belmont, CA: Wadsworth, 1973.

———. "Teaching: The Question of Personal Reality." *Teachers College Record* 80, no. 1 (1978): 23–35.

———. "Toward a Pedagogy of Thought and a Pedagogy of Imagination." New York: Maxine Greene, 2007. https://maxinegreene.org/library/maxine-greene-library/works-by-maxine- greene

———. "Toward Wide-Awakeness: An Argument for Arts and Humanities in Education." *Teachers College Record* 79, no. 1 (1977): 119–125.

———. "Voices and Powers." New York: Maxine Greene, 2007. https://maxinegreene.org/library/maxine-greene-library/works-by-maxine-greene.

———. "We Who Are Teachers Know That Imagination Has This Multiple Power," In *Variations on a Blue Guitar: The Lincoln Center Institute Lectures on Aesthetic Education*, 80–85. New York: Teachers College Press, 2001.

Grossman, Pam, Christa Compton, Danielle Igra, Matt Ronfeldt, Emily Shahan, and Peter Williamson. "Teaching Practice: A Cross-Professional Perspective." *Teachers College Record* 111, no. 9 (2008): 2055–2100.

Grumet, Madeleine. *Bitter Milk: Women and Teaching.* Amherst, MA: University of Massachusetts Press, 1988.

———. "The Politics of Personal Knowledge." *Curriculum Inquiry*, 17, no. 3 (1987): 319–329.

———. "Restitution and Reconstruction of Educational Experience: An Autobiographical Method for Curriculum Theory." In *Rethinking Curriculum Studies: A Radical Approach*, 115–130. Edited by M. Lawn and L. Barton. London: Croom Helm, 1981.

Gunzenhauser, Michael. *The Active/Ethical Professional: A Framework for Responsible Educators.* New York: Continuum, 2012.

———. "Care of the Self in a Context of Accountability." *Teachers College Record* 110, no. 10 (2008): 2224–2244.

———. "From Empathy to Creative Intersubjectivity in Qualitative Research." In *Qualitative Research: A Reader in Philosophy, Core Concepts, and Practice*, 57–74. Edited by Phil Carspecken, Lucy Carspecken, and Barbara Dennis. New York: Peter Lang, 2011.

———. "Normalizing the Educated Subject: A Foucauldian Analysis of High-Stakes Accountability." *Educational Studies* 39 (2006): 241–252.

———. "Resistance as a Component of Educator Professionalism." *Ohio Valley Philosophical Society*, 38 (2007): 23–26.

Harding, Sandra. "Feminism, Science, and the Anti-Enlightenment Critiques." In *Feminism/Postmodernism (Thinking Gender).* Edited by Linda Nicholson. New York: Routledge, 1990: 83–106.

———. *Science and Social Inequality: Feminist and Postcolonial Issues.* Urbana: University of Illinois Press, 2006.

Hartsock, Nancy. "The Feminist Standpoint: Developing Ground for a Specifically Feminist Historical Materialism." In *Discovering Reality: Feminist Perspectives on Epistemology, Metaphysics, Methodology, and Philosophy of Science.* Edited by Sandra Harding and Merrill B. Hintikka. Boston: D. Reidel Publishing Co., 1983: 283–310.

Henderson, James. *The Path Less Taken: Immanent Critique in Curriculum and Pedagogy.* Troy, NY: Educator's International Press, 2010.

Henderson, James G. and Colleagues. *Reconceptualizing Curriculum Development: Inspiring and Informing Action.* New York: Routledge, 2015.

Hiebert, James, Anne Morris, Dawn Berk, and Amanda Jansen. "Preparing Teachers to Learn from Teaching." *Journal of Teacher Education* 58, no. 1 (2007): 47–61.

Holmes, Barbara. "True Self Relating: The Community Called Beloved." Lecture, Living School of the Center for Action and Contemplation. Albuquerque, NM. April 6, 2021.

hooks, bell. *Talking Back: Thinking Feminist, Thinking Black.* Boston: South End Press, 1989.

Howard, Gary. *We Can't Teach What We Don't Know: White Teachers, Multiracial Schools.* New York: Teachers College Press, 2006.

Howe, Florence, ed. *Women and the Power to Change.* New York: McGraw Hill Book Company, 1973.

Huebner, Dwayne. "Curriculum as Concern for Man's Temporality. In *Curriculum Theorizing: The Reconceptualists,* 227–249. Edited by William Pinar. Berkley, CA: McCutcheon, 1975.

Jackson, Philip W. *Life in Classrooms.* New York: Teachers College Press, 1990.

Jackson, Sandra. "A Matter of Conflicting Interests? Problematizing the Role of Schools." In *Education Under the Security State,* 55–72. Edited by David Gabbard and E. Wayne Ross. New York: Teachers College Press, 2004.

Jagla, Virginia. "Teachers' Everyday Imagination and Intuition." In *Teacher Lore: Learning from Our Own Experience,* 61–80. Edited by William Schubert and William Ayers. New York: Longman, 1992.

Kaestle, Carl. *Pillars of the Republic: Common Schools and American Society, 1780–1860.* New York: Hill and Wang, 1983.

Kendi, Ibram X. *How to Be an Anti-Racist.* New York: One World, 2019.

Kerber, Linda. "The Republican Mother: Women and the Enlightenment—An American Perspective." *American Quarterly* 28, no. 2 (Summer, 1976): 187–205.

Kilbourn, Brent. "Fictional Theses." *Educational Researcher* 28, no. 12 (1999): 27–32.

Kliebard, Herbert. "The Rise of Scientific Curriculum-Making and Its Aftermath." In *The Curriculum Studies Reader,* 37–46. Edited by David J. Flinders and Stephen J. Thornton. New York: RoutledgeFalmer, 2004.

Kohl, Herbert. *I Won't Learn from You: And Other Thoughts on Creative Maladjustments.* New York: New Press, 1994.

Ladson-Billings, Gloria. "Can We at Least Have Plessy? The Struggle for Quality Education. Keynote address to the North Carolina Law Review Symposium, 2006. http://heinonline.org/HOL/LandingPage?handle=hein.journals/nclr85&div=39&id=&page=

———. *The Dreamkeepers: Successful Teachers of African American Children.* San Francisco: Jossey-Bass, 1994.

———. "Fighting for Our Lives: Preparing Teachers to Teach African American Students." *Journal of Teacher Education,* 51, no. 3 (2000): 206–214.

———. "Preparing Teachers for Diverse Student Populations: A Critical Race Theory Perspective." *Review of Research in Education,* 24 (1999): 211–247.

———. "Pushing Past the Achievement Gap: An Essay on the Language of Deficit." *The Journal of Negro Education* 76, no. 3 (2007): 316–323.

———. "Toward a Theory of Culturally Relevant Pedagogy." *American Educational Research Journal* 32, no. 3 (1995): 465–491.

Lagemann, Ellen. *An Elusive Science: The Troubling History of Educational Research.* Chicago: University of Chicago Press, 2000.

Lake, Robert. *A Curriculum of Imagination in Era of Standardization: An Imaginative Dialogue with Maxine Greene and Paulo Freire.* Charlotte, NC: Information Age Publishing, 2013.

———. "Letters as Windows into a Life of Praxis: Using the Epistolary Genre to Explore the Tensions between the Private Self and Public Action." In *Challenging Status Quo Retrenchment: New Directions in Critical Qualitative Research.* Edited by Tricia Kress, Curry Malott, Brad Porfilio. Charlotte, NC: Information Age Publishers, 2012.

Lake, Robert, ed. *Dear Maxine: Letters from the Unfinished Conversation.* New York: Teachers College Press, 2010.

Landinsky, Daniel, trans. *The Gift: Poems by Hafiz, the Great Sufi Master.* New York: Penguin Press, 1999.

Lather, Patti. *Getting Lost: Feminist Efforts Toward a Double(d) Science.* Albany, NY: SUNY Press, 2007.

L'Engle, Madeleine. *A Circle of Quiet.* San Francisco: HarperSanFrancisco, 1972.

———. *Walking on Water: Reflections on Faith and Art.* Colorado Springs, CO: Shaw Press, 1980. Reprinted, Colorado Springs: WaterBrook Press, 2001.

Lieberman, Ann "The Meaning of Scholarly Activity and the Building of Community," *Educational Researcher* 21, no. 6 (1992): 5–12.

Llewellyn, Marilyn. "Embracing a Language of Spiritual Inquiry." In *The Authority to Imagine: The Struggle Toward Representation in Dissertation Writing.* Edited by Noreen B. Garman and Maria Piantanida. New York: Peter Lang, 2006: 97–112.

Logsdon, Marjorie. "Writing Essays: Minding the Personal and Theoretic." In *The Authority to Imagine: The Struggle Toward Representation in Dissertation Writing.*

Edited by Noreen B. Garman and Maria Piantanida. New York: Peter Lang, 2006: 155–166.

Lucas, Christopher. *Teacher Education in America: Reform Agendas for the Twenty-First Century*. New York: St. Martin's Press, 1997.

Mathison, Sandra and E. Wayne Ross. "The Hegemony of Accountability." In *Education Under the Security State*. Edited by David Gabbard and E. Wayne Ross. New York: Teachers College Press, 2004: 91–100.

Mattingly, Paul. *The Classless Profession: American Schoolmen in the 19th Century*. New York: New York University Press, 1975.

McClintock, Robert. "Toward a Place for Study in a World of Instruction," *Teachers College Record* 73, no. 2 (December 1971), 161–205.

McDonald, Joseph. *Teaching: Making Sense of an Uncertain Craft*. New York: Teachers College Press, 1992.

McMahon, Patricia. "Narrative Yearnings: Reflecting in Time Through the Art of Fictive Story." In *The Authority to Imagine: The Struggle Toward Representation in Dissertation Writing*, 183–200. Edited by Noreen B. Garman and Maria Piantanida. New York: Peter Lang, 2006.

Menakem, Resmaa. *My Grandmother's Hands: Racialized Trauma and the Pathway to Healing our Hearts and Bodies*. Las Vegas, NV: Central Recovery Press, 2017.

Merleau-Ponty, Maurice. *Phenomenology of Perception*. London: Routledge and Kegan Paul, 1962.

Merton, Thomas. *The Sign of Jonas*. New York: Harcourt, 1953.

Miel, Alice. *Cooperative Procedures in Learning*. New York: Teachers College Press, 1962.

Miller, Janet. "Autobiography and the Necessary Incompleteness of Teachers' Stories." In *A Light in Dark Times: Maxine Greene and the Unfinished Conversation*. Edited by William Ayers and Janet Miller. New York: Teachers College Press, 1998.

———. *Creating Spaces and Finding Voices: Teachers Collaborating for Empowerment*. Albany, NY: SUNY Press, 1990.

———. "Epilogue—'Coming Together to Act on the Possibility of Repair': Conversations with Maxine Greene." In *Dear Maxine: Letters from the Unfinished Conversation*, 159–160. Edited by Robert Lake. New York: Teachers College Press, 2010.

———. *Sounds of Silence Breaking: Women, Autobiography, and Curriculum*. New York: Peter Lang, 2005.

———. "Teachers' Spaces: A Personal Evolution of Teacher Lore." In *Teacher Lore: Learning from Our Own Experience*, 11–24. Edited by William Schubert and William Ayers. New York: Longman, 1992.

———. "Women as Teachers: Enlarging Conversations on Issues of Gender and Self-Concept." *Journal of Curriculum and Supervision* 1, no. 2 (1986): 49–62.

Millies, Palma Suzanne George. "The Relationship Between a Teacher's Life and Teaching." In *Teacher Lore: Learning from Our Own Experience*, 25–43. Edited by William Schubert and William Ayers. New York: Longman, 1992.

Murray, Frank. *The Teacher Educator's Handbook: Building a Knowledge Base for the Preparation of Teachers*. San Francisco, CA: Jossey-Bass, 1996.

Nicholson, Linda, ed. *The Second Wave: A Reader in Feminist Theory*. London: Routledge, 1997.

Nieto, Sonia. *Affirming Diversity: The Sociopolitical Context of Multicultural Education*. White Plains, NY: Longman Publishers, 1996.

Noddings, Nel. "An Ethic of Caring and Its Implications for Instructional Arrangements." *American Journal of Education* 96, no. 2 (1988): 215–230.

———. *Philosophy of Education*. Boulder, CO: Westview Press, 2007.

Pagano, Jo Anne. *Exiles and Communities: Teaching in the Patriarchal Wilderness*. Albany, NY: State University of New York Press, 1990.

Palmer, Parker J. *The Courage to Teach: Exploring the Inner Landscape of a Teacher's Life*. San Francisco: Jossey-Bass, 2007.

———. *A Hidden Wholeness: The Journey Toward an Undivided Life*. San Francisco, CA: Jossey-Bass, Inc., 2004.

———. A New Professional: The Aims of Education Revisited" *Change* (Nov/Dec 2007). http://www.changemag.org/Archives/Back Issues/November-December 2007/full-new-professional.html

———. *To Know as We Are Known: Education as a Spiritual Journey*. New York: HarperCollins, 1983.

———. *The Promise of Paradox: A Celebration of Contradictions in the Christian Life*. South Bend, IN: Ava Maria Press, 1980. Reprinted, San Francisco, CA: Jossey-Bass, Inc., 2008.

Paul, Richard. "Ethics Without Indoctrination." *Critical Thinking: What Every Student Needs to Survive in A Rapidly Changing World*. Dillon Beach, CA: Foundation for Critical Thinking, 1993. http://www.criticalthinking.org/pages/ethics-without-indoctrination/494

Piantanida, Maria. "Speculation on the Personal Essay as a Mode of Curriculum Inquiry." In *The Authority to Imagine: The Struggle Toward Representation in Dissertation Writing*, 167–182. Edited by Noreen B. Garman and Maria Piantanida. New York: Peter Lang, 2006.

Piantanida, Maria and Noreen Garman. *The Qualitative Dissertation: A Guide for Students and Faculty*. Thousand Oaks, CA: Corwin, 2010.

Pierce, Charles. "What Does the Netflix Guy Have to Say About Public Education?" *Esquire* (March 17, 2014). http://www.esquire.com/news-politics/politics/a27836/billionaires-education-reform-031713

Pinar, William. *Autobiography, Politics and Sexuality: Essays in Curriculum Theory, 1972–1992*. New York: Peter Lang, 1994.

———. *The Character of Curriculum Studies: Bildung, Currere, and the Recurring Question of the Subject*. New York: Palgrave Macmillan, 2011.

———. "Currere: Toward Reconceptualization." In *Curriculum Theorizing: The Reconceptualists*, 359–383. Edited by William Pinar. Berkley, CA: McCutchen Publishing, 1975.

———. *The Synoptic Text Today and Other Essays: Curriculum Development after the Reconceptualization.* New York: Peter Lang, 2006.

———. *What is Curriculum Theory?* Mahwah, NJ: Lawrence Erlbaum Associates, 2004.

———. *What is Curriculum Theory?* 2nd ed. New York: Routledge, 2012.

Pinar, William, ed. *The Passionate Mind of Maxine Greene: "I am ... not yet."* London: Falmer, 1998.

Pinar, William and Madeleine Grumet. *Toward a Poor Curriculum.* Dubuque, IA: Kendall Hunt Publishing, 1976.

Pinar, William, William Reynolds, Patrick Slattery, and Peter Taubman, eds. *Understanding Curriculum: An Introduction to the Study of Historical and Contemporary Curriculum Discourses.* New York: Peter Lang, 1995.

Popham, W. James. "Objectives." In *The Curriculum Studies Reader,* 71–84. Edited by David J. Flinders and Stephen J. Thornton. New York: RoutledgeFalmer, 2004.

Purpel, David. *The Moral and Spiritual Crisis in Education: A Curriculum for Justice and Compassion in Education.* New York: Bergin and Garvey, 1989.

Putman, Ralph and Hilda Borko. "What Do New Views of Knowledge and Thinking Have to Say about Research on Teacher Learning?" *Educational Researcher* 29, no. 1 (2000): 4–15.

RAND Corporation. "Teachers Matter: Understanding Teachers' Impact on Student Achievement." Santa Monica, CA: RAND Corporation, 2012. http://www.rand.org/pubs/corporate_pubs/CP693z1-2012-09.html

Richardson, Laurel and Elizabeth St. Pierre. "Writing: A Method of Inquiry." In *The Sage Handbook of Qualitative Research* 3rd ed., 959–978. Edited by Norman Denzin and Yvonna Lincoln. Thousand Oaks, CA: Sage Publications Ltd., 2005.

Ricoeur, Paul. *Hermeneutics and the Human Sciences: Essays on Language, Action, and Interpretation.* Translated by John Thompson. Cambridge, UK: Cambridge University Press, 1981.

Rich, Adrienne. "Diving into the Wreck," *Diving into the Wreck: Poems 1971–1972.* New York: W.W. Norton and Company, 1973.

———. "Taking Women Students Seriously." In *The Broadview Anthology of Expository Prose,* 210–220. Edited by Laura Buzzard, Julia Gaunee, Don LePan, Mical Mosner, and Tammy Roberts. Petersborough, ONT, Canada: Broadview Press, 2011.

———. "When We Dead Awaken: Writing as Re-Vision (1971)." In *On Lies, Secrets, and Silence: Selected Prose, 1966–1978,* 35. New York: W.W. Norton and Company, 1979.

Ripley, Amanda. "Bootcamp for Teachers." *The Atlantic* (July/August 2012). http://www.theatlantic.com/magazine/archive/2012/07/boot-camp-for-teachers/309029

Rios, Carmen. "Debunking the 'Pull Yourself Up by Your Bootstraps' Myth." *Everyday Feminism,* (May 17, 2015). http://everydayfeminism.com/2015/05/debunking-bootstraps-myth

Robinson, John and Linda Hawpe. "Narrative Thinking as a Heuristic Process." In *Narrative Psychology: The Storied Nature of Human Conduct.* Edited by TR Sarbin (New York: Praeger, 1986).

Saltman, Kenneth. "The Securitized Student." In *Education Under the Security State,* 157–174. Edited by David Gabbard and E. Wayne Ross. New York: Teachers College Press, 2004.

Sartre, J. *Being and Nothingness.* New York: Philosophical Library, 1956.

Schiebinger, Londa. "The Exclusion of Women and the Structure of Knowledge." In Feminism: Critical Concepts in Literary and Cultural Studies Vol. 1. Edited by Mary Evans. London: Routledge, 2001.

Schubert, William. "Foreword: More Teacher Lore." In *Becoming a Teacher: Using Narrative as Reflective Practice,* ix–xvii. Edited by Brett Elizabeth Blake and Robert Blake. New York: Peter Lang, 2012.

———. "Teacher Lore: A Basis for Understanding Praxis." *In Stories Lives Tell: Narrative and Dialog in Education,* 207–233. Edited by Carol Witherell and Nel Noddings. New York: Teachers College Press, 1991.

———. "Teacher Lore: A Neglected Basis for Understanding Curriculum and Supervision." *Journal of Curriculum and Supervision* 4, no. 3 (1989): 282–285.

———. "Teacher and Student Lore: Their Ways of Looking at It." *Contemporary Education* 65, no. 1(1993). 42–46.

Schubert, William and William Ayers, eds. *Teacher Lore: Learning from Our Own Experience.* New York: Longman, 1992.

Schubert, William and Ann L. Lopez. "Teacher Lore as a Basis for In-Service Education of Teachers." *Teaching and Teachers' Work* 1, no. 4 (1993): 1–8.

Schubert, William, Patricia Hulsebosch, Mari Koerner, Suzanne Millies, Thomas P. Thomas, Jenny Wojcik, Georgiana Zissis. "Teaching About Progressive Education: From Course to Study Group" *Teaching Education* 1, no. 2 (1987): 77–81.

Schwandt, Thomas. "Three Epistemological Stances for Qualitative Inquiry: Interpretivism, Hermeneutics, and Social Constructionism." In *The Handbook of Qualitative Research,* 189–213. Edited by Norman Denzin and Yvonna Lincoln. Thousand Oaks, CA: Sage Publications, 2000.

Shulman, Lee. "Those Who Understand: Knowledge Growth in Teaching." *Educational Researcher* 15, no. 2 (Feb., 1986): 4–14.

Sidorkin, Alexander. *Beyond Discourse: Education, the Self, and Dialogue.* Albany, NY: State University of New York, 1999.

Sirotnik, Kenneth, ed. *Holding Accountability Accountable: What Ought to Matter in Public Education.* New York: Teachers College Press, 2004.

Spelman, Elizabeth. "Aristotle and the Politicization of the Soul." In *Discovering Reality: Feminist Perspectives on Epistemology, Metaphysics, Methodology, and Philosophy of Science,* 17–30. Edited by Sandra Harding and Merrill B. Hintikka. Boston: D. Reidel Publishing Co., 1983.

Spring, Joel. *The American School: 1642–2004.* Boston: McGraw Hill, 2004.

———. *Deculturalization and the Struggle for Equity: A Brief History of the Education of Dominated Cultures in the United States.* Boston: McGraw-Hill, 2009.

———. *The Sorting Machine: National Education Policy Since 1945.* New York: David McKay, 1976.

Stenhouse, Lawrence. *Curriculum Research and Development in Action.* London: Heinemann Educational Books, 1980.

Strauss, Valerie. "Business Leaders Inject Themselves into School Reform." Answer Sheet (blog). *Washington Post* (October 25, 2011). http://www.washingtonpost.com/blogs/answer-sheet/post/business-leaders-inject-themselves-in-school-reform/2011/10/24/gIQArm5mFM_blog

Sutton, John. "Memory." In *The Stanford Encyclopedia of Philosophy.* Edited by N. Zalta. (2004). http://plato.stanford.edu/archives/win2012/entries/memory

Tanesini, Alessandra. *An Introduction to Feminist Epistemologies.* Malden, MA: Blackwell Publishers, 1999.

Taubman, Peter. "Canonical Sins." In *Understanding Curriculum as Racial Text: Representations of Identity and Difference in Education.* Edited by L. Castenall Jr. and William Pinar. Albany, NY: State University of New York Press, 1993.

———. *Teaching by Numbers: Deconstructing the Discourse of Standards and Accountability in Education.* New York: Routledge, 2009.

Taylor, Kate and Motoko Rich. "Teachers' Unions Fight Standardized Testing, and Find Diverse Allies." *The New York Times* (April 20, 2015). http://www.nytimes.com/2015/04/21/education/teachers-unions-reasserting-themselves-with-push-against-standardized-testing.html

Teresa of Avila. "Interior Castles." In *The collected works of Saint Teresa of Avila.* Trans. Kiernan Kavanaugh and Otilio Rodriguez. Washington DC: Institute of Carmelite Studies, 2017.

Todd, Sharon. *Learning from the Other: Levinas, Psychoanalysis, and Ethical Possibilities in Education.* Albany, NY: SUNY Press, 2003.

Tyack, David. *The One Best System: A History of American Urban Education.* Cambridge, MA: Harvard University Press, 1974.

Tyack, David and Elizabeth Hansot. *Learning Together: A History of Coeducation in American Public Schools.* New Haven, CT: Yale University Press, 1990.

Tyler, Ralph. "Basic Principles of Curriculum and Instruction." In *The Curriculum Studies Reader,* 51–60. Edited by David J. Flinders and Stephen J. Thornton. New York: RoutledgeFalmer, 2004.

Urban Intellectuals. "Front Page." www.urbanintellectuals.com. Last accessed April 3, 2021.

Urban, Wayne. *Why Teachers Organized.* Detroit: Wayne State University Press, 1982.

Urban, Wayne and Jennings Wagoner, Jr. *American Education: A History.* Boston: McGraw Hill, 2004.

Vinz, Ruth. "Culturally Responsive Teaching." In *Encyclopedia of the Social and Cultural Foundations of Education*. [Electronic version] Sage Knowledge, 2008.

Weiler, Kathleen. "Feminist Analyses of Gender and Schooling." In *The Critical Pedagogy Reader*. Edited by Antonia Darder, Marta Baltodano, and Rodolfo Torres. New York: RoutledgeFalmer, 2003: 269–295.

Westbrook, Robert. *John Dewey and American Democracy*. Ithaca, NY: Cornell University, 1991.

Williams, Helen, Martin Conway and Gillian Cohen. "Autobiographical Memory." In *Memory in the Real World*. Edited by Gillian Cohen and Martin Conway. New York: Psychology Press, 2008.

Willinsky, John. *The Access Principle: The Case for Open Access to Research and Scholarship*. Cambridge, MA: MIT Press, 2006.

Zembylas, Michalinos. "Interrogating 'Teacher Identity': Emotion, Resistance, and Self-Formation. *Educational Theory* 53, no. 1 (2003): 107–127.

Index

Apple, Michael   20, 51, 87, 88, 154, 185, 186
Ayers, William   18, 19, 49, 50, 52, 67, 72, 73, 85, 88–90, 179, 180

Bahktin, Mikhail   52
Becoming/being   35, 48, 69, 137, 174, 198
   educational growth   48
Block, Alan   48, 51, 189, 199

critical pedagogy   16, 18
critical theory   16, 23, 27, 52, 185
critical thinking   8, 11, 13, 14, 27, 48, 49, 99, 119, 157
   see also Bloom's taxonomy   121
Currere   61, 64–66, 75, 76, 79, 86, 87
curriculum studies   3, 5, 7, 15, 47, 50, 62–64, 70, 77–80, 88, 150, 137, 143, 151, 179, 199
   complicated conversation   50, 84, 92, 179, 199
   public curriculum   151
   reconceptualize/reconceptualization   63, 86, 87

Delpit, Lisa   17, 51, 159, 160, 162–164, 187, 188
democracy   13, 18–20, 49, 52, 85, 98, 113, 115, 142, 146, 147, 157, 172, 180
democratic education   11, 69, 113, 146
Dewey, John   11, 18, 19, 22, 27, 34, 48, 49, 51–53, 60, 67, 69, 85, 87, 88, 97, 113, 137, 180, 183, 189, 197
dialogic   6, 11, 19, 22, 26, 27, 46, 49, 52, 60, 61, 66, 69, 71, 72, 74, 78, 79, 84, 139, 143, 150, 156, 178, 187, 192, 196
dialogue   3–5, 12, 16, 19, 21–23, 25–27, 39, 45, 46, 55, 59, 66, 71, 74, 78, 84, 85, 137, 139, 158, 174–177, 180, 189, 191, 192, 194–197

epistemology   12, 14–18, 20, 21, 24, 45, 46, 49, 63, 75, 80, 85, 87, 88, 90, 92, 155, 191
   ways of knowing   24, 46, 64, 155
ethics/ethical   12, 14, 16, 19, 20, 48, 50, 52, 59, 61, 82, 178, 189, 199
   alterity   82, 172, 174
   calling   13, 15, 158
   feminist   172, 173
   intersubjectivity   11, 42, 46, 49, 50, 52, 86, 91, 189

relational   69, 88, 92
existential   3, 23, 27–29, 31–35, 39–41, 43, 45, 48, 49, 53–56, 59, 65, 74, 75, 81, 86, 138, 178–180
   single one   41, 86

feelings associated with Naming   138
   disquietude   6, 10, 15, 37, 46, 47, 81, 82
   weary   45
   weight   35, 37
   yucky   193
feminized profession   62, 86, 150, 170
   feminization of teaching   152
Ferguson, Ann Arnett   159, 165–169, 187–189
Foucault, Michel   2, 23, 24, 27, 28, 33, 52, 53, 83, 91, 187, 188
freedom   6, 10–13, 18, 19, 23, 23, 26–28, 30–35, 37, 39, 40, 44, 45, 47–49, 52, 54, 55, 64, 65, 75, 81, 83, 86, 87, 121, 136, 137–139, 143, 145, 151, 156, 172, 177, 178, 180, 181, 183, 184, 192
Freire, Paolo   26, 27, 30, 32, 34, 53, 88

Garman, Noreen   11, 16, 19, 49, 51, 52, 74, 76, 77, 85, 86, 88, 90–92, 170
Grumet, Madeleine   85–87
Gunzenhauser, Micheal   11, 23, 49, 51, 52, 54, 189

hidden curriculum   51, 157, 166, 187
   anti-racist   159, 199
   critical race theory   159, 187
   (mis)behavior   159

imagination   3, 32, 34, 40, 44–47, 52, 54, 55, 60, 86–89, 172, 180, 192
   social   36, 40, 41, 52, 54
interpretation   5, 28–30, 39, 42, 44, 47, 53–55, 60–63, 65, 69, 71–81, 83–85, 91, 93, 139, 140, 143–145, 156, 162, 163, 167, 169–171, 177–181, 184
   critical   32, 34, 40, 54, 69, 81

Jackson, Philip   20, 51, 116, 157, 186

Ladson-Billings, Gloria   17, 87, 159–161, 187, 188
Lake, Robert   6, 47, 49, 54, 92

INDEX

Lowenburg Ball, Deborah   14, 49, 50, 143, 150, 181

McClaren, Peter   187
McClintock, Robert   51, 199
Miller, Janet   32, 36, 49, 54, 55, 67, 71–73, 75, 87–91, 155, 179–181, 186
moral   9, 12, 16, 22, 30, 36, 45, 48, 49, 51, 58, 69, 142, 145–147, 149, 151, 152, 165, 170, 173, 176, 182, 187, 188, 199
multiple interpretations   5, 39, 61, 62, 72, 73, 75, 83, 143
multiple perspectives   20, 38, 39, 40, 44, 52, 55, 61, 66, 75, 78, 115, 116, 139, 140

Naming   1, 4, 5, 7, 10, 14, 16, 21, 24, 26–28, 32, 34–37, 39–42, 44–48, 53–55, 59, 65, 66, 73, 74, 76, 77, 79, 81–84, 130, 138–140, 150, 153, 156–159, 169–178, 187, 189, 192–195, 198
  discursive   143
Noddings, Nel   26, 49, 53, 88, 89, 172, 173, 189
norm/normative/normalization   23, 37, 40, 50, 72, 77, 79, 81, 83, 91, 144, 148, 160, 170, 177, 181

obstacles (to Becoming)   1, 10, 12, 14, 30, 32, 34–39, 44–46, 50, 52, 86, 91, 139, 161
  apathy   30, 31, 40
  gaps   38, 46, 62
  paralysis   30, 40
  submergence   30, 45
ontology   11, 12, 16, 18, 21–24, 26, 46, 49, 76, 83, 143, 192
  dialogic   22, 27
  feminism/feminist discourses   24, 25, 77, 91, 172, 181, 185
  subjectivity   11, 23, 26

reflection   2, 6, 16, 25–27, 38, 45, 48, 67, 69–71, 79, 123, 136, 177, 194, 195

Palmer, Parker   10, 11, 16, 48–50, 82, 91, 171, 172, 180, 189
paradox   3, 7, 10–12, 48, 82, 83, 91, 171, 172, 174, 175, 189, 195, 197, 198
  dualism   195
  see also tension
phenomenology   28, 31, 33, 37, 40, 48, 53, 59, 65, 70, 74, 87, 138
  consciousness   28, 32, 34, 37, 39, 180

Pinar, William   11, 17, 18, 47–53, 64, 80, 85–92, 155, 179, 181, 184–186, 199
power   17, 23, 24, 28, 31, 33, 36, 52, 53, 55, 62, 73, 82, 86, 144, 146, 148–153, 155, 156, 158, 160, 162, 165, 167, 176, 181, 182, 184, 185, 187–189, 193
  agency   2, 48, 60, 65, 72, 86, 95, 96, 153, 164, 176, 178, 180
  authority   82, 140
  compliance   82, 140
  control   168, 182
  discipline   53
  professional responsibility   82, 140
praxis   34, 44, 55, 67, 71, 76, 180, 198
  Naming   1, 5, 26, 40, 45, 47, 54, 55, 59, 66, 79, 82, 139, 177, 192, 193, 198
  teachers'   46, 70, 73, 76

research   57–92
  autobiographical   47, 58, 59, 61–67, 70–72, 75, 77–80, 86–89
  education   85, 129
  feminist   62, 63, 65, 67, 79, 86, 185, 186, 189
  interpretive (inquiry)   74, 76, 78, 85
  narrative   4, 80
  post-structural(ist)   76
  scientific   59, 85

Schubert, William   50, 67, 72, 75, 88, 89, 179, 180
Shulman, Lee   14, 49, 50
Sidorkin, Alexander   11, 22, 27, 49, 52, 86, 181
Social Foundations of Education   3, 5, 15, 16, 50, 52, 77, 137, 143, 159
spiritual   22, 47, 98, 191
standard/standards (perceived for teachers)   17, 20, 21, 23, 24, 31, 78, 84, 127, 136, 141, 142, 145, 148, 157, 165, 167, 170, 173, 175, 176, 183, 184, 187, 204, 214
  best practice   31, 76, 142, 174
  classroom (mis)management   141
  professional   148
  professional expertise   141
  racial   160, 167, 187
  responsibility   138, 140, 141, 146, 153, 156
standardization   54, 68, 72, 86, 140, 148, 154, 184, 214
study (conceptual)   11, 18, 50–52, 72–84, 192–196, 199

Teacher, American   83, 144–155, 157–162, 164, 165, 168–170, 173, 174, 177, 181, 182, 185, 197
  genealogy of   83, 185
  reform   72, 73, 148, 149, 183, 184, 186
teacher inquiry   66, 76
teacher knowledge   4, 5, 50, 66, 90
  acquisition of knowledge   16, 17
  rational mind   51, 178
  teacher thinking   70, 73, 89, 154

teacher lore   50, 66–73, 75–77, 79, 88–90, 179–181
tension   10–12, 35, 37, 46, 47, 64, 80–83, 119, 121, 122, 125, 138, 142, 155, 156, 170–174, 187, 193–196, 198

wide-awakeness   32, 36, 43, 177, 189, 192, 197, 198
will, lack of   19, 20, 40
  question of being able   31

Printed in the United States
by Baker & Taylor Publisher Services